City Taxes, City Spending

STUDIES IN FISCAL FEDERALISM AND STATE–LOCAL FINANCE

Series Editor: Wallace E. Oates, *Professor of Economics, University of Maryland and University Fellow, Resources for the Future, USA*

This important series is designed to make a significant contribution to the development of the principles and practices of state–local finance. It includes both theoretical and empirical work. International in scope, it addresses issues of current and future concern in both East and West and in developed and developing countries.

The main purpose of the series is to create a forum for the publication of high quality work and to show how economic analysis can make a contribution to understanding the role of local finance in fiscal federalism in the twenty-first century.

Titles in the series include:

Local Public Finance in Europe
Balancing the Budget and Controlling Debt
Edited by Bernard Dafflon

Political Economy in Federal States
Selected Essays of Stanley L. Winer
Stanley L. Winer

Public Finance in Developing and Transitional Countries
Essays in Honor of Richard Bird
Edited by Jorge Martinez-Vazquez and James Alm

Federal Intergovernmental Grants and the States
Managing Devolution
Shama Gamkhar

State and Local Finances under Pressure
Edited by David L. Sjoquist

The Property Tax, Land Use and Land Use Regulation
Edited by Dick Netzer

Restructuring Local Government Finance in Developing Countries
Lessons from South Africa
Edited by Roy Bahl and Paul Smoke

Reforming Intergovernmental Fiscal Relations and the Rebuilding of Indonesia
The 'Big Bang' Program and its Economic Consequences
Edited by James Alm, Jorge Martinez-Vazquez and Sri Mulyani Indrawati

City Taxes, City Spending

Essays in Honor of Dick Netzer

Edited by

Amy Ellen Schwartz

New York University, USA

STUDIES IN FISCAL FEDERALISM AND STATE–LOCAL FINANCE

Edward Elgar

Cheltenham, UK • Northampton, MA, USA

Published by
Edward Elgar Publishing Limited
Glensanda House
Montpellier Parade
Cheltenham
Glos GL50 1UA
UK

Edward Elgar Publishing, Inc.
136 West Street
Suite 202
Northampton
Massachusetts 01060
USA

A catalogue record for this book
is available from the British Library

Library of Congress Cataloguing in Publication Data
City taxes, city spending : essays in honor of Dick Netzer / edited by Amy Ellen Schwartz.
p. cm. — (Studies in fiscal federalism and state–local finance)
Includes bibliographical references.
1. Local taxation—United States—Congresses. 2. Local finance—United States—Congresses. 3. Netzer, Dick, 1928– I. Schwartz, Amy Ellen. II. Netzer, Dick, 1928– III. Series.

HJ2385.C57 2004
336.01473–dc22 2004041842

ISBN 1 84376 381 8

Printed and bound in Great Britain by MPG Books Ltd, Bodmin, Cornwall

Contents

Figures

Tables

Contributors

Charles T. Clotfelter, Sanford Institute of Public Policy, Duke University.
Joseph J. Cordes, Elliot School of International Affairs, The George Washington University.
Barbara Edwards, Congressional Budget Office, Washington, DC.
Ingrid Gould Ellen, Wagner School of Public Service, New York University.
Edward L. Glaeser, Department of Economics, Harvard University.
Andrew F. Haughwout, Research and Market Analysis Group, Federal Reserve Bank of New York.
Helen F. Ladd, Sanford Institute of Public Policy, Duke University.
Therese J. McGuire, Kellogg School of Management, Northwestern University.
Thomas Nechyba, Economics Department, Duke University.
Wallace E. Oates, Department of Economics, University of Maryland.
Katherine O'Regan, Wagner School of Public Service, New York University.
John M. Quigley, Department of Economics, University of California at Berkeley.
Andrew Reschovsky, La Follette School of Public Affairs, University of Wisconsin–Madison.
Michael H. Schill, School of Law, New York University.
Robert M. Schwab, Department of Economics, University of Maryland.
Amy Ellen Schwartz, Wagner School of Public Service, New York University.
David L. Sjoquist, Department of Economics, Andrew Young School of Policy Studies, Georgia State University.
Robert M. Solow, Department of Economics, Massachusetts Institute of Technology.
Ioan Voicu, The Furman Center for Real Estate and Urban Policy, School of Law, New York University.
Sally Wallace, Department of Economics, Andrew Young School of Policy Studies, Georgia State University.

Acknowledgments

This volume consists of papers presented at a conference held in honor of Dick Netzer at New York University in New York City on 12 October 2001. The conference was sponsored by the Lincoln Institute of Land Policy and hosted by the Wagner School of Public Service at New York University. This conference would not have been possible without their support. I am particularly indebted to Joan Youngman, of the Lincoln Institute, for her guidance and support, Linda Wheeler Reiss, whose advice and assistance was critical to the success of the conference, and to Zuzanna Kobrzynski, for her expert and patient assistance with the preparation of this volume.

The fall of 2001 was a difficult time to travel in the United States and to come to New York City in particular. It was a difficult time to focus on research and academe. That so many came and participated and contributed their papers and thoughtful comments is a testament both to them and to their high regard for Dick Netzer. In the end, the festschrift was a success because of their efforts, which are much appreciated.

1. Introduction

Amy Ellen Schwartz

In 1952, Dick Netzer was awarded the PhD from Harvard University with a dissertation titled 'Pricing the Transportation Services of State and Local Governments'. That same year, his first academic article, 'Toll Roads and the Crisis in Highway Finance', was published in the *National Tax Journal*. It was to be the first of many articles, chapters and books on a wide range of topics in public finance, urban economics and, later, the economics of the arts and not-for-profit organizations. The hallmark of this work is the application of microeconomics to real world problems and the careful and thoughtful use of economic data and statistical analysis.

Dick is, undoubtedly, best known among academics for his work on the property tax. *The Economics of the Property Tax,* published in 1966, provided a comprehensive analysis of property taxation, discussing incidence, distribution and the economic effects on housing and cities. Dozens of articles and papers followed, exploring and addressing questions and problems regarding property taxation and state and local public finance more generally. *The Economics of the Property Tax* has become a classic, still found on the shelves of public finance economists and on course syllabi more than 35 years later. His article, 'The Incidence of the Property Tax: Revisited', published in 1973, earned him a spot in the *National Tax Journal*'s Hall of Fame in 1997,[1] which included the top ten most cited articles published in that journal.

Of course, Dick is also well known for his work on urban economics, including both the financing of local government and the provision of public services, and the New York City economy in particular. This has included academic research as well as public service that is impressive both for its depth and for its breadth. In 1965, Dick contributed a chapter to a volume entitled 'Urban Research and Education in the New York Metropolitan Region'. He began, 'Research on urban economic phenomena and problems in the New York Metropolitan Region, as in most of the country's other urban concentrations, is sporadic, fitful and disconnected. Organizations, often of a temporary nature, and isolated individuals work on particular bits and pieces of urban economics when and as needed to cope with particular policy issues or as a diversion from other areas of research.'[2] He concluded with a call for the community of scholars to meet their responsibilities to the larger community in which they reside and, as a true empirical researcher, for an improvement in the quality and availability of data. These themes still resonate today.

In the years that followed, Dick strove admirably to meet this responsibility. Since his return to New York City in 1960, he has served as consultant, advisor and economic guru for a wide range of civic organizations, public officials, commissions and councils, as well as academic organizations. Notable examples include more than 20 years of service as a member of the Board of Directors of the Municipal Assistance Corporation for the City of New York, of the Board of Economic Advisors for the New York State Assembly Ways and Means Committee, and as a member of the Board of Directors of the Citizens Union Foundation. He has served on editorial boards for the *Journal of Urban Economics* and *Public Finance Review*, among others. Equally important have been his contributions to public debate in books, newspaper articles and, memorably, the editorial pages.[3]

Perhaps most impressive is the way he has been able to interweave academic investigation with the practice of public finance. His research and writing clearly reflect the lessons learned and insights gained from practical applications to problems facing cities. His public service clearly reflects the expertise and analytic acumen honed in scholarly research and engagement. In this, he is a role model for subsequent generations of public finance and urban economists seeking to balance academic inquiry and research with public service and practice.

Finally, Dick Netzer is well known for his pioneering work on arts organizations. In 1978, *The Subsidized Muse: Public Support for the Arts in the United States*, was published, again, the first of many publications dealing with the economics of arts organizations and government policy toward the arts. Although much more common now, there was, at that time, relatively little serious academic research by economists dealing with the not-for-profit sector as a whole, much less the arts sector specifically.[4]

The papers in this volume were written for a conference held in October of 2001 in New York City in honor of Dick Netzer. The topics mirror those addressed by Dick in the course of his career: financing local government, the economics of urban public services and the economics of not-for-profit organizations. Further, they follow in the tradition of Dick's work by utilizing the theoretical tools of economics and public finance and the best empirical methods and data available to gain new understanding of important problems.

The first paper, by Wallace Oates and Robert Schwab, *What should local governments tax: income or property?*, explores the relative merits of two alternative tax bases for local government: property and income. It begins with a brief description of the actual use of the two taxes by local governments in the United States. It then considers the basic theory of efficient taxation in a local setting, the incidence of the two taxes, and addresses various administrative and institutional issues. New empirical work explores the relative disparities in tax base per pupil under income and property taxation for school districts in four large states. The results suggest that tax-base disparities are significantly larger under local property taxation. Thus a move to local income taxation would yield a sizeable reduction in tax-base disparities. The paper concludes that, on balance, local government can probably function reasonably well using either tax base. Both taxes can provide workable and reasonably efficient sources of local revenues. Although the authors do not find either tax base clearly and consistently superior to the other, they note that reliance upon a local property tax may well be preferred if the 'separation of sources' of tax bases – in which local governments rely upon the property tax while federal and state governments rely primarily upon income taxation – enhances local control and accountability.

The second paper, by David Sjoquist, Sally Wallace and Barbara Edwards, *What a tangled web: local property, income and sales taxes,* considers a related question in local public finance, exploring the impact of alternative taxes on the property tax. In particular, the authors examine whether the adoption of local sales and income taxes have led to reductions in property taxes. The paper begins with a discussion of the theory and existing empirical literature regarding the effect of tax-base diversification on existing taxes. Using a pooled time-series, cross-sectional sample of the largest 101 US cities across the period 1963 to 1990, they find that the adoption and presence of a local sales or income tax leads to a decrease in the level of property taxes per capita.

The paper by Andrew Haughwout explores the land value tax, long advocated by followers of Henry George because of its efficiency, as a possible revenue source for New York City (*Land taxation in New York City: a general equilibrium analysis*). The centerpiece of the analysis is a computable general equilibrium model of the New York City economy, calibrated to the city's fiscal and economic environment, that can be used to simulate revenues, economic growth and employment outcomes over alternative tax schemes. The effects of replacing part or all of the city's current tax system with a land tax are simulated and suggest that significant increases in overall output in the city are possible. Since some of the key underlying parameters are unknown, the paper describes the research that is needed for a thorough evaluation of such a policy change. The paper concludes with a discussion of the benefits of moving to land taxation in New York, including a discussion of the political economy of local taxation.

Two papers consider aspects of the expenditure side of the city budget. Ingrid Gould Ellen, Michael H. Schill, Amy Ellen Schwartz and Ioan Voicu (*The role of cities in providing housing assistance: a New York perspective*) evaluate the case for city intervention in the housing market, specifically by providing housing subsidies. The increasing reliance upon states and cities to implement social policy makes it particularly important to consider how the responsibility for housing policies should be divided among federal, state and local governments. This paper examines available theory and evidence and concludes that the role of cities is determined, in large part, by the nature and magnitude of external benefits; the federal government should play the central role in funding housing programs aimed at redistribution. The authors then turn to estimating the magnitude of these benefits for New York City's housing investments in the last two decades of the 20th century. The results suggest that investment in affordable housing generated significant external benefits. The implication is that cities have a potentially important role to play in housing assistance, based upon the spillover effects of housing construction and rehabilitation in distressed neighborhoods.

Public ownership in the American city, by Edward Glaeser, addresses a related question that seems particularly important to consider in the modern rush to privatize the provision of public services: why do many American city governments directly provide public services, when public provision is so often linked with waste and inefficiency? Glaeser both presents theoretical models to explain public ownership and examines the history of public ownership in New York City to understand the causes and consequences of direct provision. American local governments own and manage a wide portfolio of enterprises, including gas and electricity companies, water systems, subways, bus systems and schools. Existing theories of public ownership, including the presence of natural monopolies, can explain much of the observed municipal ownership. Glaeser argues, however, that the history of America's cities suggests that support for public ownership came from corruption then associated with private ownership of utilities and public transportation. Private firms that either buy or sell to the government will have a strong incentive to bribe government officials to get lower input prices or higher output prices. Because municipal ownership dulls the incentives of the manager and decreases the firm's available cash, public firms may lead to less corruption. On the other hand, public ownership may lead to inefficiency and excessively large government payrolls.

The final two papers turn their attention to the not-for-profit sector. *The nonprofit sector in K-12 education*, by Charles Clotfelter, considers the role of the not-for-profit sector in providing and shaping primary and secondary education in the United States, specifically addressing the implications for segregation and equity. In 1999, private schools enrolled 5.4 million students, representing 11 per cent of all elementary students and 8 per cent of secondary school students in the United States. In contrast to many other nonprofit organizations, the services provided by private schools are best viewed as substituting for the corresponding public services, rather than supplementing them. The implications of this distinction are important. Private schools increase the sorting of individuals across schools as families choose schools according to their tastes, thus serving to increase school segregation. Whether the effects are beneficial (because of positive effects of decreased residential segregation) or deleterious (because of adverse effects of racial or economic segregation) is a critical question to consider, particularly in light of the public support given to private schools, through tax advantages, and the additional support contemplated by voucher advocates. Clotfelter begins with a review of relevant theoretical and empirical research, focusing on the potential for the nonprofit sector to induce segregation. Empirical analysis suggests that private schools increased racial segregation and, quite likely, economic segregation also. Clotfelter concludes that the likely impact of private schools on public schools is negative, because of the impact on the peer group in public schools, undermining the case for government subsidies to private schools.

In *The partially subsidized muse: estimating the value and incidence of public support received by nonprofit arts organizations*, Joseph Cordes considers the nature and distribution of the subsidies for not-for-profit organizations, focusing particularly on the tax benefits. The paper discusses conceptual and measurement issues that arise in estimating the value of these subsidies, and uses a new comprehensive data set on the financial characteristics of more than 7000 nonprofit arts organizations to estimate the economic value and incidence of direct and indirect subsidies to the arts. The estimates indicate that in 1999 these organizations received on the order of $3 billion in direct and indirect subsidies, of which about two-thirds is attributable to tax incentives for giving, and the nonprofit exemption from income and property taxes. Art museums and media-related arts providers seemed to benefit more from these subsidies than did other providers. As in other areas of American social policy, the estimated pattern of subsidies, both direct and indirect, results from a host of decentralized decisions made by federal, state and local governments, private donors and not-for-profit organizations. As Cordes notes, these are unlikely to be identical to the patterns that would emerge from a more direct subsidy program of equal magnitude. The paper concludes with a discussion of the relative merits of a more direct system of public support for the arts.

Taken as a whole, the papers in this volume address important issues in financing local government, the economics of urban public services and not-for-profit organizations. Following in the tradition of Dick Netzer's work, they bring to bear both theoretical and empirical tools in an effort to provide analysis that illuminates problems and make progress in identifying solutions. At the same time, the papers suggest that more work needs to be done. What is the appropriate tax mix for local governments? What role might a land value tax play? What is the implication of relying upon the private sector to produce or provide public services? How large are external effects and what efficiency gains might be obtained by accounting for them, whether these externalities derive from public services, such as housing, or from peer group effects in education? What role should government play in supporting not-for-profit organizations? It is hoped that this volume will inspire others to follow the example set by Dick Netzer in endeavoring to provide answers.

NOTES

1. See Slemrod (1997).
2. Chapter X, 'Urban Economics: Research and Training Needs', p.1.
3. Dick Netzer contributed many letters to the editor of the *New York Times,* typically displaying his sharp wit, logical thinking and strongly held views on public policy issues, sometimes on issues of culture or history and, not uncommonly, attracting an indignant response from the wounded subject. I am aware of no instance in which he admitted being in the wrong.
4. *The Voluntary Nonprofit Sector: An Economic Analysis*, by Burton Weisbrod, for example, was only published in 1977.

REFERENCES

Slemrod, Joel (1997), 'The NTJ Hall of Fame', *National Tax Journal*, **50** (4), 751–3.

Weisbrod, Burton A. (1997), T*he Voluntary Nonprofit Sector: An Economic Analysis*, Lexington, US: Lexington Books.

2. What should local governments tax: income or property?

Wallace E. Oates and Robert M. Schwab*

INTRODUCTION

The property tax has long been the primary source of tax revenues for local government in the United States. As John Wallis (2001) has documented in his excellent history of the property tax in the USA, the tax has a long and rich history, dating back to the origins of our nation. In fact, in the 18th and 19th centuries, the tax was used, at various junctures, by all the various levels of government, but, over the course of the 20th century, its use became associated nearly exclusively with local government.

At the same time, local property taxation has long been a contentious issue. The tax has been the source of continuing dissatisfaction from many quarters. During the latter part of the 20th century, for example, a forceful judicial attack called into question the constitutionality of local property taxation as a source of finance for public schools. The basic charge has been that the tax base is distributed unequally among local jurisdictions, giving rise to unjustifiable fiscal disparities in the funding of public education. This has led several states to restructure their systems of school finance so as to place less reliance on property taxation.

The primary candidate as an alternative tax base to that of property for local governments is income.[1] Indeed, some students of local finance have argued that local income taxation would offer a more efficient and equitable source of local tax revenues than does property taxation. It is our purpose in this chapter to review this debate. In addition to the more traditional arguments, some recent analysis of taxation sheds new light on the issue. We find that the new 'double-dividend' literature from environmental taxation has an interesting application here that suggests that the standard excess-burden argument against the 'pyramiding' of local income tax rates on top of state and federal rates may not have much force. But this

* We thank Jennifer Godwin for her excellent work as our research assistant on this project. We are also grateful to Helen Ladd, Ian Parry and Andrew Reschovsky for some very helpful comments on an earlier draft of this paper.

must be balanced against the older and more traditional administrative argument for the 'separation of sources'.

We begin our study with a brief review of the actual use of property and income taxation by local government in the USA. (In fact, the income tax is little used by local governments; in only a few states does its use reach outside some major cities.) We then move on to a conceptual analysis of the workings of the two taxes in a setting of local government finance. Here we find that modern fiscal analysis offers some provocative insights into the comparative appeal of the two taxes to set alongside more traditional considerations.

In addition to our conceptual analysis, we have undertaken one new piece of empirical research in which we try to answer the disparities question. The legality of local property taxation for purposes of financing public schools, as we noted, has been called into question because of the disparities in the distribution of the property tax base across local school districts. A natural question that arises in our study is whether or not a shift away from local property taxation to the income tax would resolve this problem. In short, the question here is whether or not the distribution of the tax base among school districts under a local income tax is more or less equal than under a property tax. We answer that question, making use of a rich database from four large states in the USA.

Finally, we point out that our study has one important and basic premise: the need for local government to finance a substantial portion of its budget from own revenues. Therese McGuire has recently raised the question: 'Do local governments need a major own-tax source?' (2001, p.306). With increased reliance in the USA on state aid for local school finance and in view of the heavy dependence of local government in much of western Europe on intergovernmental transfers, McGuire questions whether it is necessary or important for local government to be fiscally autonomous: that is, to finance a large part of its own spending.

For the purposes of this chapter, we take the answer to this question to be yes. Local taxes provide a crucial fiscal link that encourages jurisdictions to weigh the benefits of proposed programs against their costs. If local expenditures are financed by transfers from above, this link is broken and expenditure decisions become largely a matter of negotiations between local authorities and higher-level agencies that provide the funding. This is not to say that local governments need finance the entirety of their budgets from own revenues. Some fraction of revenues may surely come in the form of intergovernmental grants in order, for example, to alleviate the problem of fiscal disparities. But it is especially important that decisions at the margin be funded locally. When decisions are being made to expand or contract programs, local funding promotes the weighing of benefits against costs. We thus take it as given, for the purposes of this chapter, that local governments require a source of own revenues with which to finance a substantial share of their expenditures.

We are especially pleased to contribute this chapter to a festschrift in honor of Dick Netzer. Netzer's research and writing on issues in local taxation and finance, spanning several decades, have guided and illuminated work in this field. His splendid book, *Economics of the Property Tax* (1966), is still a valuable resource for work on property taxation; we have drawn on it in this chapter. We are grateful for the opportunity to salute and celebrate his past and continuing contributions to public finance.

LOCAL TAXATION IN PRACTICE

It will be helpful at the outset simply to examine the structure of local revenue systems in the USA to get some sense of the role that property taxation and income taxes have actually played in local finance. Table 2.1 provides a historical description of the percentage shares of various sources of revenues for local governments and calls to our attention several noteworthy features of local finance in the USA. First, we find that, over the course of the past century, intergovernmental grants have come to have increasing importance to local government. These transfers accounted for only about 6 per cent of local government revenues in 1902; by 1980, this had risen to almost 40 per cent of local revenues, with substantial increases occurring during the period of judicial attacks on local revenue systems in the 1970s. This trend, however, stopped after 1980, with a decline in the share of grant revenues to about 34 per cent by 1996.

Second, we see the primacy of property taxation in systems of local taxes. Property taxes have always accounted for the lion's share of local tax revenues, and they continue to do so. It is true that the share of property tax revenues in total local revenues has fallen significantly over the past century, from about two-thirds of local revenues in 1902 to around one-quarter of local revenues in 1996. But property tax receipts continue to constitute over two-thirds of local tax revenues.

Third, we see in Table 2.1 that income taxes have never played a large role in US local finances. Nonexistent in 1902, they came into being over the course of the century, but have never accounted for more than 2 per cent of local revenues. These figures mask the wide variation in use across different states. As we see in Table 2.2, most states make no use of local income taxation. For the country as a whole (including the 50 states and the District of Columbia), they are the source of less than 6 per cent of local tax revenues. Moreover, the significant use of local income taxation is confined to

Table 2.1 Sources of local government revenues as a percentage of total local government revenues for selected fiscal years

Year	Intergovernmental grants	Own sources	Taxes	Property taxes	Sales taxes	Income taxes
1902	6.13	93.87	77.02	68.27	0	0
1932	13.10	86.90	69.02	67.17	0.42	0
1950	27.50	72.50	49.59	43.74	3.01	0.40
1960	27.10	72.90	48.44	42.33	3.59	0.68
1970	33.14	66.86	43.59	37.00	3.44	1.83
1980	39.65	60.35	33.44	25.40	4.67	1.93
1990	32.87	67.13	34.67	25.81	5.31	1.96
1996	33.65	66.35	33.67	24.82	5.33	1.99

Source: Tax Foundation, *Facts and Figures on Government Finance*, 31st edn (Washington, DC, 1997), Table F19, p.261.

a few states and the District of Columbia.[2] In only four states and the District of Columbia do local income taxes make up more than 15 per cent of local tax revenues. Maryland places the heaviest reliance on this source of revenues, where counties (the major unit of local government in the state) 'piggyback' onto the state income tax. In Pennsylvania, Philadelphia (the largest city in the state) employs a wage tax in which unearned income is excluded and the tax is paid at a flat rate directly by employers in the city on their wage bill; some other cities and school districts in Pennsylvania also use a tax on earned income. In contrast, the District of Columbia and New York City make use of more conventional forms of the income tax that tax all forms of income with a progressive rate structure. In Kentucky, two cities, Lexington and Louisville, and county governments tax earned income at a flat rate while, in Ohio, many municipalities and school districts use a tax on earned income and corporate net profits. School districts in Iowa simply piggyback on the state income tax. Thus, even with its limited use in the USA, we find a variety of forms and administration of local income taxation. But the tax is not a major feature of local fiscal structure in the USA.

TAXATION AND EFFICIENT LOCAL FINANCE

There is now an enormous literature, reaching back to the seminal Tiebout (1956) paper nearly 50 years ago, whose evolution has produced a well-defined (if still contentious) view of efficient local public finance. In a

Table 2.2 Local income tax receipts as a percentage of total local tax collections for fiscal year 1996

State	Percentage	State	Percentage
Alabama	2.8	Nevada	0
Alaska	0	New Hampshire	0
Arizona	0	New Jersey	0.2
Arkansas	0	New Mexico	0
California	0	New York	10.4
Colorado	0	North Carolina	0
Connecticut	0	North Dakota	0
Delaware	9.2	Ohio	23.8
Florida	0	Oklahoma	0
Georgia	0	Oregon	0
Hawaii	0	Pennsylvania	17.7
Idaho	0	Rhode Island	0
Illinois	0	South Carolina	0
Indiana	9.3	South Dakota	0
Iowa	1.0	Tennessee	0
Kansas	0	Texas	0
Kentucky	24.8	Utah	0
Louisiana	0	Vermont	0
Maine	0	Virginia	0
Maryland	30.3	Washington	0
Massachusetts	0	West Virginia	0
Michigan	7.3	Wisconsin	0
Minnesota	0	Wyoming	0
Mississippi	0		
Missouri	5.6	District of Columbia	27.8
Montana	0		
Nebraska	0	Total US	5.9

Source: Tax Foundation, *Facts and Figures on Government Finance,* 34th edn (Washington, DC, 2000), Table F27, pp.306–7.

Tiebout world, with a large number of local communities offering a wide array of outputs of local public services, households choose a community of residence that satisfies their preferences for local services. These services are financed by local taxes that play the role of prices in guiding individual choices so that, as in a private market, the equilibrium outcome is one in which marginal benefits equal marginal costs.

What is of central importance for our purposes is the nature of local taxation in this world. Tiebout himself had little to say about this, but the subsequent literature has devoted much attention to the tax issue. In principle, what is needed is for local governments to charge a head tax to each resident household equal to the marginal cost of supplying the particular level of local services available in the community. But such head taxes are not normally a part of the public finance landscape. In an ingenious extension of the Tiebout model, Bruce Hamilton (1975) showed that the introduction of a local zoning rule that specifies a minimum level of housing consumption effectively converts the local property tax into a head tax of precisely the sort required to generate an efficient Tiebout outcome. In a Tiebout–Hamilton world, households choose a community of residence that offers their preferred levels both of public services and of housing. In equilibrium, Tiebout communities are thus homogeneous in both public service and housing consumption. Although the requirements for such a model are, in the limit, very demanding, a number of authors (for example, Fischel, 1992) have argued that this view of local finance is a sufficiently close approximation to reality to have real predictive and normative significance.

More recently, William Fischel (2001) has extended the model to incorporate 'politics'. Fischel's argument is that local communities, operating in the context of a local property tax, function in certain crucial ways like corporations. In short, the Fischel world is one in which local officials (behaving analogously to corporate boards of directors) choose the mix of spending, taxes and land-use regulations so as to maximize the value of homes in the community. This implies that local fiscal and land-use decisions will employ a benefit–cost criterion: officials will put in place measures (including levels of local outputs or zoning regulations) for which the benefits to the community exceed their costs. This follows since any net benefits (positive or negative) become capitalized into house values.

Capitalization is the centerpiece of this view, since local property values are taken to mirror faithfully the benefits and costs of local policy choices.[3] As Fischel puts it, 'local governments are very different from state and national governments, primarily because voters at the municipal level know taxes and services affect their home values. This difference makes the property tax a benefit tax at the local level and a source of deadweight loss at the state or national level' (2001, p.34).

The interesting question for our purposes here is how this analysis is affected by the substitution of local income taxation for property taxes. Let us return first to the original Tiebout world, a world of mobile households without any local zoning measures to constrain housing consumption. Oates (1972, pp.131–40) has examined this case. As an efficient benchmark, consider a setting in which a large set of local communities finances a broad array of local outputs with a head tax equal to the marginal cost of financing services for an additional household. Here the head tax plays precisely the same role as a price in a private market.

Now let us introduce a local property tax as the instrument to finance local spending in lieu of the head tax. It is straightforward to see that this introduces a distortion that takes the form of underconsumption of housing. The point here is that the price of housing now incorporates the cost of local services. A household contemplating an expansion in its housing consumption finds that such a choice will mean a higher property tax liability. And this tax component of the price of housing will induce the household to purchase too little housing. This phenomenon, incidentally, is well understood in the literature; it is central to the so-called 'new view' of the property tax (for example, Zodrow, 2001). Morever, as shown first by Zodrow and Mieszkowski (1986), this can also result in communities choosing a suboptimal provision of local public services.[4]

As a further complication, local property taxation can also distort locational choices and raise issues concerning the existence and stability of equilibria. The point here is that a household's tax-price for local services now depends on the value of the property in the community. Communities with highly valued property can finance a given budget with a lower tax *rate*. Thus it is in the interest of a household to locate in a property-rich jurisdiction with low tax rates per unit of services so as to obtain these services at a lower tax-price. This can, in principle, generate a game of fiscal 'musical chairs', as people chase one another from low property value, to high property value, communities.[5]

But, as we have noted, these distortions can be remedied under a system of local property taxation by the introduction of a zoning ordinance taking the form of Hamilton's minimum housing consumption requirement. This converts the local property tax back to a benefit tax and restores both efficiency and stability to equilibria in the local public sector.[6]

What about an income tax? Let us assume that, instead of a head tax, local governments finance their spending through the use of a proportional income tax. Here the familiar basic distortion involves the work–leisure choice: the tax discourages work effort by reducing the net return below the productive value of labor. But, in a system of local finance, there will be further distorting consequences. First, note that a household's tax-price will now depend upon its income; under a proportional income tax, the higher the income, the higher the household's tax bill for any given level of public services and tax rate. This serves to reinforce the basic work–leisure distortion under the income tax, as individuals will now have an enhanced incentive to avoid additional work effort. Second, we get much the same sorts of locational distortions and stability problems as under the property tax. Here households will have an incentive to seek out jurisdictions composed of high-income residents, where the large tax base will result in relatively low tax rates. We can again envision some kind of fiscal musical chairs with lower-income households pursuing high-income residents who, in turn, themselves seek to escape to higher-income jurisdictions.

An interesting question here is whether or not a Hamilton zoning ordinance can restore efficiency and stability under an income tax regime. The answer would appear to be no, since such an ordinance sets a floor on housing consumption, not on income. Irrespective of their housing consumption, households would still have an incentive to seek out high-income communities of residence. But housing consumption is, of course, strongly correlated with income. In the limiting case where this positive correlation is perfect, the floor on housing consumption would become effectively a minimum income requirement and efficiency would be restored. An equilibrium in the system would be characterized by communities that are homogeneous in housing consumption and income, and this would convert the local income tax into a pure benefit (or head) tax. But in the more general case where this correlation is less than perfect, we would expect to find some efficiency losses associated with local income taxation.

An important issue here is the likely magnitude of these deadweight losses. Timothy Goodspeed (1989) has addressed this issue through the use of a general equilibrium numerical model in which he simulates the impact of local income taxation relative to a benchmark case of a local head tax. As expected, the income tax turns out to be less efficient than the head tax in this exercise, but the magnitude of the loss is modest. Moreover, the move from the head tax to the income tax achieves some income equalization. Goodspeed's sense is that the efficiency case against local income taxation may not be very strong.

Let us next return to Fischel's world which supplements Tiebout with politics. Here the argument is that, in the presence of capitalization, local property taxation induces local decision makers, in their quest to maximize local property values, to extend local programs to their efficient levels where marginal benefits equal marginal cost. The positive net benefits of these programs will then manifest themselves in an increase in local property values. But this argument seems basically applicable as well to a system of local income taxation. Other things equal, differentials across local communities in income tax rates will tend to be capitalized into local property values, just as will local differentials in property tax rates. Any program that promises more in the way of benefits than the associated tax liability should produce an increase in local property values under either system of taxation. In consequence, Fischel's politics argument does not appear to favor either system of taxation over the other.

There are two remaining issues that serve to complicate matters even further. First, the Fischel politics argument applies with its clearest force to homeowners. These are the households who see that the value of their homes depends on local fiscal decisions. It is a somewhat different matter for occupants of rental dwellings. The quality of local services and levels of local taxes will tend to manifest themselves in levels of local rents, but this is often only imperfectly perceived and may take place with a substantial time lag. Indeed, there is some evidence that suggests that renters are far more likely to support larger local budgets than are homeowners, a result perhaps of a perception by renters that they do not bear the burden of local property taxes (Oates, 1998). Roughly two-thirds of US households are homeowners, so those communities, largely suburban ones, may behave in the Fischel spirit. But the Fischel case is much less compelling for US center cities where renters constitute a major part of the population. In a city setting, a local income tax may have some real advantages in terms of visibility among residents.[7]

Second, there is another important difference between income and property taxation. The latter includes commercial and industrial property in the tax base, while the former typically taxes only resident households. And this can have some important efficiency implications. Local government provides public services not only for residents but for local business as well. Police, fire, transport, refuse collection and other public services provide important benefits for the local business sector, and in an efficient world firms should pay the marginal cost of the services that they receive from the local public sector (Oates and Schwab, 1991). An income tax on residents completely misses this part of the local public finance nexus. A uniform property tax within a local jurisdiction is unlikely to constitute a perfect benefit tax, but it at least places some tax burden on local commercial–industrial property.

Our journey through the sometimes arcane world of the theory of local finance does not seem, in our view at least, to produce an overwhelming sense that one of our two systems of local taxation is to be heavily preferred over the other on pure efficiency grounds. Property taxation seems to get the upper hand in the sense that a pure Hamilton–Tiebout equilibrium is fully efficient. But such an equilibrium, as we all recognize, can only be, at best, a very rough approximation to reality. Both systems involve the capitalization of fiscal differentials across jurisdictions. Since it encompasses both residential and commercial–industrial sources, local property taxation may get the nod here (at least in a suburban setting), but it is not clear on the basis of the discussion to this point that the efficiency differences between the two systems of local taxation are large. It is time to compare them from some other perspectives.

THE PYRAMIDING OF TAX RATES, SEPARATION OF SOURCES AND SOME SECOND-BEST ISSUES

In the debate over these two local tax bases, proponents of local property taxation sometimes call upon the so-called doctrine of the 'separation of sources'. The idea here is that the use of the income tax by local government involves a major instance of tax overlapping: the income tax is heavily relied upon by both federal and state levels of government, and its use also by local government means that three different levels of government are taxing the same base. Better, so the argument goes, for local government to have its own tax base, namely property, and leave income taxation to federal and state governments. A more desirable tax structure from this perspective is one in which different levels of government have their own sources of revenues – or, in short, where there is a separation of sources.

This argument relies, in part, on the likely increase in excess burden that results from the pyramiding of tax rates that occurs when several levels of government tax the same base. In our case, the combined marginal tax rates on income of federal and state governments can be quite high. And the existing estimates of the excess burden of marginal increases in these rates are large (Browning, 1987).

In a simple, partial equilibrium framework, it is straightforward to show that the level of excess burden varies positively and exponentially with the tax rate. More specifically, an excise tax on any good or activity, in the simplest kind of model, has an excess burden (*EB*) equal to:

$$EB = (1/2)(T^2/N)(E_d E_s)/(E_d + E_s), \tag{2.1}$$

where T is the tax rate, N is consumer expenditure on the good, E_d is the price elasticity of demand (absolute value) and E_s is the price elasticity of supply. Here we find that the excess burden of a tax varies directly with the square of the tax rate, so that the marginal excess burden rises with the level of the rate. This suggests that local government, rather than piling on yet higher combined rates of income taxation, would do better to tax an activity that is not being taxed by other levels of government.

But this line of argument is not fully compelling for at least two reasons. First, as equation (2.1) indicates, there are other parameters that determine the level of excess burden: in particular, the price elasticities of demand and supply. It is not entirely clear which way this consideration cuts. The supply of work effort overall is thought to be price-inelastic (probably more so than the supply of housing). But it is uncertain whether the price elasticity of demand is greater for labor or for housing consumption. It may be the case that the excess burden from income taxation is somewhat lower than that from property taxes because of the price-elasticities of demand and supply.[8]

Second, the analysis is partial equilibrium in character. When we put the analysis in the context of a general equilibrium system, especially one with pre-existing distortions from other forms of taxation, some new considerations arise. There is an interesting and important new literature that has arisen in the context of environmental taxes that provides some surprising, indeed startling, results. This literature has involved a reconsideration of the use of Pigouvian taxes to internalize the external costs of polluting activities.[9] In the absence of other distorting taxes, such Pigouvian taxes, equal to marginal social damage, can correct the existing distortion in polluting activities and restore a state of Pareto efficiency. However, in a second-best setting with other distorting taxes, most notably a tax on labor income, the analysis changes character. The tax on pollution, by raising the cost and price of pollution-intensive goods, now exacerbates the existing distortion in the work–leisure choice associated with the income tax by reducing the real wage (and hence the return to work effort). What is astonishing about these studies is how large in magnitude this indirect, and apparently second-order, effect can be. Numerical analyses, making use of computable general equilibrium (CGE) models, find that, in some circumstances, the second-best optimal tax on pollution is well below the level of marginal social damages. Moreover, if the revenues from the tax are not used to reduce the rates of other distorting taxes, the first-best Pigouvian levy can, under certain circumstances, even reduce total welfare. The general presumption arising from this (and earlier studies of efficiency in taxation) is that a broader tax base is likely to be preferred to a more narrow one in order to limit the potential for distorting substitution.

This line of analysis has obvious relevance to our problem, for it suggests that we should consider local property taxation in the context of a system with an existing (and large) income tax. In this setting, the property tax raises the price of housing consumption, a major item in household budgets, which reduces the return to work effort and thereby increases the welfare loss from the distortion in the work–leisure choice. More generally, there is a presumption in favor of income over property taxation because it represents a more inclusive tax base. Although we have not tried to construct a CGE model to obtain actual estimates of the magnitude of this effect, we suggest that such an exercise might prove useful. At any rate, this body of work certainly raises some reservations concerning the simple pyramiding-of-rates argument in favor of local property taxation.

INCIDENCE, TAX ADMINISTRATION AND SOME OTHER MATTERS

A central issue in the design of a tax system is the fairness or equity of the system. Invoking the ability-to-pay criterion on equity grounds, proponents of local income taxation frequently cite the progressive character of income taxes in their case against the local property tax. The income tax is a progressive tax; the property tax, in contrast, is a regressive tax, since housing expenditure makes up a smaller fraction of the income of higher-income households. Income, so the argument goes, is thus a superior measure of ability-to-pay than is the value of one's house.

On further examination, however, this argument is not so straightforward as it appears. First, local income taxes are typically not very progressive; often they are simply flat-rate taxes (such as the Philadelphia wage tax), although they may still possess some progressivity from an exempted level of income.[10] Second, the property tax may be much less regressive than it appears. Housing consumption is highly correlated with income, so that a proportional tax on property values may not differ greatly in its progression from a proportional income tax. Indeed, it has been argued that housing consumption provides a better measure of 'permanent income' than does current income. At any rate, it seems clear that the alleged regressivity of property taxation is much less when it is measured against permanent, rather than current, income (Netzer, 1966, p.42).

Yet more basic, under the so-called 'new view' of the property tax (first propounded by Peter Mieszkowski, 1972), the average rate of property taxation across all localities is seen as a general tax on capital. From this perspective, the tax becomes quite progressive, since ownership of the nation's stock of capital is strongly skewed in favor of high-income households. Thus, according to the 'new view' (which is not so 'new' now), the property tax is a progressive, not a regressive, tax.

But even this dispute can be seen in a wholly different light if we return to a Tiebout–Hamilton world of local finance. In such a setting, incidence is less relevant, for one's property tax bill directly represents the price of local services. There is no redistribution of income in the local public sector: people simply get what they pay for, just as in a private market. Redistribution is not an issue here.

The incidence issue (like the efficiency issue) is thus a complicated one for our comparison of local income and property taxation. There is, however, a related strand of argument that has some force both in principle and in practice: the life cycle and cyclical patterns of tax liability under the two forms of taxation. A case can be made for income taxation on the grounds that it provides a better match over time of tax payments with current income. Older and retired individuals, for example, sometimes find that, with their reduced retirement incomes, they are hard-pressed to meet their continuing property tax liabilities, especially if these liabilities are rising as a result of reassessments and/or increasing local budgets. Likewise, individuals who experience a temporary shortfall of income may have difficulty in paying their property tax bills. In contrast, one's tax liability under an income tax adjusts automatically, for the current tax payment varies directly with the household's level of current income. Recognizing this problem, many states have introduced 'circuit-breaker' rules that limit property tax payments as a fraction of current income. But this rather ad hoc kind of measure seems less satisfactory than simply tying current tax bills to current income.

But even this advantage of income taxes has its downside. One appealing feature of the local property tax is the stability of the revenues that it provides for local government. Property tax receipts, since they depend on assessed values that are revised only periodically, are not very responsive to cyclical changes in income. If the economy slides into recession and incomes fall, the local public sector is largely shielded from the recessionary pressures through stable property tax liabilities. Under an income tax, of course, local revenues fluctuate with the state of the economy. Thus what is good for taxpayers in terms of matching tax bills with income is not good for them in terms of maintaining a stable flow of revenues for their local governments.

Finally, the issue of tax administration and cost would seem to favor local income taxation. This is a case where tax overlapping among levels of government provides a real benefit. Since most state governments have income taxes, it can be a straightforward matter for localities simply to piggyback on the state tax and thereby rely on the existing state agency to handle the administration and collection of the tax. All the local government need do is choose the local tax rate; the state government can then collect the tax as a simple 'add-on' to the state income tax liability and refund the applicable portion to the local government. Property taxation, in contrast, involves a whole separate administrative apparatus that requires the definition and 'discovery' of the tax base and the assessment of property values. Substantial progress and improvements have been made through the years in the administration of the tax, especially in assessment procedures, but it continues to be a source of taxpayer discontent, with a host of associated legal issues (Youngman, 1994).

PROPERTY TAXATION AND SCHOOL FINANCE: THE DISPARITIES ISSUE

The property tax has long been a cornerstone of the US system of school finance. Local governments provide roughly one-half of the resources devoted to public education in the USA, and they raise nearly two-thirds of those funds through the property tax. The property tax is virtually the only source of tax revenue for independent school districts (that is, school districts that are not part of a municipality or county government).

This reliance on the property tax lies at the heart of a long string of court cases that have challenged the constitutionality of local funding of public schools. Critics have argued that the property tax is inherently unfair, because large disparities in tax bases across school districts lead inevitably to large differences in spending. In the landmark 1971 case, *Serrano* v. *Priest*, the California State Supreme Court declared the state's system of public school finance unconstitutional. In this case, the plaintiffs' attorneys showed that Beverly Hills spent more than twice as much per student as Baldwin Park, a low-income community 25 miles east of Los Angeles. Because of Beverly Hills' larger tax base, however, its school property tax rate was less than half of Baldwin Park's (Fischel, 1996). The court ordered the state to develop a system where school support did not depend on district wealth; the new system must satisfy the principle of 'fiscal neutrality'.

Litigation in other states soon followed. California is one of 43 states where opponents of local funding for primary and secondary schools have challenged the constitutionality of the system of public school finance. The courts have overturned systems in 20 states and upheld systems in 20 others; cases are still pending in the remaining three. In addition, litigation has been filed in a number of states where the state supreme court had already ruled. In New Jersey, for example, there have now been six major separate supreme court decisions in school finance cases since 1973.

State governments have offered a wide range of responses both to these legal challenges and to broad concerns over inequities in public school spending associated with inequality in property tax wealth. State legislatures have, for example, implemented or revised equalization formulas and increased their state's share of educational spending. In this section of the chapter, we look at a different strategy. Suppose school districts switched from a property tax to a local income tax. Would differences in tax bases across school districts rise, fall or remain roughly constant as a result?

The ideal data set for this analysis would include detailed information on the property tax base and income for each of the 15000 school districts in the USA. The *1990 Census School District Special Tabulation, School District Data Book* provides socioeconomic data for nearly all school districts. Unfortunately, no single source provides similar data on property wealth. As a consequence, it is very difficult to look at all districts in all states. Instead, we have chosen four large states where district-level data on property wealth are available from the state governments: Massachusetts, New Jersey, New York and Texas. (The supreme courts in three of these states, Massachusetts, New Jersey and Texas, have overturned their state's system of school finance; a New York case is still going on.) We then combined the 1990 Census data on income and the data from the states on property wealth in order to compare the inequality in the distribution of the bases for a property tax and a local income tax. We suspect that there are significant differences across the four states in the definition of property wealth. We therefore limit our analysis to within state differences in wealth and income and do not look at any differences across states. We provide a description of the data in our appendix.

Our goal is to compare the distribution of income per student and property wealth per student across school districts. District enrollments are highly skewed. Nationally, roughly one-third of all public school students are enrolled in about 2 per cent of all school districts. A similar pattern emerges in the four states we study here. For example, New York state had 687 school districts and more than 2.6 million public school students in 1992. Over 37 per cent of those students lived in New York City; 34 districts had fewer than 270 students. We therefore weight our district data by enrollment in order to account for differences in size.

We have developed two measures of the inequality in the base for a property tax and a local income tax across districts, the Theil index and the ratio of the tax base at the 95th percentile to the tax base at the fifth percentile. For tax base i (where i is either income or property wealth) and state k, the Theil index T_{ik} equals

$$T_{ik} \frac{\sum_{j=1}^{Jk} P_{jk} X_{ijk} \ln \left(X_{ijk} / \overline{X}_{ik} \right)}{\sum_{j=1}^{Jk} P_{jk} X_{ijk}}, \tag{2.2}$$

where X_{ijk} is the tax base per pupil in district j, J_k is the number of districts in state k, P_{jk} is the fall enrollment in district j in state k, and $\bar{X}_{ik}$ is the pupil-weighted mean tax base per pupil for the state. A value of zero on the Theil index indicates perfect equality in the tax base among districts. The index reaches the natural log of state enrollment when one district has the entire tax base and the rest have nothing. The effect of a transfer among districts on the Theil index depends on the ratio of tax bases for the districts. A \$100 transfer between districts with relatively equal resources will lead to a smaller drop in the Theil index than will a $100 transfer between districts with very unequal resources.

The construction of our second measure is straightforward. For each tax base, we rank districts within each state in terms of tax base per pupil. We then calculate the ratio of the tax base at the 95th percentile of this distribution to the tax base at the fifth percentile of this distribution. By construction, this second measure is insensitive to extremely large or small values. Unlike the Theil index, this measure equals one if the tax base per student is the same across all districts: that is, if we have perfect equality.

Table 2.3 95/5 ratio and Theil index: property wealth and income per pupil, Massachusetts, New Jersey, New York and Texas, 1990

	Massachusetts	New Jersey	New York	Texas
95/5 ratio				
Property wealth per pupil	4.88	7.00	6.89	7.49
Income per pupil	3.28	4.34	3.18	4.97
Theil index				
Property wealth per pupil	0.115	0.215	0.192	0.174
Income per pupil	0.068	0.104	0.064	0.086

Table 2.3 presents two sets of measures for tax base inequality per pupil. The message from the table seems quite clear: property wealth is distributed much more unequally across districts than is income. Consider first the 95/5 ratios shown in rows one and two of Table 2.3. There are significant differences in income across districts in all four states. Income per pupil in the richest districts in Texas, for example, is nearly five times as large as income per pupil in the poorest districts. In all four states, this ratio of income per pupil in the richest to the poorest districts is over three. But differences in property wealth per pupil are even larger than these differences in income. In New York, New Jersey and Texas, the property tax base per pupil in the wealthiest districts is roughly seven times as large as that in the poorest districts. In all four states, inequality in property wealth (as measured by our 95/5 ratio) is at least 50 per cent higher than inequality in income; in New York it is more than twice as high.

The Theil indices in the lower panel of Table 2.3 tell a similar story. Inequality in property wealth per pupil is roughly three times as high as inequality in income per pupil in New York, twice as high in New Jersey and Texas, and 1.7 times as high in Massachusetts.

We must admit that we found ourselves somewhat surprised by these results. We had no strong priors on the likely outcome, but, if anything, we probably expected roughly similar degrees of inequality under both tax bases. In fact, we would not have been too surprised to find less inequality in property wealth per pupil than in income per pupil. There are some quite poor residential areas in terms of income that are embedded in a heavily industrialized setting, and one might expect that such districts, although poor in income, would be relatively well off under property taxation because of a large nonresidential tax base. To investigate this issue in more depth, we examined the cases of some urban school districts. We report these findings in Table 2.4. For our first case in row one, we see that the ratio of property wealth per pupil in the New Bedford School District to property wealth per pupil in the state of Massachusetts is 0.398; for income, this ratio is 0.538. In fact, for every case in Table 2.4, property wealth per pupil is less relative to the state average than is income per pupil. The Camden District in New Jersey is a particularly striking case. Here we find that income per pupil is less than one-quarter of income per pupil in New Jersey. But the situation is far worse under property taxation: Camden's property tax base per pupil is only 11 per cent of the state average. We note that the districts that we chose to include in Table 2.4 are not outliers. If we were to

Table 2.4 *Ratio of district property wealth per pupil to state property wealth per pupil and ratio of district income per pupil to state income per pupil, selected school districts, 1990*

	Property wealth per pupil	Income per pupil
Massachusetts		
New Bedford	0.398	0.538
Springfield	0.498	0.599
Lowell	0.542	0.687
Worcester	0.654	0.795
New Jersey		
Camden	0.107	0.248
Newark	0.295	0.401
Paterson	0.323	0.498
Trenton	0.360	0.615
New York		
Buffalo	0.361	0.644
Utica	0.480	0.716
Syracuse	0.522	0.748
Rochester	0.595	0.726
Texas		
Laredo	0.232	0.321
El Paso	0.572	0.734

present similar data for all of the school districts in the four states, we would show that disparities in property wealth tax wealth between rich and poor districts are significantly greater than differences in income in nearly all cases.[11]

Our findings thus indicate with little ambiguity that tax-base disparities across school districts would be significantly less under local income taxation than under property taxation. But we should not exaggerate the importance of this. Tables 2.3 and 2.4 show that, even with local income taxation, there would remain large differences in the tax base per pupil across school districts. Local income taxation most certainly will not cure the disparities problem; it will alleviate it somewhat. But it seems to us unlikely that a shift in tax base from property to income would *in itself* provide an acceptable response to the courts' objections to existing systems of school finance.

CONCLUDING REMARKS

Our odyssey through the vast literature and wide-ranging issues associated with local income and property taxation has not, in our view, led us to a clear-cut conclusion concerning the superiority of one tax base over the other. While local income taxation may get the nod on grounds of administrative simplicity and cost, the relative merits of the two taxes are far less clear in terms of economic efficiency, equity and the critical role that local taxes play in facilitating local fiscal decision making. In fact, it is our sense that both of these taxes provide workable and reasonably efficient sources of local revenues. Local finance can probably function effectively, in the USA at least, making use of either tax.

Our major empirical finding in this chapter is the sizeable reduction in tax-base disparities that would occur under a move to local income taxation. However, as we noted, significant differences in tax base per pupil across school districts would remain. There would still be a need for equalizing transfers from the state government, although they would presumably be somewhat smaller in magnitude.

In our summing up, we want to return briefly to the issue of local fiscal choice and the tax base. There is another aspect of the separation of sources concept that has, we believe, some relevance here. In opting for local income taxation, local government in the USA becomes involved in a major instance of tax overlapping, as the income tax is a primary source of revenues at both the federal and the state levels. On the one hand, this has some advantages; as we have noted, this can serve to simplify administration and reduce collection costs for local governments. But, on the other hand, it brings with it a more subtle problem. There is a visibility issue here. With local income taxation, one's tax payment is typically lumped together with taxes paid to other levels of government in a way that serves to obscure the distinctly local component of the tax bill. And this may well weaken the link between local spending and taxes.

Under local property taxation, we have a real separation of sources. Local government has its own tax base, distinct from state and federal levels, and households and local businesses know that their local tax bills are going to finance local services. This should enhance local control and accountability. This is quite different from a system of local income taxation, where the local tax payment is bundled together with a state tax liability. This particular attraction of local property taxation is difficult to formalize in an economic model, or to quantify, but it is our sense that it is potentially significant and might well swing the balance in the choice of a system of local taxation.[12]

In addition, there is the basic maxim of taxation that 'An old tax is a good tax'. The local property tax has been around for a long time in the USA, and any radical change to replace it with local income taxation would set in motion (among other things) a widespread and major set of windfall gains and losses. But this is admittedly a transitory matter that should not weigh too heavily in our deliberations.

Finally, we want simply to note that there is a further variation on property taxation that we have not addressed in this chapter. The tax need not apply the same rate both to the value of land and to the value of the structures on the land. Some cities in Pennsylvania, for example, employ a two-tier system of property taxes under which the rate on structures is less than that on land. In the limit, of course, the tax rate on structures can be zero, thereby converting the tax into a pure tax on land value. Land-value taxation, as has long been recognized, has some very appealing properties. For one, it eliminates any distortions associated with the taxation of capital. Although this issue goes beyond the scope of our chapter, it is an appropriate matter to raise in closing, for it has been of longstanding interest to Dick Netzer (for example, 1998).

NOTES

1. A third significant source of local tax revenues is the sales tax. But this can hardly be the basic source of taxation for local government. Indeed, many local governments encompass what are strictly residential areas; they have a zero sales tax base.
2. James Rodgers and Judy Temple (1996) provide a useful description of the structure and use of local income taxation in individual states in the USA.
3. There is widespread evidence of the presence of capitalization. Since the study by Oates (1969) that found the capitalization of local tax and spending differentials across a sample of northern New Jersey communities, dozens of studies have found that many

dimensions of local structure (including taxes, local services, and land-use measures) are capitalized into local property values. In Fischel's words, 'capitalization is everywhere' (2001, p.56).

4. The idea here is that, from the perspective of a local jurisdiction, the cost of providing local public services entails not only the resource costs of these services, but a loss of local tax base that accrues to other jurisdictions (Wildasin, 1989). This can lead local officials to select a local tax rate and level of local services that are too low. More generally, a huge literature has emerged that explores this facet (and others as well) of fiscal competition among jurisdictions. For an excellent survey of the tax competition literature, see John Wilson (1999).
5. This stability problem can be mitigated to some extent through the intrajurisdictional capitalization of differentials in tax prices. See Hamilton (1976).
6. Dennis Epple and Holger Sieg (1999) describe the properties of a locational equilibrium in a model with local property taxation but without zoning. They find some empirical support for the model's predictions for household sorting by income.
7. But this also requires qualification. Under most income tax schedules, there is an exemption such that households with taxable incomes below some threshold pay no taxes. Thus some residents under an income tax regime face an effective tax-price of zero for local services.
8. As Ian Parry commented to us, there may be an efficiency argument for the property tax in light of the large subsidy to housing in the form of the deduction of mortgage interest from taxable income. The property tax, by raising the price of housing, serves to counteract the pre-existing federal tax subsidy.
9. See Parry and Oates (2000) for a review and assessment of this literature.
10. Parry has suggested to us that state–local income taxes may actually be regressive when we take account of certain exemptions (for example, non-wage compensation such as employer-paid medical insurance) and deductions (such as pensions contributions and mortgage interest). If the ratio of exemptions plus deductions to taxable income increases with income, then a proportional income tax would be regressive (aside from the basic exemption).
11. There are some interesting exceptions to this rule. Atlantic City, New Jersey, has a number of very large casinos. Property wealth per pupil in Atlantic City is more than three times the New Jersey average; income per pupil in Atlantic City is just 70 per cent of the New Jersey average.
12. The authors' home state of Maryland is, interestingly, one of the few in which local governments, counties in this instance, place a significant reliance on local income taxation. The local component of the tax is simply a percentage 'add-on' to the state tax liability with an upper rate limit. Most Maryland counties are at this limit, which essentially converts the tax into a lump-sum source of local revenues. Fiscal decisions at the margin involve rates on the property tax (although there are some county limitations here too).

REFERENCES

Browning, Edgar K. (1987), 'On the Marginal Welfare Cost of Taxation', *American Economic Review*, **77**, 11–23.

Epple, Dennis and Holger Sieg (1999), 'Estimating Equilibrium Models of Local Jurisdictions', *Journal of Political Economy*, **107**, 645–81.

Fischel, William A. (1992), 'Property Taxation and the Tiebout Model: Evidence for the Benefit View from Zoning and Voting', *Journal of Economic Literature*, **30**, 171–7.

—— (1996), 'How *Serrano* Caused Proposition 13', *Journal of Law and Politics*, **12**, 607–45.

—— (2001), 'Municipal Corporations, Homeowners, and the Benefit View of the Property Tax', in Wallace E. Oates (ed.), *Property Taxation and Local Government Finance*, Cambridge, MA: Lincoln Institute of Land Policy, pp.33–77.

Goodspeed, Timothy J. (1989), 'A Re-Examination of the Use of Ability to Pay Taxes by Local Governments', *Journal of Public Economics*, **38**, 319–42.

Hamilton, Bruce W. (1975), 'Zoning and Property Taxation in a System of Local Governments', *Urban Studies*, **12**, 205–11.

—— (1976), 'Capitalization of Intrajurisdictional Differences in Local Tax Prices', *American Economic Review*, **66**, 743–53.

McGuire, Therese J. (2001), 'Alternatives to Property Taxation for Local Government', in Wallace E. Oates (ed.), *Property Taxation and Local Government Finance*, Cambridge, MA: Lincoln Institute of Land Policy, pp.301–14.

Mieszkowski, Peter (1972), 'The Property Tax: An Excise Tax or a Profits Tax?', *Journal of Public Economics*, **1**, 73–96.

Netzer, Dick (1966), *Economics of the Property Tax*, Washington, DC: Brookings Institution.

—— (1998), *Land Value Taxation: Can It and Will It Work Today?*, Cambridge, MA: Lincoln Institute of Land Policy.

Oates, Wallace E. (1969), 'The Effects of Property Taxes and Local Public Spending on Property Values: An Empirical Study of Tax Capitalization and the Tiebout Hypothesis', *Journal of Political Economy*, **77**, 957–71.

—— (1972), *Fiscal Federalism*, New York: Harcourt Brace Jovanovich.

—— (1998), 'Property Taxation and Local Public Spending: The Renter Effect', working draft.

—— and Robert M. Schwab (1991), 'The Allocative and Distributive Implications of Local Fiscal Competition', in Daphne Kenyon and John Kincaid (eds), *Competition Among States and Local Governments*, Washington, DC: Urban Institute, pp.127–145.

Parry, Ian W.H. and Wallace E. Oates (2000), 'Policy Analysis in the Presence of Distorting Taxes', *Journal of Policy Analysis and Management*, **19**, 603–13.

Rodgers, James D. and Judy A. Temple, (1996), 'Sales Taxes, Income Taxes and Other Nonproperty Tax Revenues', in J. Richard Aronson and Eli Schwartz (eds), *Management Policies in Local Government Finance*, Washington, DC: International City/County Management Association, pp.229–58.

Tiebout, Charles M. (1956), 'A Pure Theory of Local Expenditures', *Journal of Political Economy*, **64**, 416–24.

Wallis, John Joseph (2001), 'A History of the Property Tax in America', in Wallace E. Oates (ed.), *Property Taxation and Local Government Finance*, Cambridge, MA: Lincoln Institute of Land Policy, pp.123–47.

Wildasin, David E. (1989), 'Interjurisdictional Capital Mobility: Fiscal Externality and a Corrective Subsidy', *Journal of Urban Economics*, **25**, 193–212.

Wilson, John D. (1999), 'Theories of Tax Competition', *National Tax Journal*, **52**, 269–304.

Youngman, Joan (1994), *Legal Issues in Property Valuation and Taxation: Cases and Materials*, Chicago: The International Association of Assessing Officers.

Zodrow, George R. (2001), 'Reflections on the New View and the Benefit View of the Property Tax', in Wallace E. Oates (ed.), *Property Taxation and Local Government Finance,* Cambridge, MA: Lincoln Institute of Land Policy, pp.79–111.

—— and Peter Mieszkowski (1986), 'Pigou, Tiebout, Property Taxation, and the Under-Provision of Local Public Goods', *Journal of Urban Economics*, **19**, 356–70.

APPENDIX

This appendix includes a brief summary of our school district data for Massachusetts, New Jersey, New York and Texas.

Sample

We developed a few simple rules to help us choose districts for our sample. First, we included only unified districts in the sample; second, we deleted districts with missing property, income or enrollment estimates; third, we tried to reduce reporting errors in the data by (a) deleting districts where property value per pupil or income per pupil was greater than 150 per cent of the 99th percentile or less than 50 per cent of the first percentile in the state, and (b) dropping districts with fewer than 50 students.

Property Wealth Data

Our property tax data are equalized valuations per pupil. We collected these data by contacting various government offices in each of the four states. In Massachusetts, the 1990 valuations by school district were available on a website maintained by the Municipal Data Bank Division of Local Services of the Massachusetts Department of Revenue (http://www.state.ma.us/dls/allfiles.htm#property tax). The New Jersey data were collected by the Local Property Branch of the New Jersey Division of Taxation and were included in the 'Director's Table of Equalization Valuations for 1990'. In New York, the Fiscal Analysis and Research Unit in the Office of Management Services for the New York State Education Department provided 1990 equalized value estimates for each school district in the state. The Texas data were included in Appendix B of the '1990 Property Value Study of School and Appraisal Districts' prepared by the Office of the Comptroller; we subsequently obtained an electronic version of those data from Kenneth Meier at Texas A&M University. Based on district and county names within each state, the property data were then matched to National Center for Education Statistics (NCES) school district codes and Census of Governments district codes.

Income and Enrollment Data

Total income in each district was calculated using district-level per capita income in 1989 and total district population estimates from the School District Database (SDDB). District public school enrollment estimates were also taken from the 1990 SDDB.

COMMENT

Andrew Reschovsky

The Oates and Schwab paper could not be more timely. In response to big budgetary shortfalls during fiscal years 2003 and 2004, many state governments have been making big cuts in state fiscal assistance to their local governments and school districts (Reschovsky, 2004). The result of these cuts in intergovernmental transfers will be increased pressure on local governments to seek new sources of revenue. Given the clear unpopularity of the property tax, the exploration of alternatives may become much more than an academic exercise. Especially in states with constitutional and statutory limits on property tax rates and on levy increases, the current environment is likely to increase interest in considering the income tax as an alternative source of local revenue.

Wallace Oates and Robert Schwab have written an interesting, provocative and very clear analysis of the strength and weaknesses of replacing the property tax with the income tax as the mainstay of local government finance. Following the conventional approach used by economists in evaluating tax policies, they address issues of economic efficiency, tax incidence and tax administration. They also provide interesting evidence relevant to the question of whether the replacement of the property tax by an income tax will serve to increase or reduce fiscal disparities among local governments.

On the whole, I agree with the authors' assessment that the property tax and the income tax have both strengths and weaknesses. Neither tax is clearly superior to the other as a local government tax. Each tax has its advantages and disadvantages, and the tradeoffs between the two taxes are complicated. It is likely that the aging of the baby boom generation will increase the opposition to the property tax. Thus, over the next couple of decades, political pressure may well grow to replace at least partially the property tax with the income tax.

Although Oates and Schwab clearly recognize the vast differences that exist among local governments in the United States, most of their study is a general discussion of the impact of the property tax and the income tax on local governments. In light of Dick Netzer's sustained interest in the fiscal problems of cities and his many contributions to the literature on urban public finance, it is instructive to ask whether the income tax or the property tax have particular advantages and disadvantages in urban areas, and in particular, in central cities. In my comments, I will try to point out circumstances in which the evaluation of the income or property tax may depend, at least in part, on the type of community one is considering.

The Property Tax as a Benefits Tax?

The literature on local public finance has paid a lot of attention to the question of whether the local property tax can be characterized as a benefits tax. As demonstrated by Hamilton (1975) and Fischel (1992), a system of local property taxes in a world of zoning will convert the property tax into a benefits tax. This implies that the property tax paid by households will be equivalent to the price of local public services, and thus the property tax will generate an efficient allocation of local public goods among communities. Oates and Schwab argue that, in the cases where housing consumption is perfectly correlated with income, a local income tax would also be converted into a pure benefits tax. When the correlation between housing consumption and income is less than perfect, however, a local income tax would be somewhat less efficient than a local property tax.

This characterization of local property and income taxes as benefit taxes is most appropriate in the suburbs of metropolitan areas. These communities tend to be relatively small, their populations tend to be made up largely of mobile homeowners, and their property tax base tends to consist largely of residential property. In the absence of budget referendums, only in small communities are local officials likely to be able successfully to match property tax payments to the public service mix desired by residents. Homeowners are much more likely than tenants to be aware of the link between property values and public service provision. Although the evidence is not conclusive, tenants may well face a 'renters' illusion' based on a perception that they do not fully bear the burden of the property tax. It is also difficult to make an argument that the property tax serves as a benefits tax for commercial–industrial property. Although business enterprises consume local public services, the fact that public education is such an important part of local government spending suggests that the link between property tax liabilities on business and services received is far from perfect.

Central cities and the first ring of older suburbs that surround them often have large, heterogeneous populations, have high concentrations of renter-occupied housing and substantial amounts of non-residential property. In these settings, it is hard to argue that the property tax operates as a benefits tax. In fact, in these settings, neither the property tax nor the income tax can be characterized as an efficient tax.

Most central cities can be characterized by a wide distribution of both incomes and housing values. There is no basis on which to argue that local property or income taxes paid by residents are correlated with public services received. In fact, many public services provided by urban governments are either implicitly or explicitly redistributive. In the USA, low-income households are heavily concentrated in central cities. In 2001, the average poverty rate in central cities was 16.5 per cent, a rate that was more than twice as high as the average suburban poverty rate (US Census Bureau, 2002). One important fiscal implication of the concentration of poverty in cities is that local governments generally play the role of *service provider of last resort*. For example, they are required by state governments or by the courts to provide shelter to the homeless and child welfare services to troubled families. This role of city government is more explicit in New York than in most other states because of a state constitutional requirement (Article XVII, Section 1) requiring the state and city governments to provide for 'the aid, care and support of the needy'. In most other states it is common for city governments to finance a number of direct services to poor persons, especially in the areas of public welfare and public health.

As Tom Nechyba (2001) has pointed out, different views of the property tax may hold in different settings. Thus, while the benefits view may be appropriate in suburban settings, I have argued above that the assumptions underlying the benefits view of the property tax are not appropriate in most urban settings. Likewise, the property tax is unlikely to be a benefits tax in most rural areas. The fact that in rural areas most people are tied to a job at a fixed location, such as a farm, and distance between communities can be large, makes it hard to imagine that many rural residents would move for fiscal reasons. It is interesting to note that, in 2001, nearly half the US population lived in either central cities of metropolitan areas or outside metropolitan areas. Thus, in interpreting the efficiency characteristics of local taxes, it is important to realize that the assumption that local taxes operate as benefit taxes is unlikely to hold in the communities where a substantial portion of the population lives.[1]

Which Tax is More Progressive?

The question of whether the local property tax is a benefits tax is particularly important in any discussion of tax incidence. If local taxes are benefit taxes, then they are just the price one pays for local public services, and hence, as Oates and Schwab argue 'redistribution is not an issue'. As suggested above, in many locations, such as urban areas, the property tax and the local income tax cannot be considered benefit taxes and, hence, the relative incidence of the two taxes is a potentially important issue.

Despite the conventional wisdom, at least among non-economists, that the income tax is progressive and the property tax is regressive, in reality there remains a lot of uncertainty about the incidence of the two taxes. As pointed out by Oates and Schwab, in principle it is not hard to make a local property tax more progressive and an income tax less progressive. An example of the former is Minnesota's complex system of property tax classification, and an example of the latter is the Philadelphia wage tax, which taxes earning at a flat rate with no low-income deductions or exemptions.[2]

What conclusions can be drawn about the incidence of the residential property tax and the income tax as they currently exist across the country?[3] Unfortunately there have been relatively few studies of the distribution of state and local tax burdens that have been national in scope. The well-known studies by Joseph Pechman and his colleagues at the Brookings Institution (Pechman and Okner, 1974; Pechman, 1985) are now out of date. Of more recent vintage are a study by Gilbert Metcalf (1994) and a study by Robert McIntyre *et al.* (2003). These two studies are particularly interesting because they allow us to see the importance of assumptions about tax incidence and about the measurement of income.

Metcalf accepts the 'new view' of property tax incidence and assumes that the entire burden of the residential property tax falls on the owners of capital. In contrast, McIntyre *et al.* assume that the burden of the residential property tax is borne by homeowners and, in the case of rental property, they assume that the burden is split evenly between tenants and landlords.

Typically distributional analyses have been based on data on both taxation and income from a single year. The McIntyre *et al.* study uses tax and income data for 2002. Starting with Milton Friedman (1957), a number of economists have argued that it is inappropriate to determine tax incidence on the basis of annual data. Their argument is that, if most people with low incomes are only temporarily poor, and if consumption decisions are generally made on the basis of lifetime incomes, then calculating tax burdens based on data from a single year will yield tax burdens for low-income people that are substantially higher than burdens calculated on the basis of lifetime or permanent income. They conclude that the use of annual income will create an 'annual income bias'. As a result of this bias the property tax (and other taxes) appear more regressive than they really are. Metcalf applies the lifetime approach by combining tax data for a single year with a measure of lifetime income.

While a number of recent empirical studies have used longitudinal data on individual or household income to impute lifetime income, Metcalf uses data on total consumption expenditures in a single year as a proxy for lifetime income.[4] He argues that, if one ignores bequests and if consumption is smooth over the life cycle, then annual expenditures provide a good measure of lifetime income.

Table 2C.1 Average residential property tax and personal income tax burdens, by quintile

	Residential property tax		Personal income tax	
Quintiles	McIntyre *et al.*	Metcalf	McIntyre *et al.*	Metcalf
Bottom	3.0	3.4	0.5	1.0
Second	2.2	3.7	1.6	2.1
Third	2.4	3.0	2.2	2.7
Fourth	2.4	3.2	2.7	3.0
Top	2.2	3.2	3.4	2.6

Notes: The McIntyre *et al.* study calculates tax burdens for non-elderly married couples. Quintiles are defined in terms of 2002 family incomes. Tax burdens in the Metcalf study are calculated for all households, and quintiles are defined in terms of 1989 annual expenditures. Metcalf's income tax burdens were calculated after dropping households with negative income tax liabilities.

Source: Author's calculations using data from McIntyre *et al.* (2003) and Metcalf (1994).

Table 2C.1 summarizes the results of the two studies for the residential property tax and the personal income tax. The McIntyre *et al.* study calculates tax burdens for non-elderly married couples. All taxpayers are divided into annual income quintiles, and average tax burdens are calculated for each quintile. Metcalf ranks households by annual consumption expenditure quintiles and calculates average burdens as taxes divided by annual expenditures.

The McIntyre *et al.* study shows that the residential property tax is modestly regressive, with the highest average burden found in the lowest income quintile. The personal income tax is progressive, with the average burden in the top quintile nearly seven times higher than the burden in the bottom quintile.[5] Metcalf finds that the residential property tax is close to proportional, with the average burden in the bottom quintile only 6 per cent higher than the average burden in the fourth and fifth quintiles. He demonstrates that his results are primarily attributable to his lifetime perspective. Even though he assumes that the entire incidence of the property tax falls on the owners of capital, when he calculates tax burdens based on annual incomes he finds that the tax is regressive above the third income decile. Although Metcalf finds that the incidence of the individual income tax is progressive, the degree of progressivity is substantially less than that found by McIntyre *et al.*

If we accept Metcalf's results, a shift from the property tax to a local income tax would result in only a modest increase in tax progressivity. This is particularly true if local income taxes are designed to be somewhat less progressive than state income taxes. On the other hand, if we accept McIntyre *et al.*'s finding, the shift to a local income tax would result in a substantial increase in tax progressivity.

My own view is that the true pattern of property and income tax incidence lies somewhere between the results of these two studies. The Metcalf assumption that the entire incidence of the property tax falls on capital is inappropriate when we consider that the decision of any single local government, or state, to increase or decrease its reliance on the property will have little impact on the national average rate of property taxation. This implies that the 'excise tax' effects of property taxation should dominate, and the burden of the property tax will depend on the relative mobility of capital, labor and housing consumers (McLure, 1977). Given the uncertainty about mobility, it is probably not correct to assume that the whole burden of the property tax falls either on capital or on housing consumers.

Although, at a conceptual level, a lifetime tax incidence approach has great appeal, the question is whether, as Metcalf claims, annual consumption expenditures in a single year provide a good measure of lifetime income. For several reasons, I believe that this is a poor assumption. First, people tend to have unanticipated and non-recurring expenditures. As households are ranked by annual expenditure levels, lifetime incomes will be overestimated and tax burdens biased downward for any household with higher than normal expenditures. Second, for annual consumption expenditures to be a good proxy for lifetime income, households need to be able to finance spending in a year when income is low by drawing on past savings or by borrowing against future income. For families that have few or no savings and are unable to borrow, changes in consumption are more likely to track changes in annual income than changes in lifetime income. Data from the *Survey of Consumer Finances* indicate that a substantial number of families have little in the way of financial assets and thus are likely to face severe liquidity constraints.[6] Third, for annual expenditures to be a good proxy for lifetime income all income must be consumed over the course of a lifetime, something that will be true only if individuals make no gifts or bequests. As it is reasonable to assume that, over the income distribution, gifts and bequests are a rising share of lifetime income, the failure to categorize bequests as consumption expenditures will overstate tax progressivity as measured by Metcalf by biasing tax burdens upward at the top of the income distribution.

The difficulty of measuring lifetime income should not be interpreted as meaning that the measurement of tax incidence using annual data on income and taxes provides accurate estimates of tax burdens. As long as incomes vary over time and some economic decisions, such as purchasing a home, are made on the basis of a household's long-run economic position, the use of annual data will bias tax incidence studies towards increased regressivity.

Chernick and I (1997) have argued that one way to correct for this annual income bias while avoiding most of the problems of trying to measure lifetime income is to use data on households' income and tax payments over a period of (at least several) years. Using longitudinal data on income and property tax payments covering a period of 11 years, we analyzed the incidence of the property tax on homeowners (Chernick and Reschovsky, 1993). We concluded that the bias towards regressivity due to the use of annual data is relatively small. The property tax remained mildly regressive when tax burdens were calculated using 11 years of data on income and tax payments.

I conclude from all this that a shift from local property to income taxation will result in a modest reduction in the regressivity of the state and local tax system. Whether a relatively small change in the distribution of tax burdens is a sufficient reason to abandon the property tax remains an open question. From the perspective of the residents of an individual local government, a comparison of tax burdens faced under an income tax relative to a property tax will depend in part on the portion of the total tax liability that can be exported to non-residents. As pointed out a long time ago by Helen Ladd (1975), local residents have an opportunity for exporting a portion of their tax revenue by levying a property tax on commercial and industrial property. Obviously, the extent of exporting will depend upon the competitive nature of local businesses and the residential location of their owners, employees and customers. Revenue from a local income tax can be exported to non-residents only to the extent that the tax is levied on commuters. Although an argument can be made, particularly in the case of central cities, that commuters reap direct benefits from city government services, only eight of the largest 24 central cities in the country currently utilize an income or wage tax and, with the exception of Philadelphia, those eight cities tax commuters at very low rates or not at all.

In 1999, New York City's non-resident personal income tax was repealed. This so-called 'commuter tax' was levied at a rate of 0.45 per cent on New York City income earned by non-residents (0.65 per cent for self-employment income). As nearly 40 per cent of the earned income in New York City was earned by nonresidents, the commuter tax, even at a low rate, provided an important source of revenue for the city (Chernick and Reschovsky, 2001). The repeal of the New York City commuter tax reflects the growing population and political clout of suburbs relative to central cities, and suggests that any broad movement to replace the property tax with local income taxes will probably not include much use of non-resident income taxes. As a consequence, the ability of central cities to export taxes will be reduced, presumably requiring higher rates of taxation on city residents and a potential worsening of the competitive position of central cities relative to their suburbs.

Tax Visibility

Oates and Schwab argue that the administrative costs of a local income tax would be substantially lower than the costs of operating a property tax system because local governments could 'piggyback' on the state income tax by merely adding a line to the state tax form that applies the local rate (or rate structure) to taxable income. As part of their concluding remarks, however, the authors suggest that the fact that individuals' state and local income tax payments would be lumped together in a single payment would make it difficult for them to recognize the magnitude of their local tax payment. This lack of local tax visibility would tend to obscure the relationship between local taxes and local spending, and might result in a reduction in local government accountability to local taxpayers.

They argue that the visibility problem associated with a local income tax is not an issue with the property tax, where there exists a real separation of sources since local governments are the only level of government that taxes real property. In my view, a similar visibility problem exists with respect to the property tax. Although state governments generally make no use of the property tax, in many states the property tax is used by several independent, but overlapping, units of government. For example, my own property tax bill, issued by the City of Madison, Wisconsin, includes property tax levies for four taxing jurisdictions in addition to Madison. These include a small state levy, the county government in which Madison is located, the Madison Metropolitan School District, with its independently elected school board, and the area technical college. In addition to my total property tax liability, the bill does list the five amounts that make up the total. Unless I take out a calculator, however, I would not know what share of my total bill is attributable to the City of Madison. For most people, especially those who pay their property tax into a bank escrow account on a monthly basis, the link between the property taxes they pay to a particular governmental unit and the services they receive is quite obscure.

Oates and Schwab conclude that the greater visibility of the property tax relative to the income tax is 'potentially significant and might well swing the balance in the choice of a system of local taxation'. While there are strong arguments in favor of the property tax, my sense is that the income tax is no more visible or invisible than the property tax, and to my knowledge there exists no evidence to suggest that one tax would lead to more accountable local government than the other.

Conclusions

A great deal of the discussion of property taxation in the economics literature implicitly assumes that residents of local communities are free to choose any level of property taxation that provides sufficient local tax revenue to finance, with the aid of intergovernmental transfers, their preferred level of public services. This assumption clearly ignores the fact that, 25 years after the passage of Proposition 13, limits on property tax rates, levies and assessments are widely used throughout the country. Most states also employ circuit breakers, homestead exemptions and other devices to reduce the property tax burdens on the elderly and others who are deemed in need of property tax relief. In addition, a number of states have initiated state aid programs to municipal governments and school districts that are explicitly intended to reduce reliance on the property tax. These grant programs are sometimes combined with spending limits as a way of effectively requiring that additional state aid results in property tax reductions rather than increases in local government spending.

Although these policies have certainly reduced average property tax burdens and may have contributed to a reduction in regressivity, they have also created their own set of inefficiencies and inequities. One example is the horizontal inequities and the 'lock-in effect' created by limits on property tax assessments, such as the Proposition 13 provision that property is to be reassessed at full market value only when it is sold (Chernick and Reschovsky, 1983; Sexton *et al.*, 1999).

Despite their shortcomings, property tax limitations appear to be a permanent part of the property tax system in the USA. The property tax remains an unpopular tax and, over the next decade, as the baby boom generation ages and moves into retirement, it is likely that efforts to reduce reliance on the property tax will only increase. That being said, it appears unlikely that many localities will choose to replace the property tax completely with a local income tax. More likely, we will continue a trend, that has been going on for at least the last two decades, of very slowly and incrementally reducing our reliance on the property tax and replacing it with the use of other taxes. In 1980, property taxes made up 76.7 per cent of total own-raised taxes of local governments. By 1990, their share of local government taxes had fallen to 74.6 per cent and by 2000 to 71.6 per cent (US Census Bureau, 2003).

Over the past decade the individual income tax has amounted to about 5 per cent of total local government tax collections. In the future, pressures to increase local government spending and the public's apparent aversion to the property tax suggest that political pressure will rise for increasing the role of the income tax as a source of revenue for local governments. As Oates and Schwab clearly explain, while both the property tax and the income tax have their advantages and disadvantages, there appears to be no strong reason why the income tax should not, over time, play a more important role in the financing of local governments.

NOTES

1. In states such as California, that have enacted strict property tax limitations, local residents are constrained from setting a preferred property tax rate, and thus, it is difficult to argue that, even in suburban settings, the property tax can function as a benefits tax.
2. Property tax assessment practices can also influence progressivity. Several older studies found that assessment–market value ratios were systematically higher in poor neighborhoods than in more prosperous neighborhoods. It is unclear whether in recent years increased frequency of assessment and higher quality assessments have eliminated this kind of assessment bias.
3. As local income taxes are used in relatively few states, the discussion here about the incidence of the income tax will be based on data from state income tax systems.
4. Examples of tax incidence studies using longitudinal data are Fullerton and Rogers (1991, 1993) and Lyon and Schwab (1995). Poterba (1989) also uses annual expenditures as a proxy for lifetime income.
5. These results do not take account of the fact that taxpayers who can itemize their deductions on their federal returns are able to deduct the value of their property and income tax payments, thereby reducing their net burdens. As the share of taxpayers who itemize rises with income, as does the federal marginal tax rate, the ability to itemize these taxes reduces the progressivity of both the residential property tax and the individual income tax.
6. In 2001, the median value of the total financial assets held by families in the lowest income quintile was under $2000, while the median value of financial assets of those in the second quintile of the income distribution was less than $8000 (Aizcorbe *et al.*, 2003).

REFERENCES

Aizcorbe, Ana M., Arthur B. Kennickell and Keven B. Moore (2003), 'Recent Changes in U.S. Family Finances: Evidence from the 1998 and 2001 Survey of Consumer Finances', *Federal Reserve Bulletin*, January.

Chernick, Howard and Andrew Reschovsky (1983), 'The Consequences of Limitations on Growth in the Property Tax Base', in John M. Quigley (ed.), *Perspectives on Local Public Finance and Public Policy, A Research Annual*, vol. I, Greenwich, CN: JAI Press Inc, pp.89–107.

Chernick, Howard and Andrew Reschovsky (1993), 'Evaluating the Long-Run Burden of the Residential Property Tax and Selected State and Local Consumption Taxes', paper presented at the Annual Conference on Taxation of the National Tax Institute, St Paul, MN, November.

Chernick, Howard and Andrew Reschovsky (1997), 'Who Pays the Gasoline Tax?', *National Tax Journal*, **50** (June), 233–59.

Chernick, Howard and Andrew Reschovsky (2001), 'Lost in the Balance: How State Policies Affect the Fiscal Health of Cities', a discussion paper prepared for the Center on Urban and Metropolitan Policy, The Brookings Institution, Washington, DC, March (available at http://www.brook.edu/dybdocroot/es/urban/chernick/chernick.pdf).

Fischel, William A. (1992), 'Property Taxation and the Tiebout Model: Evidence for the Benefit View from Zoning and Voting', *Journal of Economic Literature*, **30**, 171–7.

Fullerton, Don and Diane L. Rogers (1991), 'Lifetime Versus Annual Perspective on Tax Incidence', *National Tax Journal*, **44** (September), 277–87.

Fullerton, Don and Diane L. Rogers (1993), *Who Bears the Lifetime Tax Burden?*, Washington, DC: The Brookings Institution.

Hamilton, Bruce W. (1975), 'Zoning and Property Taxation in a System of Local Governments', *Urban Studies*, **12**, 205–11.

Ladd, Helen F. (1975), 'Local Education, Expenditures, Fiscal Capacity, and the Composition of the Property Tax Base', *National Tax Journal*, **28** (June), 145–58.

Lyon, Andrew B. and Robert M. Schwab (1995), 'Consumption Taxes in a Life-Cycle Framework: Are Sin Taxes Regressive?', R*eview of Economics and Statistics*, **77** (August), 389–406.

McIntyre, Robert S., Robert Denk, Norton Francis, Matthew Gardner, Will Gomaa, Fiona Hsu and Richard Sims (2003), *Who Pays? A Distributional Analysis of the Tax Systems of All 50 States*, Washington, DC: Institute on Taxation and Economic Policy, January.

McLure, Charles E., Jr (1977), 'The "New View" of the Property Tax: A Caveat', *National Tax Journal*, **30** (March), 69–75.

Metcalf, Gilbert (1994), 'The Lifetime Incidence of State and Local Taxes: Measuring Changes During the 1980s', in Joel Slemrod (ed.), *Tax Progressivity and Income Inequality*, New York: Cambridge University Press, pp.59–88.

Nechyba, Thomas J. (2001), 'The Benefit View and the New View; Where Do We Stand, Twenty-Five Years into the Debate?', in Wallace E. Oates (ed.), *Property Taxation and Local Government Finance; Essays in Honor of C. Lowell Harriss*, Cambridge, MA: Lincoln Institute of Land Policy, pp.113–21.

Pechman, Joseph A. (1985), *Who Paid the Taxes, 1966–85?*, Washington, DC: The Brookings Institution.

Pechman, Joseph A. and Benjamin A. Okner (1974), *Who Bears the Tax Burden?*, Washington, DC: The Brookings Institution.

Poterba, James M. (1989), 'Lifetime Incidence and the Distributional Burden of Excise Taxes', *American Economic Review*, **79** (May), 325–30.

Reschovsky, Andrew (2003), 'The Impact of State Government Fiscal Crises on Local Governments and School's, *State and Local Government Review*, **36** (Spring).

Sexton, Terri A., Steven M. Sheffrin and Arthur O'Sullivan (1999), 'Proposition 13: Unintended Effects and Feasible Reforms', *National Tax Journal*, 52 (March), 99–111.

US Census Bureau (2002), *Poverty in the United States, 2001, Current Population Reports*, Series P60-219, by Bernadette D. Proctor and Joseph Dalaker, Washington, DC: US Government Printing Office.

US Census Bureau (2003), 'State and Local Government Finances by Level of Government' (available at http://www.census.gov/govs/www/estimate.html).

3. What a tangled web: local property, income and sales taxes

David L. Sjoquist, Sally Wallace and Barbara Edwards*

INTRODUCTION

Throughout his career, Dick Netzer has been an ardent proponent of the use of the property tax for local governments. The discussion in his classic book, *Economics of the Property Tax* (Netzer, 1966), of the general sales tax as an alternative revenue source for local governments makes it clear that he believes it is an inferior alternative. However, over the past three decades, local governments have diversified their tax structures, and as a consequence local sales and income taxes have become an important part of the tax structure for many cities and other local governments across the United States.

These changes in revenue structure have likely come about for two principal reasons: pressures on the existing system of revenue in the face of increased expenditure demands, and pressures to reduce reliance on the property tax. Many individuals suggest that cities adopt sales and income taxes to finance higher levels of expenditures (Anderson, 1994). Over the past several decades, reductions in federal funds, increases in federal and state mandates, and changes in the demand for public services have put increasing pressure on local governments to adjust old revenue sources and develop new, alternative forms of revenue. Large cities are a case in point: the demand for public services has increased as central cities have taken on more of the urban poor, suffered from increased crime (at least until recently) and sought to repair their infrastructure. The existence of limits, either from mandates or from voter resistance, on the use of property taxes have required many local governments to look to nonproperty tax sources to finance these expenditures.

* The views expressed in this chapter are those of the authors and should not be interpreted as those of the Congressional Budget Office. We acknowledge the helpful comments of James Alm, Chris Bollinger, Kelly Edmiston, Therese McGuire, Amy Ellen Schwartz, Geoffrey Turnbull and Mary Beth Walker. Chris Geller, Mary Kassis, James Murphy and Drew Warwick provided technical assistance.

Local tax structures may have also been diversified in order to reduce reliance on property taxes. It has been widely argued that the more recent (post-1973) adoptions of local income and sales taxes were for the purpose of reducing reliance on property taxes (Advisory Commission on Intergovernmental Relations, 1988). There is much taxpayer dislike of the property tax, as evidenced by opinion polls and by efforts to adopt property tax limitations. In response to voter dislike of the property tax, local governments have adopted local sales and income taxes that allow, and in many cases require, local governments to reduce local property taxes through tax rate reductions, special homestead exemptions and other means.

While these may be the stated motivation for the adoption of local sales and income taxes, the actual effect on expenditures and property taxes of the adoption of these taxes, particularly several years after their adoption, is not clear. In particular, there is no agreement in the literature as to the effect on expenditures and property taxes of diversifying a local government tax structure. Some proponents of a diversified tax structure imply that non-property taxes act as simple substitutes for local property taxes and thus have no effect on expenditures. Downs (1960), however, claims that diversity in the tax structure makes citizens more aware of the costs of government and thus results in lower expenditures, while Buchanan (1967), on the other hand, argues that a diversified local tax structure will lead to fiscal illusion and thus to increases in expenditures.

In this chapter we explore whether the adoptions of local sales and income taxes have led to reductions in property taxes. The next section presents the various arguments in the literature regarding the effect of tax base diversification and discusses what the existing empirical literature says about this question. In subsequent sections we present alternative models of the effect of tax diversification on property taxes, discuss the history and use of the local sales and income taxes, and present the results of our empirical analysis. The final section summarizes the chapter and discusses the policy relevance of the findings.

THE TANGLED WEB

There are two main competing approaches regarding the question of whether the tax structure affects the level of expenditures and property tax revenue. First, models such as the median voter model (see Inman, 1978) assume that expenditure levels are driven by rational voters who make decisions based on their tax-prices, and not on the basis of the tax structure. For approaches such as the median voter model, there are at least three reasons why the tax structure could affect the level of expenditures, contrary to what proponents of a diversified tax structure suggest. First, a diversified tax structure, which implies a broader tax base and lower tax rates for a given level of revenue, could reduce the marginal excess burden at any revenue level (Advisory Commission on Intergovernmental Relations, 1988).[1] This, in turn, should reduce taxpayer resistance to further tax increases, thus increasing total taxes. Support for this argument was obtained by Becker and Mulligan (1998) and is consistent with the results of Kau and Rubin (1981). However, since local sales and income taxes are usually additions to the state tax rates, the marginal excess burden of a local 'add-on' to the state tax may be quite large.

Related to this issue of the change in excess burden is one of the reasons Netzer favors the property tax. He makes the particularly cogent argument that the property tax is a benefit tax and hence yields a socially desirable level of public expenditures.[2] Thus, if the adoption of a local sales or income tax leads to a different level of public expenditures, the level of public expenditures will no longer be the socially desirable level.

A second reason to expect that diversifying the tax structure may lead to a change in expenditures is that the percentage of taxes that are exported may differ across taxes, and hence the diversification of the tax structure may alter the value of tax prices. This should lead to a change in the level of expenditures. Third, the adoption of a sales or income tax may alter the distribution of tax prices across individual voters and hence could change the identity of the median voter, which should affect the level of expenditures.

The main alternative to the median voter approach is the Leviathan view of government (Buchanan, 1967; Buchanan and Wagner, 1977), under which government decision makers are assumed to be able to influence expenditure levels significantly beyond levels desired by the public. Buchanan and Wagner, for example, argue that a fragmented tax structure creates an illusory effect such that voters underestimate the tax price. As Wagner (1971, p.87) puts it elsewhere, a diversified tax structure leads to 'faulty fiscal perception'. To the extent that diversification results in a more complex tax structure, the Buchanan argument implies that adoption of a non-property tax will lead to an increase in expenditures.[3]

The empirical evidence of the effect of the tax structure, or characteristics of the tax structure, on the level of expenditures or the level of tax revenue is mixed. One empirical approach has been to consider the effect of diversification of the tax structure on the level of expenditures. Wagner (1976) found that cities with diversified tax structures have higher expenditures than cities with less diverse tax structures, thus providing support for the Leviathan view of government. Similar results were obtained by Breeden and Hunter (1985), who consider 37 large cities. Other research that follows a similar approach is focused on state level expenditures. Of these studies, Baker (1983), Suyderhoud (1994) and Clotfelter (1976) obtain results that are consistent with Wagner's, while Ladd and Weist (1987) do not. None of these papers considers the possibility of endogeneity that arises if the level of expenditures determine the tax structure.[4]

A related empirical approach considers whether the adoption or existence of multiple taxes results in higher tax revenue or expenditures. In an earlier piece, Deran (1968) compares cities with and without local income taxes and concludes that cities with an income tax have lower per capita taxes. Likewise, Stockfish (1985) finds no effect on expenditures as a result of the adoption of value added taxes in Europe.

Of particular relevance is Inman (1979), who models the taxing decision as a two-step process: first, the level of tax revenue needed to finance the desired level of expenditure is determined, second, the allocation of the required tax revenue across the various tax instruments is determined. In the estimation of the first equation, Inman includes a set of dummy variables that reflect the available tax options. In the regression equations, which were estimated for the largest 41 central cities (excluding Washington, DC) for fiscal year 1966–7, none of these tax dummy variables was significant.

Another theme in this literature considers whether 'automatic' increases in tax revenue result in larger expenditures: in particular, whether tax structures with higher income elasticities result in larger expenditures. Oates (1975) and Craig and Heins (1980) find a positive relationship between income elasticity of the tax structure and expenditures, while the findings of DiLorenzo (1982) and Feenberg and Rosen (1987) do not lend support to the view that expenditures increase as a result of automatic revenue increases.

MODELING THE EFFECT OF TAX DIVERSIFICATION

To investigate the question of how the adoption of a non-property tax might affect public expenditures and the property tax rate consider the following model, which assumes rational voters, i.e., no fiscal illusion or Leviathan. Consider a median voter model in which all individuals are identical; in other words, let a representative voter determine the level of the public good and the property tax rate. Since all individuals are identical, it follows that the property tax base will equal the representative voter's housing consumption times the number of voters. Let utility for the ith voter be given by the following:

$$U = U(x, h, G), \qquad (3.1)$$

where x represents an aggregate, non-housing commodity, h represents housing and G represents the amount of a pure local public good. For convenience, we suppress the subscript for the individual voter and assume that the per unit cost of G is one. We assume that the utility function exhibits all of the common properties. Let the budget equation for the representative voter be given by

$$I = P_x x + P_h(1 + t_h)h, \qquad (3.2)$$

where I is fixed income, P represents constant prices and t_h is the property tax rate. We assume that the government's budget must be balanced and is therefore given by

$$G = t_h h N, \qquad (3.3)$$

where N is the number of individual voters.

Solving (3.3) for t_h and inserting into (3.2) and rearranging yields

$$I = P_x x + P_h h + (1/N)G. \qquad (3.4)$$

Equation (3.4) implies that the property tax is a benefit tax and hence does not change the consumption of x, h or G from what it would be if a head tax were used.

Now suppose that the government adopts an excise tax at the fixed rate t_x. Since x is a composite good, the excise tax can be considered a general sales tax. The assumption of a fixed excise tax rate simplifies the analysis, but is consistent with the restrictions for most local non-property taxes that local governments have a choice of one rate. The government's budget equation is now given by

$$G = t_h P_h h N + t_x P_x x N. \qquad (3.5)$$

Again, solving (3.5) for t_h and inserting into (3.2) and rearranging yields

$$I = P_x x + P_h h + (1/N)G. \qquad (3.6)$$

Equation (3.6) is identical to equation (3.4). In other words, the tax structure is a benefit tax and hence the addition of the excise tax does not affect the consumption of G. The addition of t_x reduces t_h but does not change total revenue.

The implication of this model is clear. If a local government adopts a local sales tax, the only effect is to lower the property tax rate and property tax revenue. Alternative specifications of this basic theoretical model will affect the relationship among h, G and x. For example, if the excise tax base is fixed and the median voter chooses a level of x equal to X/N, the excise tax will increase both h and G, owing to an increase in the relative price of x. The implication of alternative models is that the effect of an excise tax on government spending is indeterminate; it depends on the underlying assumptions of the model. Likewise property taxes may or may not change, but in no case does the excise tax increase property taxes.

EXPANSION OF THE SALES TAX

Due and Mikesell (1994) date the introduction of the general sales tax in the United States to 1932, with the adoption of a 2 per cent sales tax by Mississippi. In 1933, 13 states, concerned with the effects of the Great Depression on tax revenue, followed Mississippi's lead and adopted the sales tax as a new source of revenue. By the end of the 1930s, 23 states had added a general sales tax to its tax structure. Another six states adopted a general sales tax for a temporary period during the 1930s; however, all six later reinstated it on a permanent basis. Between 1947 and 1969, another 23 states, plus the District of Columbia, imposed a general sales tax. Vermont, in 1969, was the last state to adopt the sales tax. Currently, there are just five states, Alaska, Delaware, Montana, New Hampshire and Oregon, that do not employ a general sales tax; these states accounted for only 2.5 per cent of the US population in 2000. Table 3.1 gives the year that each state adopted a general sales tax.

As of 1998, sales tax revenue accounted for about 33 per cent of state tax collections (US Bureau of the Census, 2001). Figure 3.1 shows the growth in state general sales tax revenue in real terms (left-hand scale) and as a share of total state taxes (right-hand scale) for the period 1932–98. Sales taxes as a share of total state taxes rose rapidly in the first few years, rising from zero in fiscal year 1932 to 13.6 per cent in 1936. But then the pace of increase slowed. For the past 25 years, sales taxes have accounted for between 30 and 34 per cent of total state taxes. Absolute growth in real sales tax revenue, however, increased slowly at first but then accelerated. However, the rate of growth has declined since 1960; real sales tax revenue increased at an annual rate of 9.7 per cent in the 1960s, 4.5 per cent in the 1970s, 4.3 per cent in the 1980s and 3.4 per cent between 1990 and 1998.

Two years after Mississippi adopted the general sales tax, New York City began collecting a general sales tax, over 30 years earlier than New York State's adoption of the sales tax. The adoption of local sales taxes grew

Table 3.1 Year state adopted sales tax

State	Year adopted	State	Year adopted	State	Year adopted
Mississippi	1932	Ohio	1934	Maine	1951
Arizona	1933	Arkansas	1935	South Carolina	1951
California	1933	Colorado	1935	Pennsylvania	1953
Illinois	1933	Hawaii	1935	Nevada	1960
Indiana	1933	North Dakota	1935	Kentucky	1961
Iowa	1933	Wyoming	1935	Texas	1961
Michigan	1933	Alabama	1936	Wisconsin	1961
New Mexico	1933	Kansas	1937	Idaho	1965
North Carolina	1933	Louisiana	1938	New York	1965
Oklahoma	1933	Connecticut	1947	Massachusetts	1966
South Dakota	1933	Maryland	1947	New Jersey	1966
Utah	1933	Rhode Island	1947	Virginia	1966
Washington	1933	Tennessee	1947	Minnesota	1967
West Virginia	1933	Florida	1949	Nebraska	1967
Missouri	1934	Georgia	1951	Vermont	1969

Source: Advisory Commission on Intergovernmental Relations (1968); Due and Mikesell (1994).

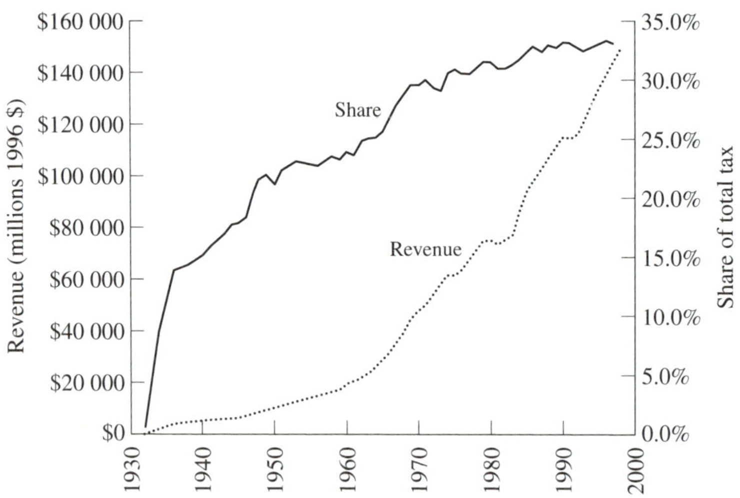

Figure 3.1 State sales tax, 1932–98

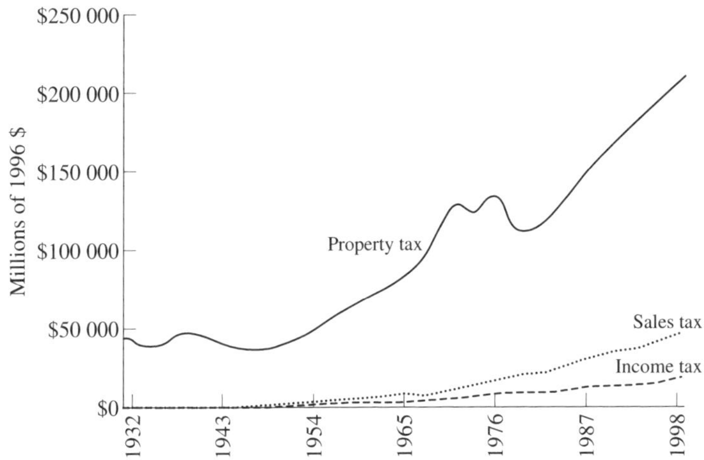

Figure 3.2 Local sales, income and property tax revenue, 1932–98

more slowly than state adoptions. By 1963, only 12 states had authorized local governments to impose a sales tax. Currently, local sales taxes are imposed in 34 states.[5] The states without local sales taxes are Connecticut, Delaware, Hawaii, Indiana, Kentucky, Maine, Maryland, Massachusetts, Michigan, Montana, New Hampshire, New Jersey, Oregon, Rhode Island, Vermont and West Virginia (American Bar Association, 2000).

In 1968, there were 2817 local governments that imposed a sales tax (Advisory Commission on Intergovernmental Relations, 1968). This rose to 4893 by 1976 and to 6579 by 1994 (Advisory Commission on Intergovernmental Relations, 1995a). In 1934, local sales and gross receipts tax revenue accounted for 0.8 per cent of local total tax revenue (Tax Foundation, 2001), increasing to 16.0 per cent by 1998 (US Bureau of the Census, 2001). Figure 3.2 shows real sales tax revenue and real property tax revenue for local governments for the period 1932–98, while Figure 3.3 shows sales, income and property taxes as a share of total local tax revenue.[6] Local sales tax revenue has grown, but property taxes have increased substantially more in absolute terms. In 1998, local real sales tax revenue was about equal to 1932 real local property tax revenue. Sales taxes as a share of local tax revenue increased to 11.1 per cent by 1998.[7] Over the same period, property taxes as a share of total local taxes decreased from 97 per cent in 1932 to 73 per cent in 1998, or by 24 percentage points.

There is wide variation in sales tax rates, both across the states and within states (Table 3.2). State sales tax rates vary from a low of 3 per cent to a high of 7 per cent. Local rates vary from a low of 0.20 per cent to a high of 7 per cent.[8] The highest combined rate is 11 per cent, in Alabama (Cornia *et al.*,

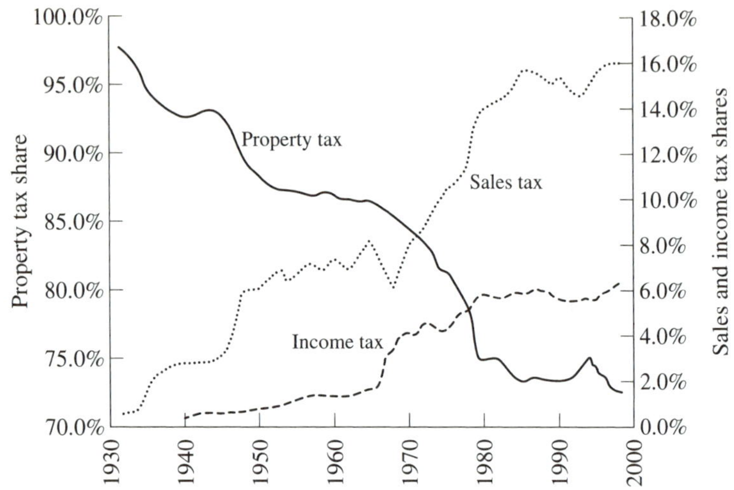

Figure 3.3 Local sales, income and property tax shares of local tax revenue, 1932–98

Table 3.2 Variations in local sales tax rates

State	Range of combined rates	State rate	Notes
Alabama	4.00–11.00	4.00	
Alaska	1.00–7.00*		No state sales tax
Arizona	5.00–8.00	5.00	
Arkansas	4.625–8.125	4.625	
California	7.25–8.50	6.00	
Colorado	3.00–9.50	3.00	
Connecticut	6.00	6.00	
Delaware			No sales tax
District of Columbia	5.75	5.75	
Florida	6.00–7.50	6.00	
Georgia	5.00–7.00	4.00	
Hawaii	4	4.00	
Idaho	6.00–8.00	5.00	
Illinois	6.25–9.00	6.25	
Indiana	5	5.00	
Iowa	5.00–7.00	5.00	
Kansas	4.90–7.65	4.90	
Kentucky	6.00	6.00	
Louisiana	4.00–10.75	4.00	

Table 3.2 (*continued*)

State	Range of combined rates	State rate	Notes
Maine	5.50	5.50	
Maryland	5.00	5.00	
Massachusetts	5.00	5.00	
Michigan	6.00	6.00	
Minnesota	6.50–7.50	6.50	
Mississippi	7.00–7.25	7.00	
Missouri	4.225–8.225	4.225	
Montana			No sales tax
Nebraska	5.00–6.50	5.00	
Nevada	4.25–7.25	4.25	
New Hampshire			No sales tax
New Jersey	6.00	6.00	
New Mexico	5.125–6.938	4.50–5.00	Partial county override
New York	6.00–8.50	4.00	
North Carolina	6.00–6.50	4.00	
North Dakota	5.00–7.00	5.00	
Ohio	5.00–7.00	5.00	
Oklahoma	4.50–9.75	4.50	
Oregon			No sales tax
Pennsylvania	6.00–7.00	6.00	
Rhode Island	7.00	7.00	
South Carolina	5.00–7.00	5.00	
South Dakota	4.00– 6.00	4.00*	*Indian reservations – supersedes state rate
Tennessee	7.50–8.75	6.00	
Texas	6.25–8.25	6.25	
Utah	6.00–7.75	4.75	City taxes may override county taxes
Vermont	5.00–6.00	5.00	
Virginia	4.5	3.50	Independent cities or counties
Washington	7.00–8.60	6.50	
West Virginia	6.00	6.00	
Wisconsin	5.00–6.00	5.00	
Wyoming	4.00–6.00	4.00	

Note: * There also are jurisdictions with zero rates. A more detailed version of this table appears in Cornia *et. al.* (2000).

Source: Calculated from data in *Vertex Sales Tax Rate Directory*, 19 November 1999.

2000). The base of local sales taxes is generally the same as for the state sales tax, although Alabama, Colorado and Georgia provide exceptions.

EXPANSION OF THE INCOME TAX

State income taxes pre-date state sales taxes. Wisconsin was the first state to adopt an income tax, in 1911. (Hawaii adopted an income tax in 1901, but of course it was not a state at that time.) By the end of 1930, 15 states (plus Hawaii) had adopted an income tax, although New Hampshire's income tax was limited to interest and dividends. Like the sales tax, use of the income tax spread rapidly during the 1930s, with 16 states adopting an income tax during that period. Not much happened for the next two decades, but during the 1960s and 1970s 11 states adopted the income tax, while one, Alaska, repealed it. The last state to adopt an income tax was New Jersey in 1979. Currently there are 43 states plus the District of Columbia with a state individual income tax. The seven states that do not have a state income tax, Alaska, Florida, Nevada, South Dakota, Texas, Washington and Wyoming, accounted for 16.1 per cent of the US population in 2000. Table 3.3 gives the year that each state adopted its income tax.

As of 1998, individual income tax revenue accounted for about 34 per cent of state tax collections (US Bureau of the Census, 2001). Figure 3.4 shows the growth in state income tax revenue in real terms (left-hand scale) and as a share of total state taxes (right-hand scale) for the period 1932–98. The pattern of income tax revenue growth is similar to that for sales tax revenue, although the initial growth was smaller – income tax revenue (in real terms) reached $20 million in 1967, while sales tax revenue reached that threshold in 1961. It was not until 1997 that state income tax revenues exceeded sales tax revenues.

The first local income tax was adopted by Philadelphia in 1938, but other adoptions by major cities did not occur until after World War II. The use of the local income tax has been concentrated in a handful of states, primarily in the mid-Atlantic and Midwest regions. In 1997, there were only 11 states in which local governments imposed the local income tax.[9] Since 1970 there has been only one state, Iowa, in which local governments have begun using an income tax, but there has been increased use within several of the 11 states. Table 3.4 shows the growth from 1970 to 1994 in the number of local jurisdictions imposing the tax. Some states, such as Alabama, Indiana, Iowa, Kentucky and Ohio, saw significant increases between 1970 and 1994 in the number of local jurisdictions imposing the tax. Most large cities that currently use the income tax adopted it by 1970.

There are two distinct periods of increased adoption of local income taxes. Adoptions were greatest in the late 1940s and the decade of the 1960s,

Table 3.3 *Year state adopted income tax*

State	Year adopted	State	Year adopted	State	Year adopted
Hawaii	1901	Oregon	1930	Colorado	1937
Wisconsin	1911	Idaho	1931	Maryland	1937
Mississippi	1912	Tennessee	1931	Alaska	1949*
Oklahoma	1915	Utah	1931	West Virginia	1961
Massachusetts	1916	Vermont	1931	Indiana	1963
Virginia	1916	Alabama	1933	Michigan	1967
Delaware	1917	Arizona	1933	Nebraska	1967
Missouri	1917	Kansas	1933	Connecticut	1969
New York	1919	Minnesota	1933	Illinois	1969
North Dakota	1919	Montana	1933	Maine	1969
North Carolina	1921	New Mexico	1933	Ohio	1971
South Carolina	1922	Iowa	1934	Pennsylvania	1971
New Hampshire	1923	Louisiana	1934	Rhode Island	1971
Arkansas	1929	California	1935	New Jersey	1976
Georgia	1929	Kentucky	1936		

Note: *Repealed in 1979.

Source: Advisory Commission on Intergovernmental Relations (1995a).

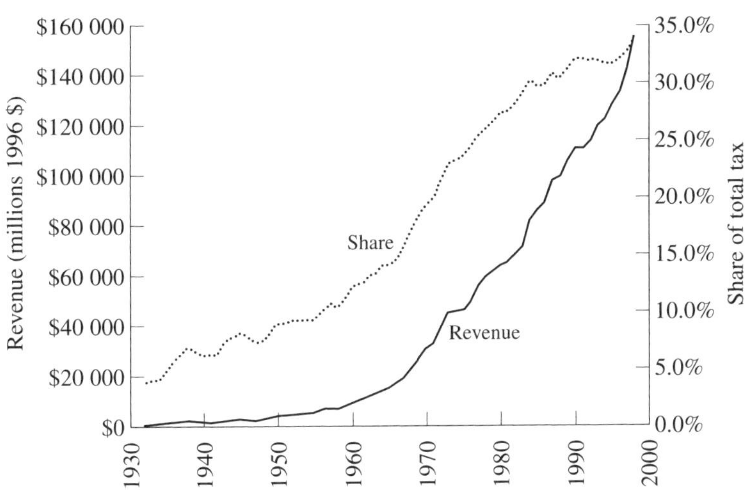

Figure 3.4 *State income tax, 1932–98*

Table 3.4 Number of local governments with income taxes[a]

State	1994	1991	1986	1981	1976	1970
Alabama	18	11	10	5	6	5
Delaware	1	1	1	1	1	1
Indiana	80	76	45	38	38	31
Iowa	379	144	61	26	3	—
Kentucky	140	114	92	67	59	36
Maryland	24	24	24	24	24	24
Michigan	20	20	17	16	16	16
Missouri	2	2	2	2	2	2
New York	2	2	2	1	1	1
Ohio	615	564	486	466	385	335
Pennsylvania	2830	2824	2777[b]	2644[b]	2553[b]	3765
Total excluding Pennsylvania	1281	873	740	688	535	451
Total with Pennsylvania	4111	3697	3517[b]	3332[b]	3088[b]	4216

Notes: [a] Payroll taxes are used locally in California, Oregon and New Jersey; [b] estimate.

Source: Advisory Commission on Intergovernmental Relations (1974; 1995a).

both periods of significant fiscal stress. The overall importance of the tax as a revenue producer is minor: as a percentage of own source revenues, it grew from 1.11 per cent in 1959 to 3.2 per cent in 1998. (In 1998, local income tax revenue was 5.2 per cent of total tax revenue.) The share leveled off somewhat after 1969 when most of the recent adoptions had been phased in. In 1998, local income tax revenues equaled about 46 per cent of the revenue from local sales taxes. Figure 3.2 shows the change over time in the sum of individual and corporate local income tax revenues and Figure 3.3 shows the change in income tax as a share of total local.

In most cases, the local income tax is a relatively simple tax. The base is some form of earned income (wages) and in some cases includes capital. In other cases (such as in the state of Maryland), the tax is coupled to state taxable income. The rates of the local income tax range from 0.5 per cent to 4.9 per cent.

EMPIRICAL ANALYSIS

The basic question we explore is whether local sales and income taxes result in lower property taxes. There is an obvious relationship between changes in property taxes and changes in expenditures; for example, if property taxes and other sources of revenue do not fall with the introduction of another tax, then expenditures must have increased. To investigate the relationship between local sales and income taxes and property taxes, we constructed a pooled time-series, cross-sectional sample of the largest 101 US cities across the period 1963 to 1990.[10] As of 1990, 18 cities in the sample had just an income tax, 42 had just a sales tax, seven had both and 34 had neither. We compared the populations and incomes of cities in our sample with and without local income and sales taxes. We did not observe any significant differences for the sales tax, but cities with income taxes are larger and are generally in the eastern half of the United States, which is not surprising since those states allow local income taxes. The data in Table 3.5 summarize this sample and the effective date of sales and income tax adoption.

Table 3.5 Sample cities

	Local Sales Tax		Local Income Tax	
Cities	Implemented?	Effective Date	Implemented?	Effective Date
Birmingham, AL	Y	1965	Y	1970
Mobile, AL	Y	1962 or earlier	N	–
Montgomery, AL	Y	1962 or earlier	N	–
Phoenix, AZ	Y	1962 or earlier	N	–
Tucson, AZ	Y	1962 or earlier	N	–
Fresno, CA	Y	1962 or earlier	N	–
Long Beach, CA	Y	1962 or earlier	N	–
Los Angeles, CA	Y	1962 or earlier	Y	1972
Oakland, CA	Y	1962 or earlier	N	–
Sacramento, CA	Y	1962 or earlier	N	–
San Diego, CA	Y	1962 or earlier	N	–
San Francisco, CA	Y	1962 or earlier	Y	1972
San Jose, CA	Y	1962 or earlier	N	–
Denver, CO	Y	1962 or earlier	N	–
Bridgeport, CT	N	–	N	–
Hartsfield, CT	N	–	N	–
New Haven, CT	N	–	N	–
Washington, DC	Y	1962 or earlier	Y	1950
Jacksonville, FL	N	–	N	–
Miami, FL	N	–	N	–
St Petersburg, FL	N	–	N	–
Tampa, FL	N	–	N	–
Atlanta, GA	Y	1984	N	–
Savannah, GA	N	–	N	–

Table 3.5 (continued)

Cities	Local Sales Tax		Local Income Tax	
	Implemented?	Effective Date	Implemented?	Effective Date
Honolulu, HI	N	–	N	–
Des Moines, IA	N	–	N	–
Chicago, IL	Y	1962 or earlier	N	–
Rockford, IL	Y	1962 or earlier	N	–
Evansville, IN	N	–	N	–
Fort Wayne, IN	N	–	N	–
Gary, IN	N	–	N	–
Indianapolis, IN	N	–	Y	1986
South Bend, IN	N	–	N	–
Kansas City, KS	Y	1978	N	–
Topeka, KS	Y	1972	N	–
Wichita, KS	N	–	N	–
Lexington, KY	N	–	Y	1952
Louisville, KY	N	–	Y	1948
Baton Rouge, LA	Y	1962 or earlier	N	–
New Orleans, LA	Y	1962 or earlier	N	–
Shreveport, LA	Y	1968	N	–
Boston, MA	N	–	N	–
Springfield, MA	N	–	N	–
Worcester, MA	N	–	N	–
Baltimore, MD	N	–	Y	1966
Detroit, MI	N	–	Y	1962
Flint, MI	N	–	Y	1965
Grand Rapids, MI	N	–	Y	1967
Minneapolis, MN	N	–	N	–
St Paul, MN *	Y	1983	N	–
Kansas City, MO	Y	1972	Y	1964
St Louis, MO	Y	1971	Y	1948
Jackson, MS	Y	1962 or earlier	N	–
Charlotte, NC	N	–	N	–
Greensboro, NC	N	–	N	–
Lincoln, NE	Y	1971	N	–
Omaha, NE	Y	1971	N	–
Jersey City, NJ	N	–	N	–
Newark, NJ	N	–	Y	1972
Albuquerque, NM	Y	1962 or earlier	N	–
Albany, NY	N	–	N	–
Buffalo, NY	N	–	N	–
New York City, NY	Y	1966	Y	1966
Rochester, NY	Y	1975	N	–

Table 3.5 (*continued*)

Cities	Local Sales Tax		Local Income Tax	
	Implemented?	Effective Date	Implemented?	Effective Date
Syracuse, NY	N	–	N	–
Yonkers, NY	Y	1970	Y	1984
Akron, OH	N	–	Y	1962
Cincinnati, OH	N	–	Y	1954
Cleveland, OH	N	–	Y	1967
Columbus, OH	N	–	Y	1947
Dayton, OH	N	–	Y	1949
Toledo, OH	N	–	Y	1946
Youngstown, OH	N	–	Y	1947
Oklahoma City, OK	Y	1966	N	–
Tulsa, OK	Y	1967	N	–
Portland, OR[a]	N	–	N	–
Erie, PA	N	–	Y	1948
Philadelphia, PA	N	–	Y	1939
Pittsburgh, PA	N	–	Y	1954
Providence, RI	N	–	N	–
Chattanooga, TN	N	–	N	–
Memphis, TN*	Y	1984	N	–
Nashville, TN	Y	1966	N	–
Amarillo, TX	Y	1971	N	–
Austin, TX	Y	1969	N	–
Corpus Christi, TX	Y	1969	N	–
Dallas, TX	Y	1969	N	–
El Paso, TX	Y	1969	N	–
Fort Worth, TX	Y	1969	N	–
Lubbock, TX	Y	1969	N	–
Houston, TX	Y	1969	N	–
San Antonio, TX	Y	1970	N	–
Salt Lake City, UT	Y	1962 or earlier	N	–
Norfolk, VA	Y	1965	N	–
Richmond, VA	Y	1966	N	–
Seattle, WA	Y	1971	N	–
Spokane, WA	Y	1973	N	–
Tacoma, WA	Y	1971	N	–
Madison, WI	N	–	N	–
Milwaukee, WI	N	–	N	–

Notes:
[a] Clackamas, Multnomah and Washington counties in the Portland area impose a local income tax. However, the revenues are not disbursed to the city for its use.
* Cities marked by a * did not have a permanent sales tax after date of adoption.

The data were obtained from *Significant Features of Fiscal Federalism* (ACIR, various years), *City Government Finances* (US Bureau of the Census, various years), *County and City Data Book*, the US Censuses of Population, and US Censuses of Government. For the earlier years, that is, the 1960s, population was not available in non-census years; other demographic variables were not available in any non-census year. To estimate the variables for the intervening years, we assumed a constant growth rate of the variables during the decade. Likewise per capita personal income was not available in all years. To estimate income in the missing years we assumed that the annual growth rate between reporting years was in proportion to the growth rate of per capita personal income for the USA. For the percentage of assessed value of property that is commercial or industrial, data were obtained for selected years and estimated for intervening years assuming a linear growth rate.

As a first step we compare property taxes in cities with and without local sales and income taxes, but without controlling for other factors that might affect the level of property taxes. In particular, we investigate whether per capita property taxes decline after the institution of a local income or sales tax. To explore this question, we created five categories of cities. We formed these separately for the local sales tax and the local income tax as follows:

1. Existing tax group (ETG): cities that instituted a local sales (income) tax before 1963.
2. Adopted tax group 1 (ATG 1): cities that instituted a local sales (income) tax between 1963 and 1990.
3. Adopted tax group 2 (ATG 2): cities with adoptions between 1967 and 1972.
4. Adopted tax group 3 (ATG 3): cities with adoptions between 1973 and 1990.
5. No tax group (NTG): a control group – cities that never instituted a local sales (income) tax.

We plotted the average annual real per capita property tax revenue (in $1000s) for each of the five groups defined above for the local sales tax (Figure 3.5) and for the local income tax (Figure 3.6). Again, we are looking for evidence of whether the use of local income and sales taxes is associated with lower real per capita property taxes.

From these figures it is difficult to discern a pattern between sales tax or income tax adoption and per capita property taxes. Cities with an early sales tax or income tax (pre-1963) demonstrate a lower level of per capita property taxes over the period 1963–90. However, for the other groups, sales tax or income tax adoption does not seem to be related to lower per

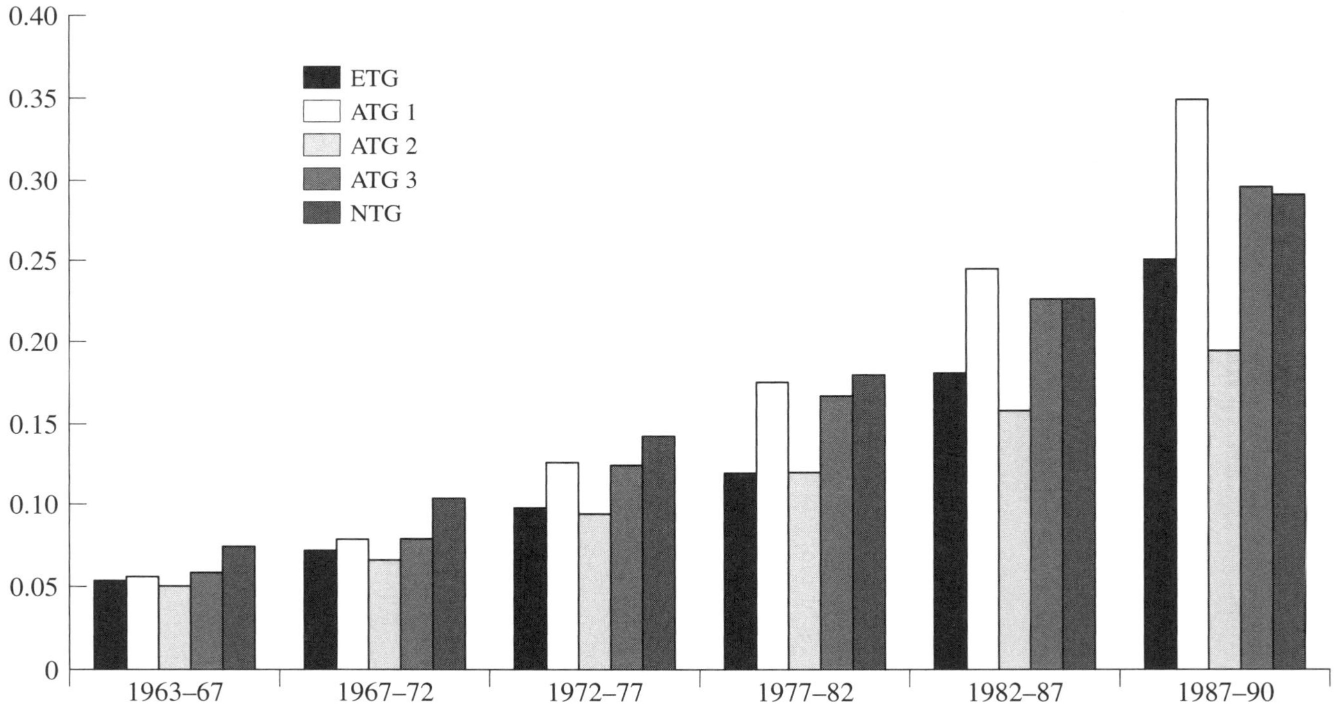

Figure 3.5 *Real per capita property tax, by sales tax adoption/use*

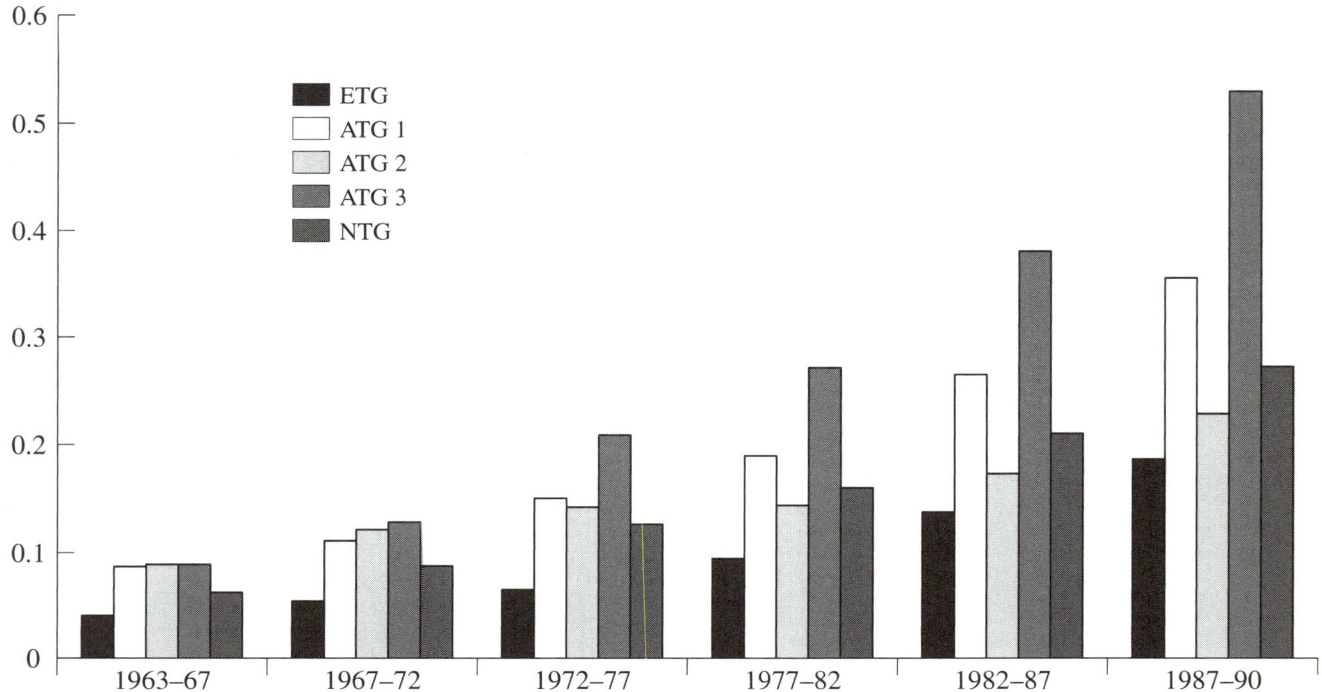

Figure 3.6 Real per capita property tax and local income tax adoption/use

capita property taxes. Thus there is no obvious evidence in the figures that sales tax or income tax adoptions lead to lower per capita property taxes.

A simple ordinary least squares (OLS) regression of property taxes as a function of various demographic, tax (local sales and income taxes) and economic variables shows no significant relationship between the adoption of the local sales and income taxes and per capita property taxes. It is possible that the existence of a sales tax or income tax may be associated with the level of property taxes; in particular, the probability of adopting local sales and income taxes may be positively related to the level of property taxes. To control for the possibility of a simultaneous relationship we estimate a model that includes an equation explaining the decision to adopt a non-property tax.

There are alternative theoretical approaches to the question of how tax structures are determined; as with expenditure determinant studies, two of the most common approaches are the median voter model (Flowers, 1977) and the Leviathan model.[11] In addition, in a series of papers, Hettich and Winer (in particular 1984, 1988 and 1999) outline a theory of tax structure in which, in essence, elected officials adopt the tax structure that maximizes the expected number of votes.

There are several empirical studies exploring the choice of tax structure. Hogan and Shelton (1973), Sjoquist (1981), Blackley and DeBoer (1987), Chicone and Walzer (1986), Biegeleisen and Sjoquist (1988), Metcalf (1993), Moomau and Morton (1992), Alm and McCallin (1996) and Norstrand (1980) all adopt, either explicitly or implicitly, a median voter model in which the choice of tax structure depends, in addition to income, tastes and control variables, on the tax prices for the various taxes, measured as the level of tax exporting, and/or some measure of the burden of each tax. Hettich and Winer (1984) assume that government agents set the tax structure in order to minimize the political cost of raising the required revenue.[12] Political cost is proxied by variables such as the level of tax exporting, revenue from the tax source, fluctuation in the base and competition from neighboring states.[13] All of the above referenced papers find that exportability, deductibility or tax burden affect the choice of tax structure.[14] All of the papers take the level of taxation as exogenous.

Feldstein and Metcalf (1987), Holtz-Eakin and Rosen (1988), and Gade and Adkins (1990), also consider whether the choice of tax structure depends upon exportability as reflected in federal tax deductibility, but they allow for the level of tax revenue and the relative use of tax instruments to be mutually determined. All find that deductibility affects the tax structure.

A related line of research equates the tax structure to a tax portfolio, where the various possible portfolios yield difference values for revenue growth, stability and equity (White, 1983; Misiolek and Perdue, 1987; Dye and McGuire, 1991; Harmon and Mallick, 1994). Thus the choice of a tax portfolio (that is, a tax structure) can be seen as a choice made over the feasible combinations of growth, stability and equity. The papers cited, however, analyze the feasible choice set of characteristics of the tax structures, but not the actual choice.

To analyze the potential simultaneous process of property tax pressure on the adoption and use of a sales tax, we utilize the following model:

$$\text{PTRPC} = f(\text{SThat, RINC, OVER65, PROPLIM, PCTPOV, OPTAX, INDPROP, LIT, YR}), \quad (3.7)$$

$$\text{ST} = f(\text{PTRPChat, LIT, RINC, RETINC, WHOLINC, PROPLIM, OPTAX, YR}), \quad (3.8)$$

where SThat is the instrument for ST, the presence of a local sales tax (=0 for no tax, =1 for a tax), PTRPChat is the instrumental variable for the endogeneous PTRPC, the real per capita property tax revenue in $1000s. LIT is a dummy variable which equals one if the city had an income tax in that year. We recognize that there are differences across cities in the structure of these taxes, and hence in their revenue raising ability. However, our interest is in whether the mere existence of such a tax will affect property taxes. Thus we did not use the level of income tax or sales tax collections as independent variables in these equations.

RINC is real per capita income (in $1000s) and is used to control for the difference in tastes for public expenditures (and thus the level of property taxes) and tax structure. PCTPOV is the percentage of population below the poverty level. This variable is expected to result in higher expenditures and hence higher property taxes, consistent with the increased need for public expenditures associated with poverty. OVER65 is the percentage of the population over 65 years of age in the city, which we expect to be negatively related to property tax level. INDPROP is non-residential property value as a percentage of total property value and is a measure of property tax exporting. We expect INDPROP to be positively related to the property tax level. OPTAX is real per capita county and school district property taxes.[15] OPTAX measures the level of competing use of the municipality's property tax base and we expect it to be negatively correlated with PTRPC. PROPLIM is a dummy variable that equals one if the city had a property tax limitation in that year and is constructed from data from ACIR (1995c). We expect PROPLIM to be negatively correlated with property tax level. YR is a set of year dummies.[16]

Equation (3.8) models the decision to adopt the sales tax. We want to control for the possibility that the adoption of a local non-property tax is in part the response to high property taxes. We assume that, as per capita property taxes increase, the probability that a city will adopt a non-property tax increases.

In our empirical investigation, we found that the results for the local income tax were not robust to alternative specifications, particularly for the equation explaining the adoption of an income tax. This could be due to the relatively small number of cities in our sample using a local income tax and the fact that most large cities that rely on the income tax adopted it prior to 1970. We therefore choose to concentrate on the potential interaction between the local property tax and sales tax. We do include a dummy variable in equations (3.7) and (3.8) to control for the presence of a local income tax.

Growing taxpayer dissatisfaction with the property tax is one impetus for diversification of revenue sources. One indication of taxpayer dissatisfaction with the local property tax is that the tax ranks as the worst tax in the latest ACIR opinion poll (ACIR, 1995b). To the extent that there is general pressure to reduce or limit the increase in property taxes, local governments may shift to other taxes. One measure of this dissatisfaction with the property tax is the presence of tax limitations. During the period covered by our data (1962–90), 33 states imposed some limitation on property tax rates or revenues.

The papers cited above suggest that the ability to export a tax is an important variable in determining the choice of taxes.[17] Thus, in addition to the level of property taxes, we include in the tax choice equation two variables to measure the exportability of the two taxes. In equation (3.8) we included retail sales and wholesale sales divided by income, denoted by RETINC and WHOLINC, respectively, to measure the exportability of the sales tax. The argument is that, the larger the city's retail and wholesale sales relative to the city's income, the greater the volume of sales to individuals and businesses from outside the city. We expect both of these variables to be positively related to the probability of adopting a sales tax. These two measures of exporting are admittedly crude, however data did not exist for better measures of exportability.

Turning to the results of Table 3.6, we find that, for equation (3.7), the coefficient on SThat is negative and significant. These results suggest that the adoption and presence of a local sales tax in the overall tax structure of a city leads to a decrease in the level of property taxes per capita.

The coefficient on the LIT variable is also negative and significant in the property tax equation. This result suggests that the local income tax has played a role in reducing property taxes per capita. The negative and significant coefficient for LIT in the sales tax equation may reflect a reluctance of cities to take on both a local income and a local sales tax.

Table 3.6 Regression results for simultaneous model (standard errors)

	Coefficient (standard error)	
Independent variable[a]	(21) PTRPC	(22) ST
Constant	−0.433* (0.053)	−0.690** (0.072)
PTRPChat	—	−1.214** (0.189)
SThat	−0.091** (0.026)	—
RINC (1 000s)	0.350** (0.005)	0.103** (0.006)
LIT	−0.045** (0.008)	−0.305** (0.020)
OVER65	−0.0007 (0.001)	—
PROPLIM	−0.060** (0.007	0.048** (0.025)
PCTPOV	0.006** (0.001)	—
OPTAX	−0.076** (0.008	−0.161** (0.030)
INDPROP	0.411** (0.026)	—
WHOLINC	—	−0.028* (0.012)
RETINC	—	0.457** (0.055)
R-sq	0.43	0.26

Notes: [a] Year dummy variables are suppressed; **significant at the 0.01 per cent level; * significant at the 0.05 per cent level.

The other variables included in equation (3.7) performed as expected, with the exception of OVER65. We expected that cities with higher elderly populations would have lower property taxes per capita since the elderly have a higher resistance to property taxes and local governments have increasingly instituted property tax exemptions for the elderly and/or low income.

The results for equation (3.8) suggest that the pressure from property taxes is not a driving factor in the adoption of a local sales tax. The coefficient on PTRPChat in the ST equation is negative and significant. In practice, as of 1990, a number of cities with relatively high property tax burdens had not adopted a local sales tax. We conclude that sales taxes are adopted as a means to diversify a local revenue structure, regardless of how high property taxes are.[18]

The adoption of the sales tax has the flavor of a natural evolution in tax policy as opposed to a crisis restructuring of local government finances. If that is a reasonable conclusion from these results, it is important to investigate what happens next. Over time, do local governments with a sales tax turn to increases in rates for further diversification (pre-crisis)? Or, once a sales tax is imposed, does it become a 'crisis tool' that is adjusted when property taxes (or other tax burdens) become too high? These questions are beyond the scope of this research, but we believe that they are important extensions.

Regarding the other results from equation (3.8), the coefficient on PROPLIM is positive and significant, as expected. One of the proxies for tax exporting, RETINC, is positive and significant. The coefficient for WHOLINC is negative and significant, which is contrary to expectations. It may be that cities with large wholesale bases do not use sales taxes in an effort to keep business competitive, or that WHOLINC is not a good measure of sales tax exportability.

CONCLUSIONS

Seventy years ago, the property tax accounted for 67 per cent of total revenue of local governments and 97 per cent of local tax revenue. It now accounts for 25 per cent of total local revenue and 73 per cent of local tax revenue. The adoption of local income and sales taxes account for much of the decline in the property tax's share of tax revenue and, along with intergovernmental grants, account for the decline in its share of total revenue. Since federal and state grants to local governments are largely financed through sales and income taxes, the overall importance of the property tax in the US fiscal system has declined significantly, from 40 per cent of combined federal, state and local revenue in 1932 to less than 8 per cent today.

In this chapter we have explored the question of whether the adoption of a local income or sales tax affects local government finance, specifically the level of property taxes. We find the property tax 'pressure', in the form of growing property tax revenue per capita, does not appear to be a cause of the adoption of a local sales tax. Our analysis of the effect on the adoption of a local income tax was too unreliable to report.

There are many ways in which the analysis of these questions could be extended. For example, one can envision that the decision to adopt a local income or sales tax could be for one of two purposes: reducing property taxes while maintaining expenditures at the same level, or expanding expenditures while maintaining property taxes at their same level. While our analysis suggests that property taxes decline with the adoption of a local income or sales tax, it is possible that some jurisdictions have one motive while others have the alternative motive to adopt local taxes. There may be some unobservable factor at work that divides the jurisdictions into these two categories.

Our analysis does not directly address the question of whether adoption of a local income or sales tax changes the level of expenditures. Thus a second extension would be to measure how the adoption of a local income or sales tax affects expenditures, both in total and in their composition. Finally, it would be useful to test the results on a specific case or cases by estimating the probability of sales tax or income tax adoptions for specific jurisdictions.

NOTES

1. Excess burden is also dependent on the price elasticity of demand, and if non-property taxes are more price elastic, then marginal excess burden might increase with their adoption.
2. For a discussion of the property tax as a benefits tax, see Fischel (2001) and Zodrow (2001).
3. Downs (1960), however, has argued that a diverse tax system makes citizens more aware of the costs of government, and that this leads to lower expenditures than with a non-diverse tax structure. In addition, Besley and Case (1995) find that state officials are less likely to be re-elected if the state's tax policy gets out of line with its neighbors', implying that politicians cannot allow taxes to increase much beyond those in neighboring states.
4. See also Munley and Greene (1978). Oates (1988), Merrifield (2000) and Hettich and Winer (1999) provide reviews of this literature.
5. Local governments in Hawaii are authorized to levy a sales tax, but no local government currently exercises that authority. Although Alaska has no state sales tax, it does allow local sales taxes.
6. It was necessary to estimate data for missing years early in the series. To do that we assumed a linear trend.
7. For early years in the 1932–99 period, only the combined total of sales tax and gross receipts tax is available.
8. The 7 per cent local rate applies to Alaska; the highest local rate in a state with a state sales tax is 5 per cent.
9. Local governments in three states, Oregon, California and New Jersey, utilize a payroll tax. Georgia and Arkansas authorize the use of the local income tax, but it is not currently used.
10. Given its unique status, Washington, DC was excluded from our sample.
11. Hettich and Winer (1999) present a brief description of each as well as other approaches, one of which is to assume that the tax structure is set so as to minimize the excess burden of taxes (Barro, 1979). Henderson (1984) develops a model of tax structure in which communities are either profit maximizers or utility maximizers.
12. Hettich and Winer (1999) provide an update of this work.

13. Inman (1989) posits a model that includes institutional, political and economic considerations. The dependent variables in the two-equation regression model are total property taxes and total fee and selected sales tax revenue. Among his findings are that the deductibility of local taxes has a significant effect on local government tax structures.
14. Chernick (1992) focuses on the determinants of one characteristic of the tax structure, its progressivity, in a one-equation model. Hettich and Winer (1999) consider the adoption of an income tax credit for property taxes paid, and do so in an empirical model that allows for the simultaneous determination of the level of income taxes.
15. To construct OPTAX we took county property taxes and allocated them to the city on a per capita basis. The city school district taxes were added, or, if the school district extended beyond the city, they were allocated on a per capita basis.
16. We estimated the model with and without city dummies. As the results were quite similar with and without the city dummies, we report the results without the city dummy variables.
17. See especially Hogan and Shelton (1973) and Gade and Adkins (1990).
18. See Turnbull and Djoundarian (1994).

REFERENCES

Advisory Commission on Intergovernmental Relations (ACIR) (1968), *Significant Features of Fiscal Federalism*, Washington, DC: ACIR.

Advisory Commission on Intergovernmental Relations (ACIR) (1974), *Local Revenue Diversification: Income, Sales Taxes, and User Charges*, Washington, DC: ACIR.

Advisory Commission on Intergovernmental Relations (ACIR) (1988), *Local Revenue Diversification: Local Income Taxes*, Washington, DC: ACIR.

Advisory Commission on Intergovernmental Relations (ACIR) (1995a), *Significant Features of Fiscal Federalism*, vol. 1, Washington, DC: ACIR.

Advisory Commission on Intergovernmental Relations (ACIR) (1995b), *Changing Public Attitudes on Governments and Taxes*, Washington, DC: ACIR.

Advisory Commission on Intergovernmental Relations (ACIR) (1995c), *Tax and Expenditure Limits on Local Governments*, Washington, DC: ACIR.

Alm, James and Nancy McCallin (1996), 'The determinants of state tax structures', University of Colorado working paper.

American Bar Association (2000), *Sales and Use Tax Desk Book: 1999–2000*, Washington, DC: American Bar Association Section on Taxation.

Anderson, John E. (1994), 'City income tax adoptions', working paper presented at the Eighty-Seventh Annual Conference on Taxation, National Tax Association, Local Non-Property Session, Charleston, SC, 14 November.

Baker, Samuel H. (1983), 'The determinants of median voter tax liability: an empirical test of the fiscal illusion hypothesis', *Public Finance Quarterly*, **11**, January, 95–108.

Barro, Robert (1979), 'On the determination of the public debt', *Journal of Political Economy*, **87**, 940–71.

Becker, Gary and Casey Mulligan (1998), 'Deadweight costs and the size of government', working paper no. 6789, National Bureau of Economic Research, Cambridge.

Besley, Timothy and Anne C. Case (1995), 'Incumbent behavior: vote seeking, tax setting and yardstick competition', *American Economic Review*, **85**, 25–45.

Biegeleisen, J. Alan and David L. Sjoquist (1988), 'Rational voting applied to choice of taxes', *Public Choice*, **57**(1), 39–47.

Blackley, Paul R. and Larry DeBoer (1987), 'Tax base choice of local governments', *Land Economics*, **63**(3), 227–36.

Breeden, Charles H. and William J. Hunter (1985), 'Tax revenue and tax structure', *Public Finance Quarterly*, **13** (April), 216–24.

Buchanan, James M. (1967), *Public Finance in a Democratic Process*, Chapel Hill, NC: University of North Carolina Press.

Buchanan, James M. and Richard Wagner (1977), *Democracy in Deficit, The Political Legacy of Lord Keynes*, New York: Academic Press.

Chernick, Howard (1992), 'A model of the distributional incidence of state and local taxes', *Public Finance Quarterly*, **20**, 572–85.

Chicone, David L. and Norman Walzer (1986), 'Factors affecting property tax reliance: additional evidence', *Public Choice*, **49**(1), 17–27.

Clotfelter, Charles T. (1976), 'Public spending for higher education: an empirical test of two hypotheses', *Public Finances*, **31**(2), 177–95.

Cornia, Gary C., Kelly D. Edmiston, Steven M. Sheffrin, Terri A. Sexton, David L. Sjoquist and C. Kurt Zorn (2000), 'An analysis of the feasibility of implementing a single rate sales tax', *National Tax Journal*, **53**(4 – Pt 3), 1327–50.

Craig, Eleanor D. and A. James Heins (1980), 'The effect of tax elasticity on government spending', *Public Choice*, **35**(3), 267–75.

Deran, Elizabeth (1968), 'Tax structure in cities using the income tax', *National Tax Journal*, **21**, 147–52.

DiLorenzo, Thomas J. (1982), 'Tax elasticity and the growth of local public expenditures', *Public Finance Quarterly*, **10**(3), 385–92.

Downs, Anthony (1960), 'Why the government budget is too small in a democracy', *World Politics*, **12** (July), 541–63.

Due, John F. and John L. Mikesell (1994), *Sales Taxation: State and Local Structure and Administration*, 2nd edn, Washington, DC: The Urban Institute Press.

Dye, Richard F. and Therese J. McGuire (1991), 'Growth and variability of state individual income and general sales taxes', *National Tax Journal*, **44**(1), 55–60.

Feenberg, Daniel R. and Harvey S. Rosen (1987), 'Tax structure and public sector growth', *Journal of Public Economics*, **32**, 185–201.

Feldstein, Martin S. and Gilbert E. Metcalf (1987), 'The effect of federal tax deductibility on state and local taxes and spending', *Journal of Political Economy*, **95**, 710–36.

Fischel, William A. (2001), 'Municipal corporations, homeowners and the benefits view of the property tax', in Wallace E. Oates (ed.), *Property Taxation and Local Government Finance*, Cambridge, MA: Lincoln Institute of Land Policy.

Flowers, Marilyn R. (1977), 'Multiple tax sources, voting equilibrium and budgetary size', *Public Finance*, **32**(2), 210–24.

Gade, Mary N. and Lee C. Adkins (1990), 'Tax exporting and state revenue structures', *National Tax Journal*, **43**(1), March, 39–52.

Harmon, Oskar Ragnar and Rajiv Mallick (1994), 'The optimal state tax portfolio model: an extension', *National Tax Journal*, **47**(2), 395–402.

Henderson, J. Vernon (1984), 'Community choice of revenue instruments', *Regional Science and Urban Economics*, **24**(2), 159–83.

Hettich, Walter and Stanley L. Winer (1984), 'A positive model of tax structure', *Journal of Public Economics*, **24**, 67–87.

Hettich, Walter and Stanley L. Winer (1988), 'Economic and political foundations of tax structure', *American Economic Review*, **78**, 701–12.

Hettich, Walter and Stanley L. Winer (1999), *Democratic Choice and Taxation: A Theoretical and Empirical Analysis*, New York: Cambridge University Press.

Hogan, Timothy D. and Robert B. Shelton (1973), 'Interstate tax exportation and states' fiscal structures', *National Tax Journal,* **26**(4), December, 553–64.

Holtz-Eakin, Douglas and Harvey S. Rosen (1988), 'Tax deductibility and municipal budget structure', in Harvey S. Rosen (ed.), *Fiscal Federalism: Quantitative Studies*, Chicago: University of Chicago Press, pp.107–26.

Inman, Robert P. (1978), 'Testing political economy's "as if" proposition: is the median income voter really decisive?', *Public Choice*, **33**(4), 45–65.

Inman, Robert P. (1979), 'Subsidies, regulations and the taxation of property in large US cities', *National Tax Journal* (June, supplement), 159–68.

Inman, Robert P. (1989), 'The local decision to tax evidence from large US cities', *Regional Science and Urban Economics*, 455–91.

Kau, James B. and Paul H. Rubin (1981), 'The size of government', *Public Choice*, **37**, 261–74.

Ladd, Helen F. and Dana R. Weist (1987), 'State and local tax systems: balance among taxes vs. balance among policy goals', in Frederick D. Stocker (ed.), *The Quest for Balance in State–Local Revenue Structures*, Tax Policy Roundtable/ Property Tax Papers Series TRP-16, Cambridge, MA: Lincoln Institute of Land Policy, pp.39–69.

Merrifield, John (2000), 'State government expenditure determinants and tax revenue determinants revised', *Public Choice*, **102**, 25–50.

Metcalf, Gilbert E. (1993), 'Tax exporting, federal deductibility and state tax structure', *Journal of Policy Analysis and Management*, **12**, 213–31.

Misiolek, Walter S. and D. Grady Perdue (1987), 'The portfolio approach to state and local tax structure', *National Tax Journal*, **40**(1), 111–14.

Moomau, Pamela H. and Rebecca B. Morton (1992), 'Revealed preferences for property taxes: an empirical study of perceived tax incidence', *Review of Economics and Statistics*, **38**, 175–208.

Munley, Vincent G. and Kenneth V. Greene (1978), 'Fiscal illusion, the nature of public goods and equation specification', *Public Choice*, **33**(1), 95–100.

Netzer, Dick (1966), *Economics of the Property Tax*, Washington, DC: The Brookings Institution.

Norstrand, Rolf (1980), 'The choice between income tax and land tax in Danish municipalities', *Public Finance*, **35** (3), 412–24.

Oates, Wallace E. (1975), 'Automatic increases in tax revenue – the effect on the size of the public budget', in W. Oates (ed.), *Financing the New Federalism: Revenue Sharing, Conditional Grants, and Taxation*, Baltimore MD: Johns Hopkins University Press, pp.129–60.

Oates, Wallace E. (1988), 'On the nature and measurement of fiscal illusion: a survey', in Geoffrey Brennen, Peter Groenewegen and Bhajana S. Grewal (eds), *Taxation and Fiscal Federalism*, Sydney: Australian National University Press.

Sjoquist, David L. (1981), 'A median voter analysis of variations in the use of property taxes among local governments', *Public Choice*, **36**(2), 273–85.

Stockfish, J.A. (1985), 'Value added taxes and the size of government: some evidence', *National Tax Journal*, **38**, 542–7.

Suyderhoud, Jack P. (1994), 'State–local revenue diversification, balance, and fiscal performance', *Public Finance Quarterly*, **22**(2), 168–94.

Tax Foundation (2001), *Facts & Figures on Government Finance*, 35th edn, Washington, DC: Tax Foundation.

Turnbull, Geoffrey K. and Salpie S. Djoundarian (1994), 'The median voter hypothesis: evidence from general purpose local governments', *Public Choice*, **81**(3–4), 223–40.

US Bureau of the Census (various years), *City Government Finances*, Washington, DC: US Bureau of the Census.

US Bureau of the Census, (various years), *Government Finances*, Washington, DC: US Bureau of the Census.

US Bureau of the Census (2001), *Government Finances* (http://www.census.gov/govs/estimate/9800us.html).

Wagner, Richard E. (1971), *The Fiscal Organization of American Federalism*, Chicago: Markham.

Wagner, Richard E. (1976), 'Revenue structure, fiscal illusion, and budgetary choice', *Public Choice*, 25 (Spring), 45–61.

White, Fred C. (1983), 'Trade-off in growth and stability in state taxes', *National Tax Journal*, **36**(1), 103–14.

Zodrow, George R. (2001), 'Reflections on the new view and the benefit view of the property tax', in Wallace E. Oates (ed.), *Property Taxation and Local Government Finance*, Cambridge, MA: Lincoln Institute of Land Policy.

COMMENT

Therese J. McGuire

The authors explore the impact of alternative local taxes on the level of local property taxes. They summarize theories that relate the level of expenditures or overall taxes to the degree of tax diversification and describe the related, limited, empirical literature. In general, this literature points to a positive relationship between expenditure levels and tax diversification. This literature does not focus on the level of one tax, as the authors do, but rather on the level of total expenditures or total revenues. In addition, the existing empirical studies of the effect of tax diversification on overall spending or tax levels do not control for the likely endogeneity of the tax structure.

To focus the analysis on the level of property taxes, the authors develop a simple model of the simultaneous choice of spending and tax structure. One can question the realism of the assumptions, but in the model the effect of the adoption of an excise (sales) tax is a reduction in property tax revenues. The authors thus establish a prior for finding a negative relationship between the adoption and reliance on local sales taxes and the level of the local property tax.

Before they turn to estimating the relationship implied by their model, the authors present historical, descriptive statistics on the levels of, and reliance by state and local governments on, property, sales and income taxes. This section is interesting, although the amount of attention paid to state taxes is surprising, given the focus of the authors on local tax diversification. (As a minor note along these lines, because of their very limited tax on capital income, many observers do not classify New Hampshire and Tennessee as having state income taxes.) The main findings from this section of relevance to the chapter are that, since the mid-1930s, local sales and, to a lesser extent, local income taxes have become increasingly important as sources of revenue for local governments, but that the property tax share of local taxes continues to be over 70 per cent.

The primary interest of the authors is in answering the empirical question of 'whether the adoptions of local sales and income taxes have led to reductions in property taxes' (p. 43). To address this question they gather data on the largest 101 cities in the USA over the period 1963 to 1990. They first look for a bivariate relationship between the adoption of a local income or local sales tax and the level of property taxes. To accomplish this, they divide the cities into five groups: those with a local sales (income) tax in place at the beginning of the period; those that adopted a local sales (income) tax between 1963 and 1966; those that adopted a local sales (income) tax between 1967 and 1972; those that adopted a local sales (income) tax between 1973 and 1990; and those that never adopted a local sales (income) tax during the period. The authors do not motivate the particular cut-off dates for the groups, nor do they motivate how real property taxes per capita – their measure of the property tax level – should vary across these groups in any one year or over time. In fact, they do not find any systematic relationship. A perhaps more revealing cut at the data would be to graph (draw a disjointed line between) five observations (one for each time period) for each of the five groups and look for a break in the time trend at the point when each group adopts a local income or sales tax (or no break in trend for the two groups whose local revenue structure is unchanging over the entire period).

The authors specify a sensible multivariate regression in equation (3.7). They postulate that real property taxes per capita are a function of whether a city has a sales or an income tax, real income per capita, percentage of the population in poverty, percentage of the population over 65, percentage of the property that is non-residential, real county and school district property taxes per capita, and whether a city faces a property tax limitation. The authors construct a pooled data set, but they have to extrapolate for many of the variables in non-census years. It is not made clear how many variables this is true for. It might be useful to estimate the equation on just the census years when data are available for all cities for all variables.

As mentioned earlier, the choice of tax structure is very likely to be endogenous to the level of property taxes, so the authors estimate equation (3.7) using two-stage least squares. The authors are unable to estimate with any confidence the decision to adopt a local income tax, so they focus on estimating sales tax adoption. The specification of the equation for the adoption of a local sales tax (equation (3.8)) is sensible for the most part, although they obtain a few unexpected coefficients.

The authors find a negative, significant coefficient on the sales tax adoption variable in the equation explaining real property taxes per capita. Thus revenue diversification in the form of sales tax adoption appears to result in lower property taxes, as expected. The results are silent on the question addressed in the previous literature of the effect of revenue diversification on overall taxes or expenditures. Perhaps in future work the authors will link their present result on the effect of sales tax adoption on property tax levels to the overall effects of revenue diversification on the size of government.

4. Land taxation in New York City: a general equilibrium analysis

Andrew F. Haughwout*

Few topics have so engaged public finance scholars, among them Dick Netzer, as the land value tax.[1] Since at least Henry George (1879), economists have urged the efficiency of a land tax, particularly relative to the current primary local tax, that on property value. Over the years, the land value tax has served admirably as a lesson in humility for economists: despite its highly touted efficiency benefits, policy makers have virtually never adopted it. This dissonance between research and practice has been so persistent that it has itself become a major theme of economists' recent discussions of the land tax (see, for example, the collection of papers in Netzer, 1998).

This chapter explores the consequences of adopting a land value tax in New York City, the city that has also been among Netzer's major intellectual projects of the last 40 years. New York, with its enormous public sector and complex local taxation system, is unique in the American federal system. Yet in other aspects, particularly its essentially complete openness to factor movements and trade, New York is like other local economies in the United States and elsewhere. This chapter develops and calibrates an equilibrium model of the New York City economy and provides simulations of the effects of adopting a land value tax in place of parts or all of the current local tax system. We believe that an application to a single municipality is instructive both as a contrast to the current academic literature and as a description of the actual arrangement of fiscal institutions in the USA. Given the significant local control of local taxes, there is a high likelihood that the adoption of land taxation, if it is to take place at all, will occur on a locality-by-locality basis, albeit with authorization from the states.

The chapter is organized as follows. The first section describes the model and its calibration to the New York City economy in 1997, the most recent

* I am indebted to the participants at the conference in honor of Dick Netzer, New York, October 2001, and especially to Tom Nechyba and Amy Ellen Schwartz for helpful comments on a preliminary version of this chapter.

year for which complete fiscal data are available. The second section discusses the effects on the equilibrium of replacing some or all of the current tax system with a land value tax. The third section discusses the results and their implications for the political economy of land value taxation in New York and, by extension, other localities.

MODEL AND CALIBRATION

Model

We specify an equilibrium open city model with endogenous local factor prices. The model is described in detail in Haughwout and Inman (2001); here we provide an overview of its structure and important features before discussing calibration to the New York City economy in some detail.

We consider a single heterogeneous jurisdiction that we will call *the city*, which hosts producers, resident workers and an exogenously determined population of non-working residents within a fixed land area. The city's workforce may also include commuters, who work at city firms but consume housing and other goods in other jurisdictions. The city is a small, open part of the larger national and world economies.

Households

The population of the city is made up of two major groups: an endogenous number of resident workers (n), who work, live and consume in the city, and are paid an endogenously determined local wage, W; and dependent households (d), who do not work, but receive an exogenous transfer income, $\bar{Y}$. Dependent populations are exogenously given, and contain both poor and elderly households.

The city workforce also contains commuting managers (m), who work in the city but consume housing and composite good in the suburbs. Managers are supplied perfectly elastically to the city at the exogenously determined managerial wage s.

All households have a common set of preferences for land (l_r), housing capital (h), composite non-housing consumption (x) and a local public good (G): $U = U(x, h, l, G)$. We measure units of housing capital and the composite good such that their prices = 1. Working households' choice of consumption is made subject to the constraint that their annual gross-of-tax expenditure not exceed annual wages (W) less taxes.

$$(1+\tau_s)x + (r+\tau_p)h + (r+\tau_p)(R/r)l_r = (1-\tau_w)W. \tag{4.1}$$

Here τ_i represents the local tax rate on sales ($i=s$), property ($i=p$) or income ($i=W$), R is the price of land and r is the discount rate. For dependent households, expenditure is constrained by the size of the exogenously determined transfer payment, $\bar{Y}$. We assume that dependent households are exempt from income taxes, but must pay sales and property taxes.

Firms

Private businesses in the model combine land (ℓ_f), resident labor (n), commuter-managers (m) and capital (k) to produce the composite output good X. We assume that production technology exhibits constant returns to scale across the private inputs, but is enhanced by the public good, G, which acts as a Hicks-neutral external scale economy. Firms choose their private input mix so as to minimize gross-of-tax unit costs, subject to the production function:

$$C=(1+\tau_p)R/r\cdot\ell_f+W\cdot n+(1+\tau_p/r)k+(1+\tau_m)m \qquad (4.2)$$

We measure units such that the prices of the composite output good (P_x), private capital (P_k) and managerial labor (s) are equal to 1.

Government

City government produces the public good G from pre-existing public infrastructure stocks (G_0), aid from higher levels of government (Z), income from pre-existing financial assets (A) and locally-generated tax revenues (T). Local governments also bear the local share of transfer costs ($\psi\cdot\bar{Y}$), the costs of depreciation (at annual rate σ), and remaining interest due on G_0, at annual rate r^o. Aggregate public good availability is then determined by the public sector budget constraint

$$G=\frac{\{T+Z+A-\psi\bar{Y}\}/(r+\sigma)+[(r-r^o)/(r+\sigma)]G_0}{C}, \qquad (4.3)$$

where $T=\Sigma_i\tau_iB_i$ ($i=X, s, p, W, m$) is aggregate local tax revenue and C is the unit cost of public sector output.

City equilibrium

Our equilibrium concept is identical to that in Roback (1982) and the subsequent literature: mobile households (firms) cannot earn excess utility (profits) simply by virtue of their locations. In our context, resident workers are the mobile group, and their bids in local land and labor markets reflect their evaluations of each location and determine the shape and position of

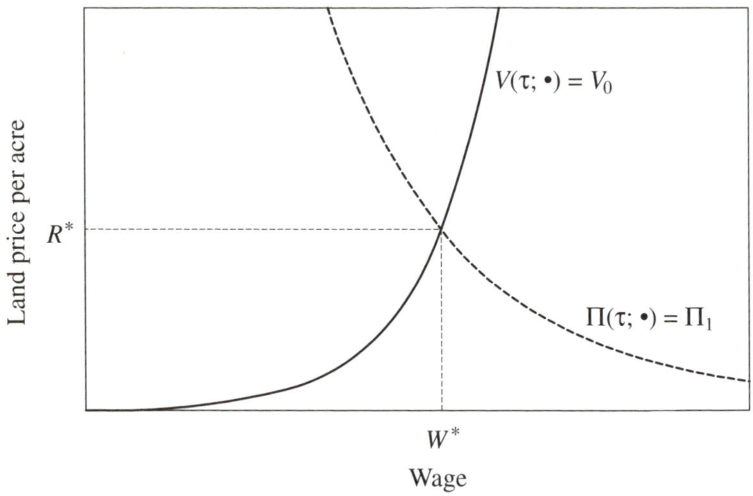

Figure 4.1 Wage and land price equilibrium

the household indifference curve V(·) in Figure 4.1. Dependent household utility, by contrast, is endogenous in the model.

The city is one of many places in which firms and households may locate. In order to attract firms and households, the city must offer at least the level of profits and utility that prevail elsewhere in the economy. As in Roback (1982) and the subsequent 'quality of life' literature (see Gyourko *et al.*, 1999 for a review), land and labor price adjustments provide the mechanism which allows both attractive and unattractive places to host activities.

Figure 4.1 provides the standard depiction of the equilibrium. The upward sloping curve is a household indifference curve in the price space. In order to be left indifferent, households must be compensated for higher wages with a higher land price. For firms, both wages and land rents are costs that must be traded off. Thus the firm iso-profit function is represented by the downward sloping curve in Figure 4.1. At (W^*, R^*), both firms and households are in equilibrium, earning zero locational rents.

Local fiscal policies, including both taxes and spending, have the potential to exert importance influences over local equilibrium prices (Gyourko *et al.*, 1999). Consider two otherwise identical cities levying a tax that is legally incident on both firms and households (in New York and many other localities the property tax has this character). Figure 4.2 depicts the effect of differences in this tax, holding public good provision constant. For a given city, this kind of difference in constant service tax rates might be created by differentials in grants-in-aid from the state. Across cities, differential historical public investment that has led to differing surviving

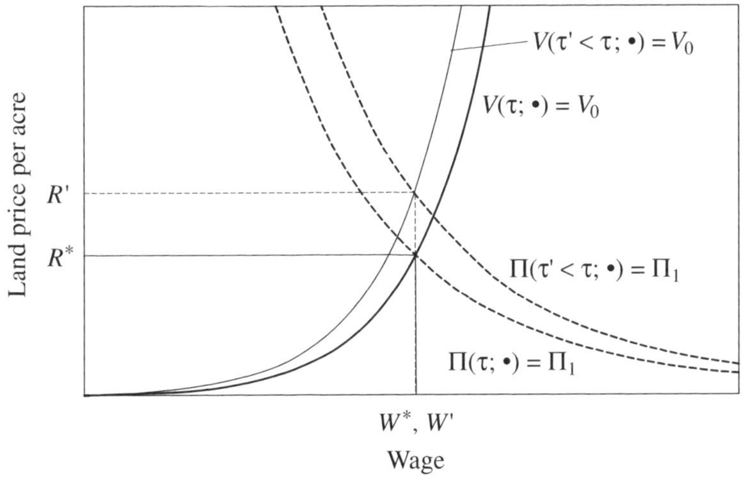

Figure 4.2 *Wage and land price equilibrium with lower taxes* (ceteris paribus)

city infrastructure stocks will also shift the curves. As shown in the figure, the city with the lower tax rate will, *ceteris paribus*, have higher land prices and potentially higher or lower wages, depending on parameters of production technology and working household preferences. Analogous arguments can be constructed for increases in public goods, taxes constant (Haughwout, 2002).

Of particular note here is the effect of distortionary taxation on the local price equilibrium. When local public services are financed with distortionary tax instruments, their cost is increased, because a \$1 increase in public spending comes at the cost of \$$(1+\eta)$ in private utility, where η measures the excess burden of the tax. Eliminating this excess burden by shifting to a more efficient tax system reduces the marginal cost of public funds, allowing more public services to be provided for a given local tax burden. Put another way, a more efficient tax system acts like a tax cut, with public services unchanged. We discuss the details of the efficiency of local taxation below, but for now note that Figure 4.2 may also be viewed as a depiction of the effect of reduced distortions from local taxation. Thus we would anticipate that replacement of some or all of the local tax structure by a land tax would increase local land prices and have ambiguous effects on local wages.

Prices, of course, have important effects on behavior. When local land prices go up, residents and firms are encouraged to economize on land. Assuming that no land is vacant in the city (that is, ignoring brownfields and counting speculative landholding as a business investment), this implies that more efficient taxation is associated with increased city density. Similarly, higher wages induce firms to move out of labor and into other factors of production. Household behavior will likewise be affected as incomes and land prices change. Finally, local public goods simultaneously reflect and affect the local economy. As prices and quantities change, so will tax revenue and public spending. Since public spending affects prices, the cycle begins again. Formally, the model contains 18 endogenous variables, which are listed in the appendix. Readers interested in the details are referred to Haughwout and Inman (2001).

SOLVING THE MODEL

The solution procedure begins with parameterizations of household preferences and firm production technologies which are then solved for expressions for the model's endogenous variables as functions of the city's exogenous fiscal and economic characteristics. These specifications and data are shown in Table 4.1 and are discussed further below. Note that taxes are exogenous in the model; when combined with local tax bases, these rates determine local public services through equation (4.3). Since the public and private sectors are interdependent, we initially solve the model for an arbitrary level of public spending. This yields a set of private market outcomes which yields a new equilibrium level of public services, and the process is repeated until the model converges. Convergence is achieved when the public sector equilibrium yields household utility and firm costs that are within 0.1 per cent of their equilibrium values.

CALIBRATING THE MODEL TO NEW YORK CITY IN 1997

Calibration of the basic simulation model to New York City requires identification of the exogenous determinants of the New York City economic, fiscal and demographic environment. This section describes the setting and provides the functional and numerical inputs required to solve for the model's 18 endogenous variables. The appendix lists the required variables.

Technology and Preferences

The city's firms' technology is represented by a Cobb–Douglas specification between land (L) and a composite joint labor–capital input produced by a

Table 4.1 Assumptions and parameterization

Production technology

$X = L_f^{0.05}\,[0.5N^{0.4} + 0.5\,(0.5K^{-0.5} + 0.5M^{-0.5})^{\,0.4/(-0.5)}]^{\,0.95/0.4}G^{0.04}$ (no congestion)

or

$X = L_f^{0.10}\,[0.5N^{0.4} + 0.5\,(0.5K^{-0.5} + 0.5M^{-0.5})^{\,0.4/(-0.5)}]^{\,0.90/0.4}\frac{G}{N^*}^{0.04}$ (full congestion)

Household preferences

$U = x^{0.7}h^{0.2}\ell^{0.1}G^{0.05}$ (no congestion)

or

$U = x^{0.7}h^{0.2}\ell^{0.1}\frac{G}{N^*}^{0.05}$ (full congestion)

New York City, FY 1997

τ_p, property tax rate = 0.0283*	Z, aid from other governments = \$5783 per household
τ_s, sales tax rate = 0.04	G_0, surviving infrastructure stock = 94479 million
τ_w, income tax rate = 0.0446	A, net income from assets = −649 per household
τ_m, commuter tax rate = 0.0045	r^o, interest cost per dollar of surviving city debt = 0.0052
Y_d, = 5\$13500/dependent household	ψ, local share of dependent income = 0.095
r_m, municipal interest rate = 0.04	L_S, available land = 110734 acres
D, dependent pop. = 831068	

World economy

P, price of composite output = 1.00	V_0, reservation utility level = 1.00
r, discount rate = 0.05	Π_0, equilibrium profit rate = 0.00
S, suburban wage = \$53000	

Note: * 0.0295 on firm capital.

Constant Elasticity of Substitution (CES) combination of resident workers (N), commuter workers (modeled as managers, M), and firm capital (K). Firm capital is specified as a complement to managerial labor, while city labor is substitutable with the composite input of capital and managers:

$$X = L_f^a[\mu_1 N^{0.4} + \mu_2(\lambda_1 K^\rho + \lambda_2 M^\rho)^{\varepsilon/\rho}]^{(1-a)/\varepsilon}G^c, \tag{4.4}$$

where μ_s and λ_s are parameters which determine factor income shares and a and c determine the marginal productivities of land, the labor–capital composite input and public infrastructure. Within the labor–capital composite input, the elasticity of substitution between capital (K) or managers

(M) and labor (N) is $1/(1-\varepsilon)$, while the elasticity of substitution between capital and managers is specified by $1/(1-\rho)$.

Our specification for the degree of complementarity between M and K and substitutability between N and the M–K composite are from Krusell *et al.* (2000), and are shown in Table 4.1. We assume that capital and managers are complements, and that both are substitutes for city labor. Complementarity between capital and managers requires that $\varepsilon > \rho$; see Fallon and Layard (1975). The specification in Table 4.1 meets this requirement as $\varepsilon = 0.40 > -0.50 = \rho$. The relative weights on K and M within the capital/manager composite input and then the relative weight between N and the capital/manager composite are selected to approximate national income shares among these three inputs; see Table 4.2. The Cobb–Douglas exponent on land, a, is set equal to 0.05 in the baseline model, following Mieszkowski (1972), Arnott and MacKinnon (1977) and Sullivan (1985); to our knowledge more recent estimates of the role of unimproved land in firm production are not available. The final elasticity measuring the marginal contribution of public infrastructure (G) to firm output is set equal to 0.04 using estimates from Haughwout (2002) for a sample of 33 US cities, but excluding New York. We model G in two ways: as a pure public good and as a congestible public service, a distinction we discuss further below.

Households' preferences are represented by a Cobb–Douglas utility function, implying unitary price and income elasticities of demand for the all-purpose consumption good ($x_{r,d}$), for housing structures ($h_{r,d}$), and for residential land ($l_{r,d}$); see Rosen (1979) and, more recently, Gyourko and Voith (2000) for evidence consistent with this assumption of elastic demand for residential housing and land. Work effort by resident workers is exogenous and suppressed in the specification of U(·); dependent residents do not work. Resident workers and dependent residents are assumed to have the identical preferences for x, h, and l but, of course, not identical utilities in equilibrium. Preferences are specified as shown in Table 4.1:

$$U = x^{\alpha} h^{\beta} l^{(1-\alpha-\beta)} G^{\gamma}. \tag{4.5}$$

Households allocate 70 per cent of their annual after-wage tax income to the all-purpose consumption good ($x_{r,d}$), 20 per cent to housing structures ($h_{r,d}$), and 10 per cent to land ($l_{r,d}$). These after-tax budget shares are chosen to approximate actual share allocations for typical New York homeowners. Local public goods (G) are also included in resident-worker and dependent-resident utility, with the budget share set equal to 0.05, again based upon the recent empirical work in Haughwout (2002).[2] City residents in our model take city G as exogenous.

What are the functional forms of firm and household demands for city

Table 4.2 *Calibration to NYC economy, 1997*

	Public good congestibility			
	Full congestion	No congestion	Actual data	Data source
Wage (resident workers, $ per year)	39172	36125	30000	NY City Housing and Vacancy Survey, 1999 data, median
Median home value ($)	143392	88159	151920	NY City Housing and Vacancy Survey, 1996 data, median*
Output ($ million per year)	167446	150370	299548	NY City Comptroller's Office (1998)
Jobs	3073053	2941060	2953900	NY State Dep. of Labor
Resident workers	2025898	2026042	2429732	Estimated using Census Journey to work data
Commuters	1047155	915018	524168	
Productive capital stock per worker ($)	97820	89312	79083	National data from *Survey of Current Business* (1998)
Tax revenues ($ per household)	9581	8185	5763	New York City, Comptroller's Office, 1997
Income	1320	1143	1532	
Property and Corporate	7416	6182	3203	
Sales	839	783	1028	

Notes: * Calculated as present discounted value of median rent, using a 5 per cent real discount rate and 1 per cent annual depreciation rate; approximately 70 per cent of occupied NYC housing units are rented.

land? A key determinant of the response of the city's public and private economies to the elimination of distortionary taxation is the response of city residents (and potential residents) to changes in land prices (Nechyba, 1998). In both the firm (eq. 4.4) and household (eq. 4.5) specifications adopted here, land demands are unitary price-elastic; that is, the price elasticity of demand is equal to −1.0. In spite of the importance of these parameters for policy analysis of the sort conducted here (as well as estimating the effects of many other local policy changes), little is known about them. Extremely careful recent work by Gyourko and Voith (2000) indicates that price elasticity of the demand for residential land is −1.6. But there is little evidence of which we are aware on the demand for land by firms.

In addition, experimentation with the current model demonstrates that the results are sensitive to the relative importance of land (l) and housing capital (h) in consumption. When housing makes up a smaller share of resident worker and non-worker expenditures than is assumed here, the simulated benefits of a switch to land taxes are much larger than those reported below. Households' responses to the elimination of distortionary taxation are determined in part by what happens to local wages. When wages and/or land prices rise, as they do with the elimination of sales and capital taxes (see Table 4.3), the extent to which households change their use of land and housing capital is determined by the share of these goods in consumption. Assumption of a relatively low housing share (15 per cent instead of the current model's 30 per cent) leads to much more dramatic city-level effects of the elimination of distortionary taxes (Haughwout, 2001).

One test of the assumptions is whether the model can replicate actual policy changes. Haughwout and Inman (2001) find that a model using a parameterization very similar to the one used in this chapter fits the tax change data for Philadelphia quite well. Nonetheless, given the lack of evidence on this front, the results here must be evaluated with care. Lower price elasticities or a lower housing share in consumption would reduce the simulated benefits of a shift to land taxation from those reported here and higher elasticities or shares would increase them (Nechyba, 1998, Haughwout, 2001). One clear implication is that more empirical work is needed here. We return to this issue in the conclusion.

The City

Table 4.1 describes the fiscal and economic assumptions made in the implementation of the model. New York is, of course, the nation's largest city, and has arguably its most complex local government. As a consolidated city made up of five counties, New York, like several other US cities (among them Philadelphia, San Francisco and Baltimore) performs both municipal

Table 4.3 Eliminating NYC sales, capital and income taxes (percentage changes from baseline)

	Public good congestibility	
	Full congestion	No congestion
City wage (W^*)	−3	3
City land price (R^*)	118	68
Capital per unit of land ($[K^* + H^*]/L$)	228	88
Jobs ($N^* + M^*$)	133	24
Residents (N^*)	126	16
Commuters (M^*)	146	41
Population ($[N + D]$)	89	11
Poverty rate (δ)	−47	−10
Dependent population utility (V_d)	−1	−8
Per capita tax revenue (T)	−74	−73
Relevant public good provision (G^*/N^* or G^*)	−65	−44
Aggregate output (X^*)	127	27

Note: Figures in the table are the percentage increases from the relevant baseline level. Simulations set sales, capital and income tax rates to zero, but leave land tax rates at their baseline levels. See the text.

and county functions. In addition to this distinction, New York has a unique political culture which has contributed to an unusual set of fiscal institutions in the city. One result of these institutional and cultural traits is that New York spends much more per resident than most other cities. In the fiscal year 1993–4, for example, New York's general expenditure amounted to nearly \$5600 per capita, roughly 3.5 times as much as the average expenditure of the nation's 23 largest cities in that year (Haughwout, 1997).

Helping to finance these expenditures is a complex revenue system centered upon four major taxes, described in Table 4.1. A few complications arise in the context of city taxes. In addition to the taxes specified in Table 4.1, New York levies a general corporate tax that has a dual structure. A corporation must pay the maximum of either an 8.85 per cent levy on its net income (defined as revenue minus allowable expenses) or a 0.15 per cent levy on the value of its capital assets in the city. Since we ignore the purchase of intermediate inputs, net income is not clearly defined in our model. We thus treat the general corporation tax as an additional tax on business capital. Thus the effective capital tax rate for firms is 2.95 per cent in the simulations.

New York's property tax base is divided into four classes. Each class has different assessment rules, and by implication different effective tax rates.

Data limitations make it impossible for us to distinguish these bases here, and we thus apply the weighted average rate to all capital and land in the city. Finally, the city's income tax, as noted above, is progressive. Earlier empirical research indicates that the incentive effects of income taxation in New York are dominated by the top marginal rate, which is the measure used for the calibration (Haughwout *et al.*, 2000). Future research could refine the treatment of these taxes.

In 1997, New York City received over \$16.5 billion in aid from the state and national governments, or about \$5800 per household (New York City Comptroller's Office, 1998). The city owned a public capital stock valued at almost \$95 billion in that year, while outstanding debts were costing the average household \$649 annually (Haughwout and Inman, 1996, updated). We set the municipal interest rate at 4 per cent, and the city's share of the (assumed) \$13500 annual transfer payments to dependent households at 9.5 per cent (Haughwout and Inman, 2001). Total city land available for private development was 110734 acres (New York City Department of City Planning, 1995).[3]

The World Economy

The simulation model requires values for the price of the composite output good X, equilibrium utility available to households in other cities, and the equilibrium profit rate. In addition to these normalization rules (shown in Table 4.1), we measure private capital such that its annual rental price is \$1 per unit, assume a discount rate of 5 per cent, and a suburban wage S of \$53000, the average income earned by residents of the Nassau-Suffolk and Newark Metropolitan Statistical Areas (MSAs), as reported in the 1990 Census.

How Public are City Services?

Models like the one described here must confront the difficult question of the degree of congestibility of the goods and services produced by the public sector. The definition of public goods requires that they be 'non-rivalrous', implying that congestion is not an issue in the analysis of public goods. Yet it is clear that many publicly funded programs are subject to at least some congestibility: a police officer can be at only one crime scene at a time, for example. Previous estimates of the congestibility of large city public capital stocks (Haughwout, 2002) find modest evidence that they are not congested at current levels of usage. Yet the model here includes the entire public sector, not just the capital stock, and research has indicated that some urban public services are indeed congested at the margin.

Further, the tax changes modeled here result in large increases in economic activity in New York. That one might argue that the 1990 infrastructure stock of the city was sufficient for its 1990 population is not much comfort when one considers a situation in which the city's population is substantially higher.

Because public spending is endogenously determined within the model, aggregate city revenues increase as the city grows. But how much the city grows and the value of the additional public services that growth creates will be determined in part by how congestible public goods are. We address this issue by conducting two sets of simulations, each with a different specification of the way public spending enters into utility and production. In the 'no congestion' specification, public spending is treated as a pure (local) public good: all city firms and residents share equally in the spending generated by the public sector. In the 'fully congestion' simulations, public goods are treated as equivalent to private goods. (See Table 4.1 for the specifications.) This approach allows the reader to see the extreme cases; the reality is likely somewhere in between.

Model Results and Actual Outcomes

Table 4.2 compares the model's results with actual outcomes in New York in 1997. For most of the endogenous variables, the model performs reasonably well. The model predicts a resident wage (\$36000–\$39000 in the 'no' and 'full' congestion baselines, respectively) that is between the city's actual median (\$30000) and mean earned incomes (\$48285). The model simulates median home values that bracket the city's median price in 1996. Aggregate output figures for municipalities are notoriously difficult to generate. The Comptroller's Office estimate provided here is produced with a methodology based on resident incomes. It shows gross city product (which presumably includes housing services and other components not measured as output in the model) considerably higher than the private business output estimate produced by the model. While the model predicts aggregate jobs relatively closely, it simulates a higher ratio of commuters to resident workers than is true in reality. The simulations indicate that the typical New York City worker has access to more private capital than her counterpart in the rest of the country, as expected.

The model does a relatively good job of predicting sales and income tax revenues per household, but is too high on property and corporate tax revenues. There are three sources of error likely to arise here. First, the model treats all capital as if it were new, whereas most of the city's private capital stock is in fact depreciated. Second, not all business capital is in fact taxable under the property tax. Some, like office machines, is generally excluded.

Other business capital escapes taxation because of special deals offered by the city, whose value is difficult to estimate (NYC IBO, 2001). Finally, the city's actual general corporation tax allows firms to choose their filing method (8.85 per cent of net revenue or 0.15 per cent of city capital stock). Assuming that firms choose the method that minimizes their tax liability, the predictions of the model (which assume that all firms pay the property base liability) will be an overestimate of corporate tax payments. Overall, however, the baseline simulation provides a reasonable starting place from which to get a sense of the effects of a change in the structure of city taxation.

REPLACING THE NEW YORK CITY PROPERTY TAX WITH A LAND TAX

Fixed Tax Rates

Table 4.3 reports the results of replacing the city's sales, income, property and general corporation taxes with a land tax, under the baseline assumptions about technology and preferences. In these simulations, the current tax on property (and the surcharge on business capital) is set at zero, and the current land tax rate (2.83 per cent) is left unchanged. With no change in the rate of tax on land, the elimination of other taxes results in two principal effects on the city. First, the elimination of tax distortions to decisions and the overall reduction of tax burdens make the city more attractive to both firms and households. On the other hand, reducing taxes reduces revenues and public good provision.

The results are consistent with expectations, and indicate that substantial benefits are available from this elimination of distortionary taxation in New York. Turning to the first (full congestion) column of Table 4.3, note the increases in private output and land values (>100 per cent), private capital stock (>200 per cent) and population (over 80 per cent) that are simulated to accompany this change. Note also that aggregate public good provision and per capita tax revenues each fall by over 50 per cent.

The second column of Table 4.3 identifies one source of the magnitude of these results. The public good congestibility parameters in the firm (eq. 4.1) and household (eq. 4.2) behavioral equations have substantial effects on the magnitude of the local benefit from the elimination of capital taxation. Virtually all of the outcomes reported in the table are less responsive to the elimination of distortionary taxes when public goods are modeled as non-congestible.[4] Nonetheless, the increases in land values and capital intensity shown in the no congestion column remain rather impressive.

In both the simulations reported in Table 4.3, dramatic reductions in poverty rates occur as workers enter the city. Yet, since local dependent workers pay little in local taxes, they benefit little from the elimination of distortionary taxes. Meanwhile the tax system is shifting from one which they partially escape (because of their assumed exemption from income tax) to a land tax, which they face fully. The second potential effect on the well-being of non-working households is the reduction in public good provision engendered by the change in the city's tax structure. We would thus expect, and indeed get, negative effects on the poor. In all of the simulations reported here (Tables 4.3 and 4.4), however, such effects are relatively small, and other simulations (not reported) indicate that landowners could compensate dependent households for their lost utility.

Fixed Tax Revenues

Table 4.4 reports, for the full congestion scenario only, results for the land tax simulations when aggregate tax revenues are constrained to their baseline level. The additional line at the top of the table reports the required land value tax rate, 21.7 per cent. At this rate of tax, aggregate revenues would remain unchanged, but revenues per capita fall as population rises. Again, many of the city aggregate indicators, especially its private capital

Table 4.4 Eliminating NYC sales, capital and income taxes without changing aggregate tax revenue

	No congestion
Required land tax rate	21.7
City wage (W^*)	4
City land price (R^*)	−28
Capital per unit of land ($[K^* + H^*]/L$)	168
Jobs ($N^* + M^*$)	84
Residents (N^*)	72
Commuters (M^*)	112
Population ($[N + D]$)	51
Poverty rate (δ)	−34
Dependent population utility (V_d)	−8
Per capita tax revenue (T)	−34
Aggregate public good provision (G^*)	0
Aggregate output (X^*)	91

Notes: Figures in table are the percentage increases from the relevant baseline level. Simulations set sales, capital and income tax rates to zero, and change the land tax rate to keep aggregate tax revenue at its baseline level. See text for more information.

stock, increase sharply. One interesting feature of Table 4.4, however, is that land values are estimated to *fall* when the public sector is constrained to remain the same size, the removal of distortionary taxes makes the city less attractive overall as a place to live and do business. We return to this apparent anomaly in the next section, where we discuss these results in the context of the literature.

Comparison with Recent Literature on Local Taxation

These results are near the tops of the ranges reported by Nechyba (1998) using a similar model applied to the US state–local public sector as a whole. In those simulations, Nechyba finds that (depending on the elasticity of substitution between land and capital), capital stock would rise between 14 and 122 per cent, with output increasing by 10–90 per cent. Why would our results for New York be at the high end of Nechyba's ranges?

The most obvious place to look is in the specifications of the current model when compared with Nechyba (1998). The production and preference functions represented in Table 4.1 assume a unitary elasticity of substitution between land and other inputs (in production) and other goods (in consumption); see above. Nechyba (1998) points out that this elasticity is an important determinant of the benefits predicted from adoption of a land tax. While we argue that the (admittedly modest) empirical evidence supports this specification, it is clear that more empirical estimation of land demand functions is required to enhance the precision of the model. Land expenditure's shares of firm costs and household budgets also have an important effect on the simulated benefits of a land tax. Other things equal, lower land shares lead to higher estimated benefits, as firms and households use city land more intensively; see Haughwout (2001). Finally, the congestibility of public goods and services has important effects on the estimated benefits of a reduction in tax distortions.

While these technical factors surely explain part of the high benefits simulated here, there may be also good political economic reasons to expect the real New York economy to react more strongly than the average US locality to an increase in the efficiency of its tax policy. In particular, New York is a city with a very large public sector and concomitantly high levels of distortionary taxation. In previous work, Haughwout *et al.* (2000) found that New York is very near the peak of its revenue schedule (local Laffer curve) on three of the four taxes modeled here (property, sales and income). This suggests that the excess burden of local taxation (η) is very high in New York, and that reductions in tax distortions may have especially large economic efficiency payoffs.

This empirical result also helps explain how the sign of the land price effect in Table 4.4 can be negative in the face of a reduction in distortionary taxation. Recalling that public goods enter production technology and preferences as a pure public good, the public good level produced by this high tax rate levied on a very large tax base is not worth its cost. This problem would be even worse (that is, land prices would be even lower) were this large public sector to be financed by distortionary taxes. Indeed, from a rate of 21.7 per cent, the net effect of reductions in land tax rates and public services is to increase land values.

THE POLITICAL ECONOMY OF LAND TAXATION AND CONCLUDING REMARKS

The benefits to be had from eliminating the distortion introduced by capital and labor taxation, particularly in cities in which rates (and their associated distortive effect) are high, appear to be enormous. Does the current model shed any light on the sources of opposition to a land tax?

The answer does not seem to lie in the obvious rich–poor or business–household schisms in local politics. When businesses and middle-class households are freely mobile, there are only two groups whose well-being can be directly affected by the efficiency of local taxation. Dependent households' well-being does not seem to be much affected either way, while landowners stand to gain substantially from a move to a land tax, at least under certain conditions. But it may be these very conditions in which the trouble lies: as demonstrated in Table 4.4, shifting to a land tax does not necessarily lead to an increase in land values. It is only when the structure of taxation *and the amount of revenue collected* can both be altered that landowners unambiguously benefit. But of course this means that the politics of the land tax are closely identified with the politics of local government size. Conflict over the latter is likely to remain significant, particularly in cases where city government is already 'too large' from landowners' perspectives. This suggests that the most likely candidates to adopt a land tax may not be the nation's largest cities, where preference and income heterogeneity makes these conflicts most intensive, but more homogeneous Tiebout suburbs. Unfortunately, as others have pointed out, it is in such communities that local taxation is probably least distortive (Hamilton, 1976, Fischel, 1998).

If this view is correct, then the adoption of a land tax is most likely where its alternatives are least onerous, and where its benefits are smallest. In places where it could really make a difference, it is likely to be doomed to the usual fate of dramatic policy proposals with small or uncertain benefits to crucial interest groups. The best we can hope for may be incrementalism in both kinds of places, perhaps with land taxes being the ones raised when revenue shortfalls develop, when another tax is exogenously eliminated or when crisis strikes in another form.

But what is perhaps most clear from this work is that, while theoretical public finance can offer consistent predictions of the signs of most of the effects of a shift to land taxation, we are far short of the empirical knowledge required to predict their magnitude accurately. If moving to land taxation were politically costless, it presumably would have been accomplished long ago. The range of benefit estimates presented here and in Nechyba (1998) implies that more work on the role of land in consumption and more particularly in production needs to be done before economists can make a clear and convincing case that policy makers would be well advised to pay the required costs.

NOTES

1. Netzer's contributions to the study of land and property taxes are too numerous to catalogue exhaustively here, but are nicely bracketed by early work on the economics of local taxation (Netzer, 1966) and later work on its politics (Netzer, 1998).
2. The budget share of 0.05 is also very close to the average share of income allocated to local public goods by Philadelphia suburban area households under the assumption that suburban households can choose *à la* Tiebout their preferred level of local public goods; see Inman and Ritter (1999).
3. We exclude streets, bodies of water, public land and recreational land from the definition of available land.
4. The sources of this difference are complex. In the full congestion simulations, the shift to land taxes induces land price increases and wage declines, making resident labor a relatively attractive factor of production compared to land, commuter labor and private capital. This induces firms both to increase output and to hire more resident workers per unit produced. Meanwhile, the amount of land demanded by each of these workers falls in response to lower wages and higher land prices, leaving more land available for firm production. In the 'no congestion' simulations, these relative price changes are less dramatic, as both wages and land prices increase (the latter not as much as in the congestible public goods simulations).

REFERENCES

Arnott, R. and J. MacKinnon (1977), 'The Effects of the Property Tax: A General Equilibrium Simulation', *Journal of Urban Economics*, **4**, 389–407.

Census (1990), 'Median Family Income by Metropolitan Statistical Areas (MSA): 1969, 1979, and 1989' (available at http://www.census.gov/hhes/income/histinc/msa/msa2.html), last accessed Tuesday 2 October 2001).

Fallon, P. and P. Layard (1975), 'Capital–Skill Complementarity, Income Distribution and Output Accounting', *Journal of Political Economy*, **83**, 279–301.

Fischel, W. (1998), 'The ethics of land value taxation revisited', in Dick Netzer (ed.),

Land Value Taxation: Can It and Will It Work Today?, Cambridge, MA: Lincoln Institute.
George, H. (1879), *Progress and Poverty*, 1971 edn, New York: Robert Schalkenbach Foundation.
Gyourko, J. and R. Voith (2000), 'The Price Elasticity of Demand for Residential Land', mimeo, Wharton School, University of Pennsylvania, Philadelphia, USA.
Gyourko, J., J. Tracy and M. Kahn (1999), 'Quality of Life and the Environment', in Paul Cheshire and Edwin Mills (eds), *Handbook of Urban and Regional Economics*, vol. 3, New York: North Holland Press, pp.1413–51.
Hamilton, B. (1976), 'Capitalization of intrajurisdictional differences in local tax prices', *American Economic Review*, **66**, pp.743–53.
Haughwout, A. (1997), 'After the Fall: An Examination of Fiscal Policy in New York City Since 1974', Proceedings of the 89th Annual Conference on Taxation, National Tax Association.
Haughwout, A. (2001), 'Land taxation: The effect of parameters', mimeo, Federal Reserve Bank of New York.
Haughwout, A. (2002), 'Public Infrastructure Investments, Productivity and Welfare in Fixed Geographic Areas', *Journal of Public Economics*, **83**, 405–28.
Haughwout, A. and R. Inman (1996), 'State and local assets and liabilities, 1972–1992', mimeo, Federal Reserve Bank of New York.
Haughwout, A. and R. Inman (2001), 'Fiscal Policy in Open Cities with Firms and Households', *Regional Science and Urban Economics*, **31** (2–3).
Haughwout, A., R. Inman, S. Craig and T. Luce (2000), 'Local Revenue Hills: A General Equilibrium Specification with Evidence from Four US Cities', NBER working paper 7603.
Inman, R. and G. Ritter (1999), 'Local Taxes and the Economic Future of Philadelphia', *Greater Philadelphia Regional Review*, Winter, 5–8.
Krusell, P., L. Ohanian, V. Rios-Rull and G. Violante (2000), 'Capital Skill Complementarity and Inequality', *Econometrica*, **68** (5), 1029–53.
Mieszkowski, P (1972), 'The Property Tax: An Excise Tax or a Profits Tax?', *Journal of Public Economics*, **1**, 73–96.
Nechyba, T. (1998), 'Replacing Capital Taxes with Land Taxes: Efficiency and Distributional Implications with an Application to the US', in D. Netzer (ed.), *Land Value Taxation: Can It and Will It Work Today?*, Cambridge, MA:Lincoln Institute, pp.183–209.
Netzer, D. (1966), *Economics of the Property Tax*, Washington, DC: Brookings Institute.
——(ed.) (1998), *Land Value Taxation: Can It and Will It Work Today?*, Cambridge, MA: Lincoln Institute.
New York City Comptroller's Office (1998) (http://www.financenet.gov/financenet/state/nycnet/ecodec98.htm).
New York City Independent Budget Office (2001), 'Full Disclosure? Assessing City Reporting on Business Retention Deals', Policy Brief, June.
New York City Department of City Planning (1995), 'City Land Use Facts' (available at http://www.nyc.gov/html/dcp/html/lufacts.html), last accessed Tuesday 2 October 2001.
New York State Department of Labor (2003) (http://www.labor.state.ny.us/html/nonag/search.htm).
Roback, J. (1982), 'Wages, Rents, and the Quality of Life', *Journal of Political Economy*, **90**, 1257–78.

Rosen, S. (1979), 'Wage-Based Indexes and the Quality of Life', in P. Mieszkowski and M. Straszheim (eds), *Current Issues in Urban Economics*, Baltimore: Johns Hopkins Press.

Sullivan, A (1985), 'The General Equilibrium Effects of the Residential Property Tax: Incidence and Excess Burden', *Journal of Urban Economics*, **18**, 235–50.

APPENDIX: MODEL VARIABLES AND SOLUTION PROCEDURE

Endogenous Variables (see Tables 4.2–4.4 for selected equilibrium values)

Equilibrium local prices
R^* [land rent], W^* [labor]

Equilibrium firm input use per unit output
k [private capital], l_f [land], n [resident labor], m [commuter/managers]

Equilibrium resident worker household consumption (per household)
x_r [composite good], h_r [housing capital], l_r [land]

Equilibrium dependent household consumption and utility (per household)
x_d [composite good], h_d [housing capital], l_d [land], V_d [utility]

City-level economy and demography
X [aggregate output], N + M [employment], δ [poverty rate]

City fisc
$\mathfrak{R}$ [tax revenues], G [public services, present value]

Exogenous Variables (See Table 4.1 for values)

V_0 [reservation utility level], Π_0 [equilibrium profit rate], P [price of composite output], r [discount rate], S [suburban wage], L_S [city land area], D [dependent population]; Y_d [dependent household income], Z [aid from other governments], G_0 [pre-existing infrastructure stock], A [net income from city-owned assets], r^0 [interest cost per dollar of surviving city debt], ψ [local share of dependent income] r_m [municipal interest rate], τ [tax rates].
Note: Current public services *G* are modeled as the annual services from G_0 plus current revenues less interest costs (Haughwout and Inman, 2001).

Equilibrium

An open city equilibrium exists within our model when no mobile firm, resident household or commuter has an incentive to change their location, residence or job. This means satisfying the constraints depicted in Figure 4.1 and ensuring that commuters get their after-tax wage of S. An equilibrium specifies the model's 18 endogenous variables. The 18 equations of the model specified above are sufficient to solve for each of the 18 endogenous variables, conditional on values for each of the model's exogenous parameters.

The model is solved iteratively. First, given preferences and technologies, world prices (r, 1, S) and the firms' and resident-workers' outside options (Π_0, V_0), local tax rates τ and an assumed starting value for G ($=G^{(0)}$), Figure 4.1 depicts two equations in the two unknown endogenous city prices, W and R. Initially, the equilibrium values of wages and rents will be $W=W^{(0)}$ and $R=R^{(0)}$, both conditional upon the assumed starting value of $G=G^{(0)}$.

Given $W^{(0)}$ and $R^{(0)}$, the remainder of the model can then be solved for firms' input demands, resident workers' demands and dependent residents' demands, respectively, again conditional upon $G=G^{(0)}$. Firms' and residents' demands for land and firms' demand for workers allow us to compute aggregate city output ($X^{(0)}$), aggregate resident employment ($N^{(0)}$) and the dependent population's share of total city population ($\delta^{(0)}$). Given conditional firms' and residents' demands, rents and wages, and now the dependent residents' share of city population, city's own tax revenues ($\Re^{(0)}$) can be calculated. Finally, we can now solve for a new starting value of G $=G^{(1)}$, and the solution process can be repeated.

An equilibrium is obtained when $G^{(t-1)}=G^{(t)}=G$; that is, when a starting value of G creates a private economy and subsequent public goods resources just sufficient to pay for the original starting level of G. Sufficient for an equilibrium level of G to be a locally stable equilibrium is for a small increase (decrease) in G from equilibrium to cost (save) more than any endogenous public goods resources generated (lost), *at given tax rates*, after the private economy's adjustments to that change in G. Simply put, for given tax rates increasing G cannot, in equilibrium, be a source of new wealth (that is, a 'money machine') for the city's current residents. All simulations reported here produced stable and unique equilibria.

COMMENT

Thomas Nechyba

I see it as a special privilege to be involved in this project to honor Dick Netzer who first convinced me to work on land taxation issues several years ago. Andy Haughwout's chapter on land taxation in New York City has once again sparked my interest in the topic. The chapter builds on some very interesting recent work by Andy and Bob Inman (Haughwout and Inman, 2001), work in which they propose a new model of an open city and a new way of thinking about fiscal policy within such a city. The model contains a rich set of features. Producers, resident workers and non-working residents all play a role within a fixed land area, and a city government raises tax revenues from a variety of sources to pay for public services. Andy carefully calibrates the model and then runs several simulations involving tax reforms that relate to land taxation. It should be emphasized at the outset that this is probably the richest model ever used for analyzing local land tax reforms, and Andy deserves much credit for its development. While I will argue below that the estimates of the likely impact of land tax reforms simulated in this chapter are probably too large, this does not take away from the very nice set-up and calibration that Andy has conducted. Future versions of this model are likely to give even more insight to policy makers on the impact of various types of local tax reforms, including those involving an increased role for land taxation.

Rather than belaboring details of the model and calibration, I would like to draw attention to just a few issues that may be of importance for the future direction of the research agenda launched by this chapter. First, from my own work on land taxation, I have come to appreciate the importance of two different types of elasticity assumptions in models of this kind, and of the sensitivity of results to these assumptions. While the assumptions Andy makes are well grounded in both the theoretical and the empirical literature, I believe they are nevertheless likely to be too large, thus causing the results to indicate more dramatic effects of land tax reforms than I would expect in the real world. Second, Andy specifically and carefully models New York City. Both his own work and some of my previous work on land taxation suggest that this is quite important because New York City is unique in many ways. While this means that the present chapter is particularly relevant to New York City, it also means that the results do not easily generalize to other cities. This calls for similarly careful work to be conducted for other settings to provide accurate information to policy makers elsewhere. Finally, the chapter concludes by raising the provocative question of why dramatic land tax reforms have not been conducted in New York City in light of the large benefits that are predicted in the model. This raises interesting questions regarding the political economy of tax reform, a question that can be addressed with future work using Andy's model.

The Magnitude of the Economic Responses in the Model

The benefits (for a city) of replacing current taxes with efficient land taxes arise from two primary sources: first, current tax distortions are eliminated (thus causing a more efficient use of current resources) and, second, inputs are drawn into the city as the city becomes a more attractive place for production (thus causing an increase in resources for the city). For both these effects, assumptions regarding the responsiveness of economic agents to changing conditions are central to the analysis. In the first set of simulations, Andy demonstrates the effects of simply eliminating distortionary taxes and leaving land taxes unchanged. A reduction in tax revenues from such a reform adversely affects those who are currently poor in the city (albeit by a relatively small magnitude), and it reduces the level of public infrastructure. Nevertheless aggregate output rises substantially as a result of the more efficient tax system (and the accompanying change in the use of factors). A second set of simulations then proceeds to an analysis of a city tax reform in which distortionary taxes are eliminated and land taxes adjusted so as to keep tax revenues constant. This requires an increase in land taxes from 2.83 per cent to 21.7 per cent, causing land prices to fall while increasing overall output in the city dramatically (by 91 per cent).

The direction of most of the results in the chapter is not surprising to those who have considered the possibility of land taxation. The main aim of current research efforts is therefore to quantify the magnitude of the effects in order to present policy makers with a better understanding of the likely economic and political tradeoffs implicit in different tax reform proposals. It is in this dimension that the chapter offers an important contribution. However, as Andy Haughwout explicitly states, the results presented do need to be viewed with some caution. In this work as well as other work on simulating the potential impact of land taxation, the underlying assumptions about the responsiveness (or elasticities) of different economic variables are of crucial importance, and researchers are not at this point certain of what the 'right' elasticity assumptions are. Elasticities that are of particular importance are supply elasticities of labor and capital as well as elasticities of substitution between land, labor and capital. With applications such as the one in this chapter, the economy is often considered a 'small, open' economy in which supply elasticities are infinite, while elasticities of substitution have to be assumed, based on prior empirical evidence. Andy thus assumes infinite supply elasticities and uses functional forms for production technologies that imply elasticities of substitution of one.

One approach to judging whether the magnitude of the results in the chapter is realistic is therefore to evaluate explicitly whether the underlying elasticity assumptions that drive the results are reasonable. Infinite *supply elasticities* are theoretically sound in small open economies because such economies are too small to affect the world price of factors. At the same time, this theoretically sound introduction of infinite supply elasticities is likely to represent reasonable *long-run* responsiveness measures for cities only so long as neighboring political jurisdictions do not strategically respond to policy changes around them, and such elasticities are unlikely to be correct in the short run because of mobility and adjustment costs. Two implications follow from this: first, the full magnitude of the results reported above could not be expected for some time; second, a long literature on tax competition suggests that other jurisdictions (that experience declines in capital and labor as such factors move to New York) would respond by altering their own policies, thus causing general equilibrium changes in factor prices even though New York itself is a small, open economy. One way to approximate such responses (without explicitly modeling strategic interactions) would be to deviate from the 'small, open economy' assumption to one that reflects lower supply elasticities even in the long run. The analysis in Nechyba (2001) suggests that supply elasticities implied by strategic interactions between jurisdictions might yield predictions of output growth (from land tax reforms) that could be substantially lower than what a 'small, open economy' model would predict.[1]

Similarly, results would certainly be less dramatic if *elasticities of substitution* were lower than 1. Andy correctly argues that the very limited empirical evidence suggests that elasticities of substitution in the range of 1 are not empirically implausible, but I suspect that they are too high for an analysis of the type conducted here. Even if empirical estimates of 1 are correct, these represent estimates 'on the margin'. The policy reforms simulated in this chapter are very much outside the margin in that they are dramatic and large. Constant elasticity production functions (such as those used in this chapter) necessarily assume the same elasticity throughout, but, in areas where housing and building stocks are difficult to adjust dramatically, it seems likely that the relevant elasticities for large policy changes are significantly smaller, at least in the short run. In my own work, I have focused on elasticities of substitution that are a quarter to half the size assumed in this chapter. While this still gives dramatic results, predictions of output growth (and changes in other economic variables) tend to be smaller than what is reported in Andy's simulations for New York City.

Tax Reform in New York City

While my view of the elasticity assumptions suggests that the effects of land tax reforms in New York City are overestimated in this chapter, some of my previous work also suggests that unusually large responses to tax reforms of this sort may be more readily expected in New York than in other places. Nechyba (2001) analyzes state tax reforms for each of the 50 states under assumptions that are more conservative than those made in the present chapter. One of the striking results in this analysis, however, is that results for New York appear to be outliers. In simulations that consider the elimination of all state and local taxes on capital (in revenue-neutral reforms that raise taxes on land rents), New York shows the highest increase in output of any state (and twice the increase of the average state) largely because New York has the highest initial tax rate on capital. This holds for a variety of different elasticity assumptions. In comparing these results with Andy's, I find two parallels: first, Andy suggests in this chapter as well as other work (Haughwout *et al.*, 2000) that New York's taxes are sufficiently high to be near the top of the 'Laffer curve' and that this is in part responsible for the large positive effect he simulates for reforms involving land rent taxes. My 50-state analysis suggests that this may indeed be the case. Second, while Andy's more careful analysis of the city of New York is quite instructive, it should not be generalized to other cities without the model being fully recalibrated to reflect underlying economic conditions in those cities. New York is unique in many ways, and tax reforms of the kind investigated here may therefore be significantly different in New York than in other cities.

The Political Economy of Land Tax Reforms

Haughwout's model, in line with previous work on the topic, predicts substantial gains from tax reforms that reduce distortionary taxes in favor of greater reliance on land taxes. From the theoretical literature, we know that the total 'pie' grows under such reforms, which means that, at least in principle, winners gain more than losers lose, and Pareto improvements are possible with sufficiently creative policy making. Why, then, have such reforms not been conducted, especially at the local level where benefits include not only more efficient use of existing resources but also a dramatic increase in resources drawn from other jurisdictions?

The answer offered by Andy is that revenue neutral land tax reforms will lead to reductions in land values while non-revenue neutral reforms that raise land values result in smaller city governments. Either way, there are political interests that are likely to align themselves against proposed reforms. In my own work on land rent taxation in the states, this same result holds. While it is theoretically possible for land values to rise as a result of revenue-neutral reforms shifting the tax base toward land taxes,[2] empirically plausible assumptions typically yield predictions of land value declines. At the same time, this suggests the possibility of less dramatic reforms in which the most distortionary taxes are identified for replacement by a land tax. Andy considers only a reform that eliminates all New York City taxes and replaces them with land taxes, but some of the taxes that are being eliminated are currently more harmful than others. A more detailed analysis that focuses on the reduction (or elimination) of particular taxes as opposed to all taxes might be very instructive. While the prediction of declining land values for the dramatic reform in Table 4.4 is almost certainly correct (and probably too small, given my comments on the underlying elasticity assumptions), it may be the case that a more detailed analysis will yield some types of taxes that could be replaced by land taxes with no cost or even with benefits to landowners.

Using the much more simplistic but also more conservative model of Nechyba (2001), for instance, I predicted an increase in land values for the typical state when state *corporate income taxes* are replaced by a greater reliance on land taxes. This prediction was particularly large for New York. While I predicted a modest decline in land values when *property taxes* are replaced by pure land rent taxes in the typical state, the model predicted an increase in land values for such a tax reform when it was calibrated to New York. An analysis of reforms lowering the *sales taxes* or state *income taxes* in favor of greater reliance on land taxes, on the other hand, yielded predictions of large declines in land values. While these predictions depend on different supply elasticity assumptions for labor and capital (with capital generally assumed to be more mobile), they suggest that a sharper focus on identifying particular categories of taxes for reduction under land tax increases may yield more politically feasible policy reforms that come closer to the Pareto improvement that is theoretically achievable.

My anticipation, then, is that, as simulation models of land tax reforms become more sophisticated, as they make more realistic assumptions regarding elasticities and as they incorporate more detailed analysis of specific tax reforms, the prospects for land taxes to play an important role in policy reforms seem brighter even as the estimates of the benefits become more modest. Land taxes thus retain the sweet efficiency flavor so cherished by many public finance theorists while losing some of their nourishing magnitude. They are unlikely to be the answer to all fiscal problems, but marginal changes in tax laws – especially when specifically aimed at reducing or eliminating some of the more wasteful taxes in state and local tax laws – will surely find a place for a greater reliance on land taxes, and New York City may be a particularly attractive place to contemplate such reforms. Andy Haughwout's contribution to the development of better models to evaluate reform proposals is a truly welcome addition to the literature.

NOTES

1. Nechyba (2001), for instance, suggests that results might be approximately 75 per cent smaller in magnitude.
2. This is true because, if other taxes are sufficiently high and distortionary, a reduction in such taxes can yield sufficient increase in optimal factor use on any particular land parcel to yield an increase in post-tax land rents, even when tax rates on such rents rise (Nechyba, 1998).

REFERENCES

Haughwout, A. and R. Inman (2001), 'Fiscal Policy in Open Cities with Firms and Households', *Regional Science and Urban Economics*, **31**.

Haughwout, A., R. Inman, S. Craig and T. Luce (2000), 'Local Revenue Hills: A General Equilibrium Specification with Evidence from Four US Cities', NBER working paper 7603.

Nechyba, T. (1998), 'Replacing Capital Taxes with Land Taxes: Efficiency and Distributional Implications with an Application to the US', in Dick Netzer (ed.), *Land Value Taxation: Can It and Will It Work Today?*, Cambridge, MA: Lincoln Institute, pp.183–209.

Nechyba, T. (2001), 'Prospects for Land Rent Taxation in State and Local Tax Reforms', Lincoln Institute working paper, Cambridge, MA.

5. The role of cities in providing housing assistance: a New York perspective

Ingrid Gould Ellen*, Michael H. Schill, Amy Ellen Schwartz and Ioan Voicu

The current debate over housing policy in the United States takes place against a backdrop of devolution. In recent years, the federal government has increasingly relied upon states and cities to create and administer social policy. Thus, as this devolution continues, it is useful to consider how the responsibility for housing programs and policies should be divided among federal, state and local governments and, given the severity of urban housing problems, city governments in particular. This chapter examines available theory and evidence regarding the appropriate role of different levels of government, focusing in particular on the role of cities. Studying the case of New York City, we also offer new evidence on the extent to which investments in affordable housing can help to eliminate externalities and rebuild inner city communities.

The chapter is organized as follows. In the first section we review relevant theoretical and empirical literature to distill an understanding of whether and under what conditions cities are the appropriate level of government to fund and/or administer housing subsidy programs.[1] In brief, we conclude that, although cities should play a major role in administering housing programs, they should be wary about actually funding them. Redistribution of income, a major objective of most housing subsidy programs, should generally be paid for by the federal government, not cities. In contrast, cities should consider funding housing production programs when they are part of a comprehensive strategy either to remove negative externalities or to

* Authors listed in alphabetical order. All contributed equally. The authors would like to thank the Fannie Mae Foundation and New York University's Furman Center for Real Estate and Urban Policy for funding this research. They would also like to express their gratitude to Jerilyn Perine, Richard Roberts, Harold Shultz, Calvin Parker, Ilene Popkin and Harry Denny of the New York City Department of Housing Preservation and Development for providing them with the data necessary to complete this research.

generate positive spillovers. In the second section we estimate the impact that the new housing units developed through New York City's Ten Year Plan have had on property values in immediately surrounding areas. Our estimates suggest that the city's investment in new housing generated significant external benefits. Thus, although we conclude that the federal government should play the central role in funding housing programs aimed at redistribution, our results also point to a potentially important role for cities, based upon the spillover effects of housing construction and rehabilitation in distressed neighborhoods.

SEARCHING FOR THE APPROPRIATE ROLE FOR CITIES IN HOUSING ASSISTANCE

The Provision of Housing Assistance in a Federal System

Housing assistance in the USA is provided by overlapping governments whose relationship to each other is subject to a continual process of adjustment and redefinition. At the federal level, housing subsidies are provided by the US Department of Housing and Urban Development (HUD) as well as indirectly, through favorable provisions of the tax code, by the Internal Revenue Service. In recent years, the federal government has increasingly relied upon states and cities to create and administer housing policy. As shown in Quigley (2000), the net budget authority for all housing aid administered by HUD declined sharply during the 1980s (from about \$55 billion in 1980 to a little more than \$10 billion in 1990) and has remained at relatively low levels (\$10–20 billion) throughout the last decade.

Many American cities have responded by creating new and innovative programs to promote the production of housing. In addition, community-based nonprofit organizations and private developers have stepped into the void, piecing together a variety of subsidies and funding sources to create affordable housing. The various roles played by cities in providing housing assistance to their residents are briefly summarized below.

Revenue generation

Some cities fund housing subsidies out of their own revenues. According to Basolo (1999, p.442), among 209 cities surveyed with populations of 50000 or more, slightly over one-quarter of all expenditures for housing were funded by internal sources. The sources of city revenue dedicated to housing are varied. Some spend money solely from annual tax collections; others borrow funds in the capital market. Dedicated sources of revenue have also become more commonplace in recent years. Cities such as San Francisco and Boston have created trust funds for housing with money provided by linkage fees on new development. Chicago and Houston use tax increment financing to pay for programs to rehabilitate housing in particular neighborhoods.

Program creation
Cities, even those that do not fund housing assistance out of their own revenues, nonetheless often create housing programs to meet their own particular needs. The funding typically comes from flexible federal block grant programs such as the HOME Investment Partnerships Program (HOME) or the Community Development Block Grant. These programs might include grants and loans to community development corporations to build housing or municipal provision of infrastructure improvements. Some cities, in partnership with their states, also use money from the Temporary Assistance for Needy Families (TANF) block grants to fund an array of housing programs (Wright *et al.*, 2001).

Program administration
Cities and other public authorities administer programs that are funded and created by higher levels of government. For example, the public housing program is typically administered by public housing authorities, which are usually coterminous with cities and whose board members are often selected by the Mayor and/or City Council. All of the capital costs for building the housing and virtually all of the operating subsidies are paid for by HUD, which also prescribes detailed rules and regulations to guide program operation.

The Role of Cities

Government intervention in providing housing assistance has been justified on a wide variety of grounds, some related to equity, some to efficiency. One reason for government providing housing subsidies is to address inequities in the distribution of income that leave many families unable to afford adequate housing. Although not all housing subsidies seek to transfer income from higher to lower-income households, this is probably the most frequent justification offered for rental housing programs.[2] As Tobin (1970) has noted, although Americans typically accept inequality in most aspects of life, there is a rough consensus that 'certain specific scarce commodities should be distributed less unequally than the ability to pay for them'.

Yet earmarked subsidies and in-kind redistribution are generally inefficient, both because many households would not choose to spend each additional dollar of income on housing consumption (Polinsky and Ellwood, 1979) and because administrative costs for housing programs can be extremely high. Certainly, if redistribution were the sole objective of housing policy, a more cost-effective approach would be lump-sum income transfers.

Nevertheless, while recipients may be best served by unrestricted cash transfers, taxpayers may prefer their tax dollars to be used to subsidize someone's shelter rather than other consumption. The knowledge that people are not living in desperately deteriorated and unhealthful accommodations may itself bring taxpayers positive utility and therefore serve as a consumption item for the donors rather than the recipients (Aaron, 1972; Schill, 1990; Olsen, 2001). It is also possible that the interests of recipients are in fact better served as well. First, people who prefer other goods and services to a minimum level of shelter may lack sufficient information or be unable to assess rationally the true worth of decent housing, thereby justifying societal paternalism. Furthermore efforts to provide a minimum level of housing consumption may be justified as necessary to protect children from irresponsible (or poorly informed) parents.

While these arguments help to justify some government intervention in housing markets on redistributive grounds, cities are generally not the appropriate governmental entity to fund redistribution efforts, in part because they typically lack the fiscal capacity of other levels of government. Because of state constitutional limitations, cities typically have fewer sources of revenue to call upon as compared to states and the federal government. In addition, cities are usually subject to debt limitations which, at least as compared to the federal government, further constrain their ability to raise revenue.

Perhaps most importantly, the mobility of both people and capital threatens to undermine any effort to redistribute income at the local level. This feature of our federal system has long been recognized and is well-documented in both the economic literature (Tiebout, 1956) and the political science literature (Peterson, 1981). Middle and higher-income taxpayers as well as the owners of mobile capital will have a strong incentive to exit or not enter a municipality that raises taxes for programs that do not generate corresponding benefits. This will leave the city with fewer resources and make further redistribution infeasible. At the same time cities with generous redistributive programs may become a magnet for needy households from other locations, further intensifying the problem.

Thus, although there are many reasons why housing programs whose sole or primary purpose is redistribution might be better administered or even designed by local or regional governments (for example, local governments can tailor programs to match the particular needs of their residents), there are strong reasons against these governmental entities funding these initiatives.

What about economic efficiency? Three main arguments are typically made to justify government housing assistance based upon economic efficiency objectives.[3] First, government intervention might be justified as a way to address adjustment lags in supply and demand. Because housing takes significant time to construct, there is generally a time lag between exogenous increases in demand and supply (Aaron, 1972). In some cities the problem is systemic and the result of regulatory barriers to entry, such as zoning, rent controls and building codes (Salama *et al.*, 1999). Direct provision of housing by government may theoretically solve both the short-run and systemic barriers to supply problems since governmental bodies are frequently not subject to the same regulations as private market actors, but using government housing programs to solve problems caused by barriers to supply seems analogous to killing a fly with a shotgun. To the extent that the core problem is excessive regulation, a more direct solution would be the removal of regulatory barriers rather than programs to circumvent them.

Second, government intervention might also be warranted to address discrimination in the housing market.[4] Discriminatory treatment may increase search costs, drive up the cost of housing for its victims and interfere with optimal residential location decisions. In principle, discrimination can be eliminated, or at least avoided, by direct provision of housing by government. Unfortunately, some of the most blatant acts of discrimination by landlords in the USA have been those committed by government agencies and some of the most segregated housing developments in the nation are owned by public housing authorities (Hirsch, 1983). Further, even if governments could be relied upon to operate in a non-discriminatory manner, it is unclear whether earmarked housing assistance would be the most effective method to ameliorate the effects of housing discrimination. Instead, more vigorous enforcement of the laws outlawing housing discrimination may be preferable (Schill and Friedman, 1999).

Third, in our view, the strongest efficiency-based argument for intervention rests on the presence of externalities. Because housing is fixed in space, its condition influences the value of neighboring properties. The existence of a dilapidated structure, for instance, can reduce the value of neighboring homes and may lead to disinvestment in the neighborhood. Similarly, a high-quality building might generate positive spillovers and increase values and confidence in the area. If building owners do not bear all of the costs (or benefits) generated by their properties, the private sector will underinvest in housing. Public intervention such as slum clearance or rehabilitation assistance may therefore be appropriate.

Another potential external benefit delivered by new housing in particular is the increase in population it typically invites. More people can improve neighborhood safety by increasing street traffic and providing labor for community watches. More residents can also fuel demand for retail services and promote economic development. Finally, some types of housing programs, especially those that promote home ownership, may increase neighborhood stability and provide residents who will have strong economic incentives to become active in neighborhood organizations and political affairs.

There are likely to be informational externalities too. Developers of housing, like most people, may be risk averse and prone to investing too little in some neighborhoods because of a concern that a project will fail to overcome local disamenities. Part of the problem relates to a lack of information about the neighborhood as well as the difficulty disparate actors encounter in coordinating their activities. If an entrepreneur could be assured that her investment, together with those of other developers and the city, would be spatially concentrated, this risk would be minimized. Government, through subsidies and planning, may be able to promote the flow of information about particular communities, reduce the difficulties of coordination and thereby reduce risk (Caplin and Leahy, 1998).

Despite their theoretical appeal, spillovers generated by government housing assistance programs have been difficult to document empirically. As Mills and Hamilton write, researchers 'have almost uniformly failed to find significant and consistent effects of neighboring activities on property values' (1994, p.253). This has left many economists skeptical about this justification for earmarked housing assistance. Further, public investments in housing, even those carefully planned to eliminate negative externalities or promote positive spillovers in selected communities, can have the opposite effect on other neighborhoods. The construction of new housing may promote filtering: cities with high vacancy rates and relatively stable or declining populations may see demand for housing at the bottom weakening, as households move out of their existing units for newly vacated units of better quality, possibly leading to disinvestment, abandonment and the generation of new negative externalities (Mills and Hamilton, 1994).

But to the extent that we believe government housing programs can in fact produce positive spillovers, cities would seem to have a comparative advantage. Certainly there is strong justification for these programs being created and administered by local governments. It is highly doubtful that the federal government or, for that matter, even states or regional governments, would have the in-depth knowledge required to identify neighborhoods where earmarked investments would promote neighborhood revitalization. Indeed the growth of community-based housing organizations was, in part, a reaction to the concern that even city governments were too distant from the streets of inner city communities.

Furthermore, for a neighborhood revitalization strategy to be successful, it should be part of a comprehensive effort that involves more than just housing. Selective condemnations by municipal redevelopment authorities, code enforcement by housing inspectors, infrastructure and transportation improvements by the city and increased attention to crime prevention and education all need to be coordinated. Each of these functions is typically located within local governments. Still the question remains as to whether local governments can finance neighborhood revitalization strategies without falling prey to the forces that constrain redistributive policies.

In summary, redistributive goals are likely to be best addressed at the federal level, and many of the market failures found in housing markets (such as discrimination and supply barriers) may be addressed through means other than direct provision. The strongest argument to justify local provision of housing subsidies, then, is the presence of externalities. Housing programs designed to promote neighborhood revitalization have the potential for creating spatial externalities: improving local economic conditions and generating wealth for city residents. The key question, then, is largely empirical: are these spatial externalities large enough to justify intervention? In the second section of the chapter we turn to answering this question, using the New York City experience, to explore whether the housing created through New York City's Ten Year Plan for Housing generated spillover effects on neighboring properties, and whether these spillovers were of sufficient magnitude to justify the subsidies provided. First, however, it is important to review the existing literature and the evidence amassed to date.

THE SPILLOVER EFFECTS OF LOCAL HOUSING PROGRAMS: EVIDENCE FROM NEW YORK CITY

Past Literature

Prior studies provide inconclusive evidence about the nature of spillover effects generated by investments in affordable housing. Nourse (1963) and Rabiega, Lin and Robinson (1984), for instance, find that newly developed public housing can have modest, positive impacts on neighboring property values, while Lyons and Loveridge (1993), Goetz *et al.* (1996) and Lee *et al.* (1999) find small negative effects, at least associated with certain types of federally subsidized housing. Cummings *et al.* (2000) study two place-based home ownership developments in Philadelphia and find little evidence of spillover effects of any kind. Because of data limitations it is difficult to pinpoint the direction of causality in these studies. Are subsidized sites systematically located in weak (strong) neighborhoods, or does subsidized housing lead to neighborhood decline (improvement)?

A few more recent studies have made strides to overcome this causality problem with variants of neighborhood fixed effects models. Briggs *et al.* (1999), for instance, use a census tract fixed effects model to examine price changes surrounding seven scattered-site public housing developments on property values in neighborhoods in Yonkers, New York. They find little effect on the surrounding area.

Santiago *et al.* (2001) use a similar fixed effects model to study whether the Denver Housing Authority's scattered site public housing program influenced the sales prices of surrounding single-family homes. These authors test for both changes in price levels and trends after completion, and find that proximity to dispersed public housing units is, if anything, associated with an increase in the prices of single-family homes.[5] Ellen *et al.* (2001) and Schill *et al.* (2002) use a neighborhood fixed effects model to study the impacts of selected New York City housing programs, and they too find evidence of significant, positive spillover effects. In short, while there is little consensus about the spillover effects of subsidized housing investments, these recent works, which adopt conservative methodologies, seem to emerge with more optimistic findings.

Notice that spillover benefits may well differ with the type of housing investment. Ownership housing may yield higher spillover benefits than rental housing. Similarly, multi-family housing may be destructive to communities, while single-family homes are beneficial. Finally benefits may differ between rehabilitation and new construction programs. There is little empirical work addressing any of these questions. Indeed most of the past work has examined the impact of a single program, typically limited to federally supported, new construction rental programs.[6] Two exceptions are noteworthy. Lee *et al.* (1999) report that ownership projects are associated with higher surrounding property values, but they cannot determine whether this is simply because they are sited in higher-value neighborhoods. Schill *et al.* (2001) find no statistically significant difference between the impact of ownership and rental programs, but their study included newly created housing units as well as apartments and homes getting far more modest subsidies for renovation.

Finally, as regards scale effects, there is some suggestive evidence that added units magnify effects (Lyons and Loveridge, 1993; Santiago *et al.*, 2001; Ellen *et al.*, 2001; Schill *et al.*, 2001), but more work needs to be done to understand the nature of these marginal effects.

Evidence on Spillovers from New York City

In 1985, Mayor Edward I. Koch made a commitment of over $4 billion to build or rehabilitate more than 100000 housing units over a period of five years. The initiative, commonly referred to as the 'Ten Year Capital Plan', or the 'Ten Year Plan', ultimately resulted in the expenditure of more than $5 billion and the construction or rehabilitation of over 182000 units over a period of more than 15 years, making it the largest municipally supported housing program in the history of the USA. The Ten Year Plan encompasses a wide variety of programs to stimulate the production and rehabilitation of housing (see Schill *et al.*, 2002 for more detail). In this section, we focus on estimating the spillover effects of the 66 000 new units that have been produced through the program (either through new construction or through the gut rehabilitation of vacant buildings).

Because these units represent a diversity of housing types, we also explore whether impacts vary with the type of housing. In particular, we compare the effects of ownership and rental housing, multi-family and single-family housing and, finally, newly constructed units versus those that were created through the rehabilitation of formerly vacant and uninhabitable buildings (gut rehabilitation). Before turning to data and results, we describe the methodology used.

Methodology

At the heart of our empirical work is a hedonic regression model that explains the sales price of a property as a function of its structural characteristics (such as lot size and building age) and its neighborhood surroundings. We use this model to compare the prices of properties that are within 500 feet of Ten Year Plan sites with prices of comparable properties that are outside this 500-foot ring, but still located in the same census tract or neighborhood. Then we estimate whether the magnitude of this difference has changed over time and, if so, whether the change is associated with the completion of a new housing unit. This approach weeds out any systematic differences between the neighborhoods chosen for these city housing investments and other locations around the city, and allows us to disentangle the specific effects of the housing investments from the myriad other changes occurring across neighborhoods and properties in the city. At the end, we combine these estimates with information on costs to gain some insight into the magnitude of the net benefit of these projects.

Note that caution should be exercised in interpreting the parameters of hedonic regression models as the effects of amenity changes. As discussed in Quigley (1979), 'it does not follow in general that estimates of changes in aggregate property values accurately reflect the market return to public policies that affect amenity levels', even if all consumers are identical in their demands for housing characteristics (p.402). In practice, changes in property values can be induced by a variety of forces, both inside and outside a particular neighborhood, consumers differ from one another and the benefits of the housing investment may stretch beyond the neighborhood boundaries. Our difference-in-difference methodology controls for many of the confounding factors, using census tract quarter fixed effects, and thus it is less likely that the estimates will reflect the influence of these other forces.

More formally, we estimate a regression model of the sales price of a property that can be expressed as follows:

$$\ln P_{ict} = \alpha + \beta X_{it} + \gamma Z_{it} + \Sigma\, \rho_{ct} I_{ct} + \varepsilon_{it},$$

where $\ln P_{ict}$ is the log of the sales price of property i in census tract c in quarter t; X_{it} is a vector of property-related characteristics, including age and structural characteristics, Z_{it} is a vector of locational attributes (specifically, local housing investment within 500 feet of the property); and I_{ct} is a series of dummy variables indicating the quarter and census tract of the sale. The coefficients to be estimated are α, β, γ and ρ, and ε is an error term. Notice that the ρ_{ct} will vary across census tracts and across time, which allows us to control for neighborhood conditions and local public services common to all properties within a census tract in a particular quarter.

Here the coefficients on continuous variables can be interpreted as the percentage change in price resulting from a one-unit increase in that attribute. The coefficients on dummy variables, such as 'property sold is within the 500-foot ring of a site where Ten Year Plan units are or will be built', can be roughly interpreted as the percentage difference in price between properties inside the ring and those not inside the ring but sold in the same census tract in the same quarter and year, controlling for other attributes included in the regression (see Ellen *et al.*, 2001).

Specifying the Variables

Structural characteristics of the property

We include a rich set of variables describing the structural characteristics of the properties, including building age, square footage, the number of buildings on the lot and dummy variables distinguishing 18 different building classifications such as 'single-family detached' or 'two-family home'.

Controls for neighborhoods and trends in property values

Our regressions include a different dummy variable for every census tract for every calendar quarter in our study period (for example, first quarter 1980, second quarter 1980, and so on for each census tract). These dummy variables, which we refer to as 'census tract-quarter effects', enable us to control for tract-specific trends in prices. Using quarters rather than years controls for seasonal patterns in sales prices.

Proximity to Ten Year Plan units

We include several different variables in our regression model to capture the impact of proximity and number of units created through the Ten Year Plan. We begin by including a variable (In Ring) that indicates whether the property sold would at any time be located within 500 feet of a unit created through the Ten Year Plan. (We used Geographic Information Systems (GIS) techniques to measure the distance from each sale in our database to all Ten Year Plan and other housing sites and, from these distance measures, created a variable that identified properties within 500 feet of housing investments of different types.[7]) As discussed, these subsidized units may have been constructed in particularly distressed neighborhoods, and so we want to control for this baseline effect as fully as possible.

Several variables capture the impact of the actual completion of new Ten Year Plan units on property values in the 500-foot ring. Our 'Post Ring' dummy variables indicate whether the sale is within 500 feet of some number of completed new units.[8] In addition, we include variables indicating the number of completed new units within 500 feet of the sale and the number of units squared. These terms allow us to measure the marginal effects of additional new subsidized units.

To capture any post-completion trend, we include Tpost, a continuous variable that indicates, for properties in the 500 foot ring, the number of years between the date of sale and the project completion date. For instance, the variable equals 1/365 if a sale is located within 500 feet of a new unit and occurs the day after its completion; it equals one if the sale occurs one year after the unit completion; it equals two if the sale occurs two years after completion, and so on. The Tpost coefficient will be positive if, after completion, prices in the rings continue to rise relative to prices in the census tract. We also interact Tpost with the number of completed units in the ring at the time of sale, to test whether this time trend depends on project scale.

Proximity to other subsidized housing

We also include a set of variables that control for proximity to other subsidized housing, since it is possible that the location of these other types of units is correlated with that of the new Ten Year Plan units. These include pre-1987 city-sponsored projects, housing units sponsored by the federal government (such as Section 202 and Section 8 units) and occupied units that received other rehabilitation subsidies through the Ten Year Plan. In each case, we control for both selection effects and post-completion effects.

Extension of the Model

As noted above, different types of projects may yield significantly different impacts. Thus, in a second model, we also include variables indicating the proportion of the completed units in the ring that are multi-family units (as opposed to 1–4 unit homes), the proportion that are rental (as compared to ownership) and the proportion that were created through new construction (rather than through the gut rehabilitation of vacant buildings).[9]

In the third and fourth models, we add a number of additional 'In Ring' variables to control more precisely for selection effects and therefore arrive at more precise impact estimates in turn. In particular, we allow the initial prices in the rings surrounding Ten Year Plan sites to vary for homeownership and rental projects by including separate 'In Ring' variables for properties within 500 feet of new owner units (but no new rental units), properties within 500 feet of new rental units (but no new owner units) and properties that are within 500 feet of both new owner and new rental units. (Note that these are mutually exclusive categories.) It may be, after all, that rental units were systematically sited in more distressed neighborhoods than ownership units. Since it also may be true that large projects were systematically sited in more distressed locations than smaller projects, the fourth model includes separate 'In Ring' variables for (1) properties within 500 feet of a site that ultimately received at least 100 units and (2) properties within 500 feet of a site that ultimately received fewer than 100 units.[10] Thus, in the fourth model, we end up with six mutually-exclusive 500-foot rings:

- rings with fewer than 100 units in ownership projects (and no rental projects),
- rings with at least 100 units in ownership projects (and no rental projects),
- rings with fewer than 100 units in rental projects (and no ownership projects),
- rings with at least 100 units in rental projects (and no ownership projects),
- rings with fewer than 100 units (mix of ownership and rental projects),
- rings with at least 100 units (mix of ownership and rental projects).

Comparing Costs to Benefits

Although a fully satisfying cost–benefit analysis is outside the scope of this chapter, we have made some effort to compare the magnitude of the external benefits delivered by these housing investments to their approximate costs. Specifically, we estimate the aggregate benefits that all new housing units built through the Ten Year Plan units generated within their immediately surrounding communities (again, measured as a 500-foot radius). Note that these do not provide a full accounting of the benefits derived from each new housing unit. As discussed above, the external benefits of the housing investments may not be fully capitalized into land values. Spillover benefits may also extend beyond 500 feet – in fact, our past work suggests that they do (Ellen *et al.*, 2001). Benefits may also extend to nearby commercial properties, and residents of more distant neighborhoods may also receive 'warm glow' benefits from the knowledge that there is better housing in New York City. Moreover the actual occupants of these subsidized housing units clearly receive benefits from the housing investment. These are not counted here since we focus exclusively on external, rather than private, benefits.

To simulate the aggregate benefits for all Ten Year Plan housing developments, we first identify all the residential properties within 500 feet of Ten Year Plan housing units and then assign them to one of the six rings defined above. We then assign to each property a pre-completion price, that is, an average per unit price based on the ring type and the year of earliest project completion.[11]

We then use this pre-completion price, the number of units in each property and our post-completion coefficients to estimate the increase in value enjoyed by all the properties. The sum of all of these property benefits should amount to the total benefit that all the Ten Year Plan housing delivered to residential properties located within 500 feet of new units. Formally the total benefit is computed using the formula:

$$Benefit = \sum_{i=1}^{N} u_i \bar{P}_i [\exp(\hat{\gamma}' Z) - 1],$$

where i indexes properties, N is the total number of properties in 500-foot rings, u_i is the number of units for property i, $\bar{P}_i$ is the pre-completion price assigned to property i, Z is the vector of post-completion variables, and $\hat{\gamma}$ is the vector of their corresponding coefficient estimates.

Summary of Data

To undertake the analysis outlined above, we have linked three geocoded data sources. First, we obtained data on all of the new housing created through the Ten Year Plan from the New York City Department of Housing Preservation and Development (HPD).[12] For each housing project, this data set indicates the geographic location, the year the project was completed, the type of building structure, the number of units that were built or rehabilitated, whether units were newly constructed or created from the gut rehabilitation of vacant buildings, and whether units are rental or owner-occupied. In addition, HPD staff also provided us with approximate city and state costs for each type of HPD project. Finally HPD provided us with data on federal housing built or rehabilitated in New York City during the 1980s and 1990s and on other city-subsidized housing projects, completed prior to 1987.

We supplemented our data on housing investments with data from two other city sources. First, through an arrangement with the New York City Department of Finance, we obtained a confidential database that contains sales transaction prices for all apartment buildings, condominium apartments and single-family homes over the period 1980–99.[13] In order to ensure that we did not include the sales of Ten Year Plan developments themselves, we attempted to exclude any sales that could potentially be part of a development. Unfortunately the Real Property Assessment Division databases (RPAD) and homes sales data do not identify whether a particular property received city subsidies, so we excluded any sale that occurred on the same block as a Ten Year Plan development if the sale was of a building that was constructed after the Ten Year Plan units had been completed.[14] Our final sample includes 293 803 property sales, spread across 1612 census tracts.[15] Because of the long time span of the data, and New York City's size, this is a large sample size compared with that in much of the literature.

Second, data on building characteristics were obtained from an administrative data set gathered for the purpose of assessing property taxes (the RPAD file). Unfortunately, the RPAD data contain little information about the characteristics of individual units in apartment buildings (except in the case of condominiums). Nonetheless these building characteristics explain variations in prices surprisingly well, suggesting the data are rich enough for estimating hedonic price equations.[16]

Table 5.1 shows summary statistics from the RPAD data. The first column shows the characteristics of our full sample of property sales; the second column shows the characteristics of sales that at some point would be located within 500 feet of a new unit created through the Ten Year Plan. As shown, most sales were located in Brooklyn and Queens, largely because those boroughs include a relatively large share of smaller properties, which sell more frequently than apartment buildings. Nearly two-thirds of all buildings sold were either one- or two-family homes, and 81 per cent were

Table 5.1 Characteristics of properties sold

	Percentage of all property sales	Percentage of sales within 500 feet of Ten Year Plan new housing site
Borough		
Manhattan	14.6	17.3
Bronx	13.1	14.2
Brooklyn	29.6	51.7
Queens	31.0	14.3
Staten Island	11.8	2.4
Any borough	100.0	100.0
Building class		
Single-family detached	25.0	10.8
Single-family attached	11.1	5.8
Two-family	27.6	29.8
Walk-up apartments	17.5	36.4
Elevator apartments	1.2	2.2
Loft buildings	0.1	0.1
Condominiums	14.4	9.2
Mixed-use, multi-family (includes store or office plus residential units	3.1	5.8
Any building type	100.0	100.0
Other structural characteristics		
Built pre-World War II	77.0	94.5
Vandalized	0.0	0.2
Other abandoned	0.1	0.4
Garage	31.1	12.8
Corner location	7.1	7.7
Major alteration prior to sale	3.3	7.0
N	293803	40659

Note: All sales in community districts where at least 100 Ten Year Plan units were built or rehabilitated (including units in renovated city-owned, occupied buildings).

single-family homes, two-family homes or small apartments. Almost a third of the transacting properties had garages and more than three-quarters were built before World War II. Only a handful of buildings were vandalized or otherwise abandoned.

The second column of Table 5.1 reveals some systematic differences between properties located close to Ten Year Plan sites and those that are not. Properties located within the 500-foot ring are far more likely to be in

Brooklyn and far less likely to be in Staten Island and Queens. Properties in the 500-foot ring are also much older, much less likely to be single-family homes, more likely to be walk-up apartments and, consistent with these differences, much less likely to have garages.

Table 5.2 Number of properties sold, by ring

	N	Percentage of all property sales
All property sales	293803	100.0
Sales within 500 feet of:		
Any Ten Year Plan new housing site	40659	13.8
Homeownership only site	15614	5.3
Small homeownership site	14816	5.0
Large homeownership site	798	0.3
Rental only site	13893	4.7
Small rental site	12214	4.2
Large rental site	1679	0.6
Homeownership and rental site	11152	3.8
Small homeownership and rental site	7160	2.4
Large homeownership and rental site	3992	1.4
Any completed Ten Year Plan new housing project	14344	4.9

Note: All sales in community district where at least 100 Ten Year Plan units were built or rehabilitated (including units in renovated city-owned, occupied buildings).

Table 5.2 gives a sense of the type of subsidized housing built in these rings. Using the mutually exclusive categories described above, the table shows that these properties are fairly evenly distributed among rings with new owner units (but no new rental units), new rental units (but no new owner units) and both new owner and new rental units. In terms of size, most of the properties within 500 feet of a Ten Year Plan site are located in rings where fewer than 100 units will ultimately be built. Finally, 14 per cent of the properties would at some point be located within 500 feet of a new Ten Year Plan unit, with 5 per cent of the properties already within 500 feet of a completed Ten Year Plan unit.

Regression Results

Table 5.3 shows the key coefficients and their standard errors for the ring variables for the basic model in column 1. Column 2 shows the model in which we control for the mix of units in the ring: the proportion that are

Table 5.3 Selected coefficients from regression results for models 1 and 2 (dependent variable = log of price per unit)

	Model 1	Model 2
In Ring, new units	−0.0752***	−0.0753***
	(0.0045)	(0.0045)
Post Ring, new units	0.0162	0.0364***
	(0.0108)	(0.0125)
Number of new units at the time of sale	1.7×10^{-4}	3.9×10^{-4}*
	(2.0×10^{-4})	(2.2×10^{-4})
Number of new units at the time of sale^2	-3.4×10^{-7}	-6.4×10^{-7}*
	(3.4×10^{-7})	(3.5×10^{-7})
Share of multi-family new units at the time of sale		−0.0013
		(0.0203)
Share of rental new units at the time of sale		−0.0439**
		(0.0199)
Share of new construction units at the time of sale		−0.0144
		(0.0143)
Tpost, new units	4.3×10^{-4}	0.0009
	(0.0020)	(0.0020)
Tpost* (number of new units at the time of sale)	-3.5×10^{-5}	-4.3×10^{-5}*
	(2.9×10^{-5})	(2.9×10^{-5})
Adjusted R^2	0.8712	0.8712
N	293803	293803

Notes: Both regressions include a set of variables that control for proximity to other subsidized housing: In Ring, Rehab Occupied Units Only; Post Ring, Rehab Occupied Units; Number of Rehab Occupied Units at the Time of Sale; In Ring, Federal and Pre-1987 City Units; Post Ring, Federal and Pre-1987 City Units; and Number of Federal and Pre-1987 City Units at the Time of Sale. Both regressions include the following variables capturing characteristics of the property sold: building age and its square, log square feet per unit, the number of buildings on a lot, dummies for the presence of commercial units, extension, major alteration prior to sale, location on a block corner, vandalized buildings, other abandoned buildings, and odd shape, and a set of 18 building classification dummies ('single-family detached', 'two-family home', 'three-family home', 'four-family home', 'five/six-family home', 'more than six families, no elevator', ' walk-up, units not specified', 'elevator apartment building, cooperatives', 'elevator apartment building, not cooperatives', 'loft building', 'condominium, single-family attached', 'condominium, walk-up apartments', 'condominium, elevator building', 'condominium, miscellaneous', 'multi-use, single family with store', 'multi-use, two-family with store', 'multi-use, three-family with store' and 'multi-use, four or more families with store'). Both regressions include census tract-quarter fixed effects. Standard errors in parentheses.

***denotes 1% significance level; **denotes 5% significance level; *denotes 10% significance level.

multi-family units (as opposed to 1–4 unit homes), the proportion that are rental (as compared to ownership) and the proportion that were created through new construction (rather than through the rehabilitation of vacant buildings). In this way we allow the impacts to vary according to the mix of housing created in a particular ring. The coefficients on the structural variables are not shown here, but, as in Ellen *et al.* (2001), they have the expected signs, which, combined with relatively high R^2s (of roughly 0.87), suggest that these variables provide adequate controls for the characteristics of the houses sold.[17]

The first point to make here is that the In Ring coefficient is negative and statistically significant. Specifically the coefficient indicates that, before completion of a project, the properties located within 500 feet of a Ten Year Plan site sold for roughly 7.5 per cent less than comparable properties located in the same census tract, but beyond 500 feet of an investment site. In other words, our estimates imply that the HPD investments tended to be made in the most distressed locations within already distressed census tracts.

In terms of project impacts, the coefficient on Post Ring in column 1 is statistically insignificant, indicating that, on average, the Ten Year Plan units do not appear to have generated significant external benefits. But as we see in column 2, when we control for project mix, we find a positive impact, suggesting that certain types of projects do generate significant positive benefits on surrounding properties.

Consider the three 'share' variables in model two. These variables indicate the mix of completed, city-subsidized units within 500 feet of a property sale. The coefficient on the share of units that are rental is negative and statistically significant, indicating that rental projects have significantly smaller effects than ownership projects. The coefficients on the variables showing the share of units that are in multi-family structures (as compared to 1–4 unit buildings) and the share of units that were built through new construction (as opposed to gut rehabilitation) are not statistically significant. In other words, after controlling for tenure, there is no apparent difference between the spillover impacts of units in multifamily structures v. 1–4 unit structures and between new construction and rehabilitation projects.

Recall that the model also includes Tpost variables (post completion time trends) to test whether these impacts change over time. While the coefficient on Tpost is insignificant, indicating that the effects are sustained over time, the coefficient on Tpost interacted with the number of units is negative and marginally significant, providing modest evidence that the impacts of large projects do erode somewhat over time.

Model Extensions

Although the results in model 2 suggest that ownership units generate greater spillover effects, this may be the artifact of selection. It may be, that is, that owner-occupied units are located in less distressed neighborhoods to begin with. To identify the differential impacts of ownership and rental units, we therefore include three mutually exclusive 'In Ring' variables, one indicating properties within 500 feet of new owner units (but no new rental units), one showing properties within 500 feet of new rental units (but no new owner units) and another showing properties that are within 500 feet of both new owner and new rental units. The results are shown in the first column of Table 5.4 (model 3).

The 'In Ring' coefficients suggest that the ownership projects were built in somewhat less distressed neighborhoods. In fact, after controlling for this difference in initial conditions, the coefficient on the share of rental units falls in magnitude and is no longer statistically significant. While the value of properties surrounding completed homeownership projects are higher, this appears to be because homeownership projects are sited in areas with higher property values to begin with. When including these separate in-ring variables, the estimated impact falls slightly. The post-ring coefficient falls from 0.038 to 0.030, suggesting that the initial gap between prices in the ring and in the larger census tract falls by 3 percentage points after completion.

It may also be true that large projects were systematically sited in more distressed locations than were smaller projects, which could bias our estimates of marginal impacts. Thus model 4 includes separate 'In Ring' variables for small and large projects within each of our three ring-types. The coefficients on the 'In Ring' variables show that larger projects were indeed located in micro neighborhoods that were relatively more distressed, especially in rings where only rental housing was constructed. When controlling for these selection effects, the magnitude of the coefficient on the number of new units in the ring almost doubles, and that of the coefficient on the number of new units squared increases by 50 per cent. Using these coefficient estimates, the marginal impact of the 10th city-subsidized unit increases significantly to 0.0631 percentage points $(100[(6.5\times10^{-4})+2(-9.3\times10^{-7})10])$, and that of the 100th unit grows to 0.0464 percentage points $(100[(6.5\times10^{-4})+2(-9.3\times10^{-7})100])$. We believe that this final model provides the most precise estimates of impacts. Therefore, in estimating total program benefits, we use these parameters.

Note that the fixed component of the effect (the portion of the impact that is independent of the number of completed units) is far larger than the marginal effect of additional units. (As noted above, the 'fixed' component

Table 5.4 Selected coefficients from regression results for models 3 and 4 (dependent variable = log of price per unit)

	Model 3	Model 4
In Ring, new units, owner but not renter	−0.0677***	
	(0.0053)	
In Ring, new units, owner but not renter, 1–100 units		−0.0677***
		(0.0053)
In Ring, new units, owner but not renter, 101+ units		−0.0836***
		(0.0219)
In Ring, new units, renter but not owner	−0.0843***	
	(0.0063)	
In Ring, new units, renter but not owner, 1–100 units		−0.0791***
		(0.0064)
In Ring, new units, renter but not owner, 101+ units		−0.1701***
		(0.0165)
In Ring, new units, owner and renter	−0.1015***	
	(0.0080)	
In Ring, new units, owner and renter, 1–100 units		−0.1015***
		(0.0084)
In Ring, new units, owner and renter, 101+ units		−0.1267***
		(0.0132)
Post ring, new units	0.0299**	0.0299**
	(0.0128)	(0.0128)
Number of new units at the time of sale	3.9×10^{-4}*	6.5×10^{-4}***
	(2.2×10^{-4})	(2.2×10^{-4})
Number of new units at the time of sale^2	-6.4×10^{-7}*	-9.3×10^{-7}***
	(3.5×10^{-7})	(3.6×10^{-7})
Share of multi-family new units at the time of sale	−0.0014	−0.0058
	(0.0203)	(0.0204)
Share of rental new units at the time of sale	−0.0275	−0.0306
	(0.0208)	(0.0209)
Share of new construction units at the time of sale	−0.0133	−0.0201
	(0.0143)	(0.0144)
Tpost, new units	0.0011	8.8×10^{-4}
	(0.0020)	(0.0020)
Tpost* (number of new units at the time of sale)	-4.0×10^{-5}	-3.9×10^{-5}
	(2.9×10^{-5})	(2.9×10^{-5})
Adjusted R^2	0.8712	0.8712
N	293803	293803

Note: As for Table 5.3.

of the effect is estimated to be 3 percentage points.) One interpretation of this relatively large effect is that one new housing unit is all it takes to eliminate much of the negative impact of an eyesore (whether blighted properties or land).

A Preliminary Investigation of the Costs and Benefits of Housing Investments

As noted above, we do not include a wide array of benefits associated with the programs, most notably the benefits delivered to actual residents who are able to move into the new subsidized housing. On the cost side, we use high cost estimates in order to be conservative, but we do not include the value of federal rent subsidies that some residents receive, nor do we include the forgone revenues to the city as a result of tax abatements and exemptions that all new and rehabilitated properties receive. In addition, for some of the rental properties, the value of low income housing tax credits is omitted.

In Table 5.5, we present the aggregate costs of all housing units built through the Ten Year Plan and compare them to the estimated benefits these units have delivered to their immediately surrounding communities (500-foot rings). In the first two columns, we assume that none of the loans

Table 5.5 Estimated ratio of benefits generated in 500-foot ring to costs of subsidies

	No loan repayment		30% loan repayment	
Project type	City subsidy only	Total subsidy	City subsidy only	Total subsidy
All housing units	1.11	0.72	1.59	1.02
Homeownership	2.67	1.38	3.81	1.97
Rental	0.93	0.62	1.32	0.88

provided by the city are paid back. (Virtually all the subsidies provided by the city were in the form of long-term loans.) In the second set of columns, we assume a 30 per cent repayment rate. Looking at the first row, we see that, even if we assume no repayment, the benefits generated in the 500-foot ring actually exceeded the city's investment. We think this is quite remarkable, given that we are only counting the external benefits generated within 500 feet of a project and we have ignored the value of any private benefit enjoyed by the residents of the new city housing.

Note that, when we consider total government subsidies (and include state and federal dollars too), the benefits generated in the 500-foot ring do not fully exceed costs. If we assume a 30 per cent repayment ratio, however, these benefits exactly match the costs. Looking at the bottom two rows, the table seems to suggest that homeownership programs are a better bargain for the city. This is not because their spillover effects are larger (recall regression results above). It is because the subsidies delivered to them are thinner: occupants of ownership housing, given their higher incomes, are able to shoulder a larger share of actual housing cost.

While we think these estimates are striking, it is worth stressing again that they are only meant to be suggestive. Clearly the results of the cost–benefit calculation are sensitive to the many assumptions we have made in estimating the costs and benefits.

CONCLUSION

In this chapter we have sought to shed light on the appropriate role of cities in providing housing assistance to their residents. Our analysis of the existing theory and evidence suggests that, although cities should assume an important role in administering housing subsidy programs, they should only fund them under a limited set of circumstances. Redistribution of income, an important goal of most housing subsidy programs, is likely to be best addressed at the federal, rather than local, level. Also many of the market failures present in housing markets may be better addressed by initiatives to remove the causes of the failures rather than by spending programs. Cities can, however, use housing assistance programs to promote neighborhood revitalization objectives by removing negative externalities and generating positive spillovers.

Our empirical investigation of the new construction and gut rehabilitation programs of New York City's Ten Year Plan suggest that housing programs can indeed generate positive spillover effects. We estimate that these programs were associated with higher sales prices of housing in surrounding blocks. But the existence of statistically significant, positive impacts on sales prices does not necessarily mean that the benefits generated by the development initiatives exceed their substantial costs to the city. Our preliminary analysis which compares one set of benefits (the external benefits delivered to the 500-foot ring) to one set of costs (the subsidies provided) suggests that the benefit–cost calculus for the city might well be positive. When state and federal subsidies are netted out of the cost estimates, these benefits exceed the costs by a substantial amount, especially for the homeownership programs. Thus using city revenues to fund housing programs such as those created in the Ten Year Plan is particularly attractive when non-city sources of financing are available. Since New York City used state and federal funds to build some of the Ten Year Plan units, the positive external benefits seem large compared to the city's own investment.

In the absence of an external source of subsidy, would a city such as New York wisely spend its own funds to finance housing development? In future research we will expand upon the rudimentary benefit–cost analysis we have presented here. Specifically we will seek to derive estimates concerning the imputed value of the housing to residents, the effects of the housing on property values beyond 500 feet and the tax expenditures of the city and federal governments.

NOTES

1. Our focus in this chapter is on housing assistance or subsidy programs. Cities also regulate housing markets in a number of ways, including zoning ordinances, building and housing codes and rent regulation. Although these functions are vital and affect the supply of housing in many ways (Salama *et al.*, 1999), they are not the focus of this chapter.
2. Typically, the beneficiaries of housing assistance programs must earn incomes that are less than 80 per cent of the metropolitan area median, and in practice beneficiaries have incomes that are considerably lower. The key exceptions are several provisions of the Internal Revenue Code; for example, the deduction for home mortgage loan interest, the deduction for property taxes and the favorable treatment of capital gains on the sale of a home which can be thought of as subsidies for homeowners.
3. Two other arguments are sometimes made as well. First, subsidized housing production programs have been touted as a way to increase output and provide economic stimulus. While the evidence on this is limited, many doubt that housing subsidy programs are a very effective countercyclical policy tool (Sinai and Waldfogel, 2001; Weicher, 1979). In any event, macroeconomic fiscal policy making is a role that few would consider cities capable of playing. Another argument made by some economists is that the market for rental housing may be monopolistically competitive. As Peter Arnott has pointed out, housing is highly heterogeneous, which he argues makes the market quite thin. This differentiated product, combined with asymmetric information and high search costs, may mean that landlords have market power that they can exploit (Arnott, 1995). To the extent that such monopoly power exists, it might justify public action. However most economists view the housing market as generally competitive, with many providers (Heilbrun, 1987).
4. Recent evidence suggests that black and Latino home-seekers encounter unfavorable treatment about half of the time they transact in the housing market (Ondrich *et al.*, 1999). Clearly, discrimination is troubling from an equity perspective as well, and efforts to combat discrimination have likely been motivated more by concerns about social justice than about economic costs.
5. This method is first presented in Galster *et al.* (1999).
6. Lyons and Loveridge (1993) and Goetz *et al.* (1996) examine the differential effects of a variety of federal programs, but they limit study to federal, new construction rental projects.
7. Since all buildings in New York City have been geocoded by the New York City Department of City Planning we used a 'cross-walk' (the 'Geosupport File') which associates each tax lot with an x,y coordinate (that is, latitude, longitude using the US State Plane 1927 projection), police precinct, community district and census tract. A tax lot is usually a building and is an identifier available to the homes sales and RPAD data. We

are able to assign x,y coordinates and other geographic variables to over 98 per cent of the sales using this method. For most of the HPD units, we had both tax block and tax lots. If the tax lot was unavailable, then we collapsed the Geosupport file to the tax block level (calculating the center of each block) in order to assign x,y coordinates. We were unable to assign an x,y coordinate to 6 per cent of the HPD units, largely owing to missing block information.

8. In cases where a sale was within 500 feet of more than one unit, we used the completion date of the first unit completed.
9. Note that home ownership units are defined in this chapter as units within an ownership project. Some of these units are in fact rental apartments in small, owner-occupied properties.
10. The 100 unit cut-off point defining small v. large projects is chosen so that no more than 35 per cent of the sales for a given ring type occur within 500 foot of projects larger than the threshold.
11. To arrive at pre-completion prices, we estimated six simple regressions, one for each ring type. In each case we regressed ln (price per unit) on a set of year dummies. The coefficients on the year dummies give the (unconditional) mean price (in logs) in a given year for the given ring type.
12. For the purposes of this chapter, units created under the Ten Year Plan are defined to include only those projects that were completed between January 1987 and June 2000.
13. Because sales of cooperative apartments are not considered to be sales of real property, they are not included in the data set. We should also note that most of the apartment buildings in our sample are rent-stabilized. Given that legally allowable rents are typically above market rents outside of affluent neighborhoods in Manhattan and Brooklyn during most of the period 1987 to 2000, we do not think that their inclusion biases our results (see Pollakowski, 1997.)
14. To provide a margin of error with respect to the construction dates in RPAD, we also excluded sales of buildings on the same block as a Ten Year Plan unit that were built up to two years before the Ten Year Plan units.
15. We limited the analysis to properties that are located within the 48 community districts (of the total 58) where there were more than 100 Ten Year Plan units developed that were either (1) rehabilitation of occupied, *in rem* buildings, (2) rehabilitation of vacant buildings, or (3) new construction.
16. See Ellen *et al.* (2001) for more detail on the data and parameter estimates on the building characteristics in a similar model.
17. The coefficients on control variables included in the models but not shown in Table 5.3 are available upon request from the authors.

REFERENCES

Aaron, Henry J. (1972), 'Shelter and Subsidies: Who Benefits from Federal Housing Policies?', The Brookings Institution, Washington, DC.

Arnott, Richard (1995), 'Time for Revisionism on Rent Control', *Journal of Economic Perspectives*, **9**(1), 99–120.

Basolo, Victoria (1999), 'Passing the Housing Policy Baton in the US: Will Cities Take the Lead?', *Housing Studies*, **14**(4), 433–52.

Briggs, Xavier de Souza, Joe T. Darden and Angela Aidala (1999), 'In the Wake of Desegregation: Early Impacts of Scattered-Site Public Housing on Neighborhoods in Yonkers, New York', *Journal of the American Planning Association*, **65**(1), 27–49.

Caplin, Andrew and John Leahy (1998), 'Miracle on Sixth Avenue: Information Externalities and Search', *The Economic Journal*, **108** (January), 60–74.

Cummings, Jean L., Denise DiPasquale and Matthew E. Kahn (2001), 'Inner City Homeownership Opportunities and Black Community Choice', paper presented at the American Real Estate and Urban Economics Annual Meetings, January 2001.
Ellen, Ingrid Gould, Michael H. Schill, Amy Ellen Schwartz and Scott Susin (2001), 'Building Homes, Reviving Neighborhoods: Spillovers from Subsidized Construction of Owner-occupied Housing in New York City', *Journal of Housing Research*, **12**(2), 185–216.
Galster, George C., Peter Tatian and Robin Smith (1999), 'The Impact of Neighbors Who Use Section 8 Certificates on Property Values', *Housing Policy Debate*, **10**(4), 879–917.
Goetz, Edward, Hin Kin Lam and Anne Heitlinger (1996), 'There Goes the Neighborhood? The Impact of Subsidized Multi-Family Housing on Urban Neighborhoods', Center For Urban and Regional Affairs Working Paper 96–1, Minneapolis.
Heilbrun, James (1987), *Urban Economics and Public Policy*, 3rd edn, New York: St Martin's Press.
Hirsch, Arnold (1983), *Making the Second Ghetto: Race and Housing In Chicago 1940–1960*, Cambridge, MA: Cambridge University Press.
Lee, Chang-Moo, Dennis P. Culhane and Susan M. Wachter (1999), 'The Differential Impacts of Federally Assisted Housing Programs on Nearby Property Values: A Philadelphia Case Study', *Housing Policy Debate*, **10**(1), 75–93.
Lyons, Robert F. and Scott Loveridge (1993), 'A Hedonic Estimation of the Effect of Federally Subsidized Housing on Nearby Residential Property Values', Staff Paper P93–6, Department of Agriculture and Applied Economics, University of Minnesota.
Mills, Edwin S. and Bruce W. Hamilton (1994), *Urban Economics*, New York: Harper Collins College Publishers.
Nourse, Hugh O. (1963), 'The Effects of Public Housing on Property Values in St. Louis', *Land Economics*, **39**, 433–41.
Olsen, Edgar O. (2001), 'Housing Programs For Low-Income Households', NBER Working Paper no. W8208, Cambridge.
Ondrich, Jan, Alex Stricker and John Yinger (1999), 'Do Landlords Discriminate? The Incidence and Causes of Racial Discrimination in Rental Housing Markets', *Journal of Housing Economics*, **8**(3), 185–204.
Peterson, Paul E. (1981), *City Limits*, Chicago: University of Chicago Press.
Polinsky, Mitchell A. and David T. Ellwood (1979), 'An Empirical Reconciliation of Micro and Grouped Estimates of the Demand for Housing', *Review of Economics and Statistics*, **61**(2), 199–205.
Pollakowski, Henry O. (1997), 'The Effects of Rent Deregulation in New York City', MIT Center for Real Estate, Cambridge, MA.
Quigley, John M. (1979), 'What have we Learned about Urban Housing Markets?', in Peter Mieszkowski and Mahlon Straszheim (eds), *Current Issues in Urban Economics*, Baltimore, MD: Johns Hopkins University Press, pp.391–429.
Quigley, John M. (2000), 'A Decent Home: Housing Policy in Perspective', Brookings-Wharton Papers on Urban Affairs, 53–88.
Rabiega, William A., Ta-Win Lin and Linda Robinson (1984), 'The Property Value Impacts of Public Housing Projects in Low and Moderate Density Residential Neighborhoods', *Land Economics*, **60**, 174–9.
Salama, Jerry J., Michael H. Schill and Martha E. Stark (1999), *Reducing the Cost*

of New Housing Construction in New York City, New York: Center For Real Estate and Urban Policy.

Santiago, Anna M., George C. Galster and Peter Tatian (2001), 'Assessing the Property Value Impacts of the Dispersed Housing Subsidy Program in Denver', *Journal of Policy Analysis and Management*, **20**(1), 65–88.

Schill, Michael H. (1990), 'Privatizing Federal Low Income Housing Assistance: The Case of Public Housing', *Cornell Law Review*, **75**, 878–948.

Schill, Michael H. and Samantha Friedman (1999), 'The Fair Housing Amendments Act of 1988: The First Decade', *Cityscape: A Journal of Policy Development and Research*, **4**(3), 57–78.

Schill, Michael H., Ingrid Gould Ellen, Amy Ellen Schwartz and Ioan Voicu (2002), 'Revitalizing Inner City Neighborhoods: New York City's Ten Year Plan', *Housing Policy Debate*, **13**(3), 529–66.

Sinai, Todd and Joel Waldfogel (2001), 'Do Low-Income Housing Subsidies Increase Housing Consumption?', paper presented at the mid-year meetings of the American Real Estate and Urban Economics Association, Washington, DC.

Tiebout, Charles M. (1956), 'A Pure Theory of Local Expenditures', *Journal of Political Economy*, **64** (October), 416–24.

Tobin, James (1970), 'On Limiting the Domain of Inequality', *Journal of Law and Economics*, **13**(2), 263–77.

Weicher, John C. (1979), 'Urban Housing Policy', in Peter Mieszkowski and Mahlon Straszheim (eds), *Current Issues in Urban Economics*, Baltimore, MD: Johns Hopkins University Press, pp.469–508.

Wright, David, Ingrid Gould Ellen and Michael H. Schill (2001), *Community Development Corporations and Welfare Reform: Linkages, Roles and Impacts*, Albany, NY: Nelson A. Rockefeller Institute of Government.

COMMENT

John M. Quigley

This is a really major issue, of real importance, and I want to encourage the quartet of authors to persevere in the completion of this very dense and complicated empirical project.

Almost all economists, almost everywhere, almost always conclude that the case for government provision of housing services for the poor is very weak. A major failure of the public housing program was directly attributable to government provision: the contentious issue of the siting of faculties and the politics involved meant that facilities were too large and were located in remote places, increasing the isolation of the poor. Government-subsidized new construction by private actors was subject to the kind of abuse Ed Glaeser describes in Chapter 6. Indeed Sam Pierce, HUD Secretary during the Reagan Administration, got his 15 minutes of fame for his association with monstrous abuses of the Section 8 new construction program.

Beyond this, however, there remains the technological fact that investing in new housing for low-income households is uneconomic. It is very expensive to produce dwellings emitting small quantities of housing service through new construction. This is a principle that private landlords know well. You produce slums and other forms of low-income housing from the oldest and most obsolete part of the housing stock.

Now along came Ingrid Ellen and her friends to challenge this conclusion on empirical grounds. They do not contest the line of reasoning I have just described. They simply ignore it. Indeed, a great irony in the careful benefit–cost calculations the authors perform is that they completely ignore the housing benefits enjoyed by the occupants of the dwellings produced under New York's Ten Year Plan.

The authors present a series of regression results relating the selling prices of properties to their hedonic characteristics, a set of locational measures, and fixed effects for each census tract and quarter. The locational measures are of two kinds: a set of dummy variables indicating whether a property is within 500 feet of a place where 'Ten Year Plan' units are built; and the number of new 'Ten Year Plan' units within 500 feet of a property.

These sets of variables include a variety of 'in Ring' (500 feet) comparisons – to correct, as far as possible, for selection effects – and the possibility that 'Ten Year Plan' units or larger projects of 'Ten Year Plan' units were located in different kinds of neighborhoods.

The authors conduct a careful statistical analysis disentangling the effects of these locational measures from the initial conditions at the various locations. For example, the locations chosen for 'Ten Year Plan' rental dwellings were those where initial housing prices were lower. For another example, the locations chosen for owner-occupied Ten Year Plan units were those where initial housing prices were not quite as low. For a third example, the locations chosen for large projects were those where initial housing prices were lower still. Thesc selection issues are explored skillfully and systematically, and I come away believing the results.

But this is an important finding with real implications. I have three suggestions to strengthen the analysis.

First, within the existing research design, in which all the independent variables save one or two are binary, the authors should supplement these regression results with a full-blown difference-in-differences treatment. The authors have 300000 observations on sales across 10000 census tracts – about 200 per tract. Surely there must be enough repeat sales, that is, two sales of the same property, to support a difference-in-differences estimator. Most consumers of economic empiricism would find it persuasive if the regression results were confirmed by the non-parametric differences methodology. That may be especially true in this market when many of the persistent attributes that would make a single-family house or a duplex more valuable are never measured.

Second, the authors should use more of the spatial information at their disposal. They have measured, or presumably could measure, the exact distances of properties from 'Ten Year Plan' units. In the current paper, they throw this detail away and measure the distance in two flavors. It would be quite interesting – and perhaps quite important empirically – to incorporate distance in some continuous way. According to work by Nic Tideman, a simple exponential fits some of these propinquity measures quite well. More attention to this would make the results (the effects of distance from 'Ten Year Plan' units on property values) more credible.

Third, the authors should attempt a serious cost–benefit analysis. Who knows about the 75 projects chosen? Are they representative of anything? I think before doing systematic cataloging of the myriad possible benefits, the authors should analyze the property value benefits using all projects on some systematic sample. Before trying to include the market value of the 'warm glow' citizens got from the 'Ten Year Plan,' the authors should get us credible estimates of property value externalities relative to costs, perhaps without any allowances for non-residential properties at all. If they do want to get fancy, they might consider selectivity between property values and MWTP, as illustrated in recent work by my colleague Ken Chay on air quality and home prices.

Finally, there is the more general issue: that of New York. People who study urban phenomena always think of New York as a special case, the only North American city where mass transit underground is efficient, the only city where auto ownership does not rise with income, and so on. These externalities arise from propinquity, and there is a lot of propinquity in the Big Apple. Significantly, however, most of the data for this interesting exercise actually comes from Queens and Brooklyn. Are these boroughs sufficiently similar in spatial structure to Boston, Chicago and San Francisco for us to think there is an economic analogy? We know they are not similar to Phoenix, Atlanta or Dallas!

How were these projects chosen in New York? If we order the net benefits by project, is anything systematic revealed? The extent to which these New York results illustrate a more general proposition are thus unclear at this time. But this is a fine paper, and it represents a first-rate contribution to economic scholarship.

6. Public ownership in the American city

Edward L. Glaeser

American local governments own and manage a wide portfolio of enterprises, including gas and electricity companies, water systems, subways, bus systems and schools[1]. Existing theories of public ownership, including the presence of natural monopolies, can explain much of the observed municipal ownership. However, the history of America's cities suggests that support for public ownership came from corruption then associated with private ownership of utilities and public transportation. Private firms that either buy or sell to the government will have a strong incentive to bribe government officials to get lower input prices or higher output prices. Because municipal ownership dulls the incentives of the manager and decreases the firm's available cash, public firms may lead to less corruption. Public ownership is also predicted to create inefficiency and excessively large government payrolls.

Why do many American city governments directly provide public transportation, water and even power and light? Why do so many governments pave and clean their own streets instead of using subcontractors? Government ownership is almost invariably linked with waste and inefficiency, yet government provision in these areas remains common.[2]

One traditional argument is that natural monopolies create a case for government ownership, or at least significant regulation (see, for example, Atkinson and Stiglitz, 1980), but it is not obvious that most public services are really natural monopolies. Subways may have some aspects of natural monopoly, but New York once had three competing subway lines. Certainly buses are not natural monopolies: New York once had dozens of competing bus and streetcar lines. There are times when water has been supplied privately and competitively (Koeppel, 2000). Some utilities may look like natural monopolies, but often there were competing electricity and gas providers.[3]

More recently, Hart *et al.* (1997) argue that the advantage of government ownership is that it limits perverse incentives. The weaker incentives of government operators mean that there is less incentive to cut costs and therefore cut quality. This theory helps us understand some of the examples of public ownership. For example, public provision of water may be explained by the huge problems associated with unclean water. However, this theory works much less well in explaining public transportation and electricity. It also does not work well as a theory of direct government provision of street cleaning: clean streets are very observable and easy to contract on (especially in a repeated setting).

A less benign view of public ownership is that it is an example of empire-building politicians obtaining power at the expense of public welfare. Public ownership provides large opportunities for political patronage that would appeal to any politician even if there were welfare losses from public ownership (see, for example, Shleifer and Vishny, 1994). I am certainly friendly to this view, and even if many supporters of public ownership were motivated by benign reasons, many supporters were, and are, motivated in other ways. However the cynical view does not help us to understand the widespread support for public ownership across American cities in the 19th century. Many progressive reformers who supported public ownership were unconnected to governments and clearly had nothing to gain from public ownership.

The history of America's cities provides a fourth theory of public ownership that is complementary to the other three: public ownership may reduce bribery and corruption. In the 19th century, private firms that either sold to the government or bought from the government would frequently bribe government officials to get favorable prices. The city of New York massively overpaid for the construction of the Tweed Courthouse. Transit companies bribed politicians to get extended (that is, perpetual or 999-year) rights to public streets for nothing. Private companies had huge incentives to bribe politicians and they acted consistently on those incentives.

Indeed progressive era reformers called for public ownership as a solution to this problem of corruption. As Leonard Darwin wrote in 1907, 'One of the points which here appears to tell most in favour of municipal ownership is the belief that it would tend, if extensively adopted, to purify civic life.' A few pages later, he continues describing the progressive argument for public ownership 'the worst frauds attributed to civic administrators have been committed in connection with the franchises granted to private corporations; abolish these franchises by means of the introduction of direct municipal labour and this type of fraud must disappear completely' (Darwin, 1907).

This chapter presents three models of public ownership that formalize this argument. The first two models examine situations where firms sell to the government (such as street cleaning contractors) or buy from the government (such as railroads). In these models, corruption led governments to overpay for their purchases and undercharge for their sales. Public ownership eliminates this problem because the public manager is only weakly incentivized and will not risk prison for profits that he does not himself enjoy. This chapter follows Glaeser and Shleifer (2001) in emphasizing that large private firms subvert the government – the corruption of the Gilded Age came from the increases in the scale of firms (and government) – and that there are scale economies in corruption. The reforms of the progressive era, including public ownership, can be seen as responses to increase in scale.

Of course, public ownership does not eradicate corruption. When governments own firms, the corruption just moves upstream. Public firms will still overpay for inputs if those inputs are privately provided, because private providers will bribe the officials in charge. Even if the firms just use labor, which is the case that I consider, there will be corrupt bargains between workers and firms. Public firms will overpay workers who will reciprocate either with direct kickbacks or through in-kind service (such as campaigning for Tammany Hall or votes). Such direct, or indirect, kickbacks have been quite common, particularly before Civil Service Reform. This explains why reformers saw public ownership and Civil Service Reform as strong complements and why Tammany Hall politicians were quite happy with public ownership as long as they could eliminate civil service reform.

Since both public and private ownership create losses from different sorts of corruption, the model gives us conditions under which public ownership is desirable. A key determinant is whether the firm sells or buys significantly from the government. If the firm is particularly labor-intensive, then large kickbacks from workers may deter public ownership. If it is hard to create corrupt bargains with large volumes of workers, public ownership becomes more attractive.

A third model explains why government ownership, rather than subsidization, may be an appropriate response to externalities. In a world of massive corruption, subsidies will be roundly abused. For example, in the 19th century, land grants and tax abatements were used to address the externalities supposedly coming from railroads. In practice, the subsidies to railroads seem to have been related more to the size of the bribes of railroad officials than to the merits of the case. If government subsidies are going to be perverted through corruption, then public ownership may provide a solution. Of course, government ownership will again bring its own forms of corruption.

After presenting a model of corruption and public ownership, I examine the history of public ownership in New York City (and to a lesser extent other American cities) for the major local government services: water supply, sanitation, street maintenance, power and light utilities, and public transportation. In these histories, I evaluate the importance of the four theories of public ownership: natural monopoly, maintaining quality through soft incentives, public empire building and eliminating corruption. Water supply, some utilities and the subway system all have some aspects of natural monopolies. Certainly many of the contemporary observers arguing for public ownership thought that there were substantial scale economies that suggested natural monopoly.

The best example of the Hart *et al.* (1997) model is public provision of water supply, where poor quality seems to have been the biggest problem with private provision. Other services also have quality problems, but it is not obvious whether poor quality occurs because of standard contracting problems or because of corruption. For example, there were huge quality problems when private contractors handled street cleaning in the 19th century. Low quality is the result of corruption combined with rules restricting politicians to take the lowest bid. When politicians are forced to take the low bid, accepting low quality is a means by which bribed politicians can overpay for services.

In almost all of these five areas, the desire to eliminate corruption seems to have played some role in public provision. Eliminating corruption seems to have been least important in the provision of water, and probably most important in public transportation. While I am not sure that it was the dominant factor leading to public ownership in any of the sectors, the history seems to suggest that it was a sizeable factor in all of the sectors.

CORRUPTION IN THE CITY

This section describes the principal forms of 19th-century municipal corruption. The municipal ownership movement hit its stride during the early 20th century as a response to the events of the late 19th century. For example, in 1902, 22.5 per cent of the electric light and power stations in the country were owned by municipalities; by 1927, 50.7 per cent of these utilities were municipally owned. Municipal stations grew in absolute numbers even as commercial ones decreased. The 1912 census of electric railways cites only two cities that own their own street railways. By 1922, 16 cities had their own street railways. Between 1880 and 1903, 22 cities bought waterworks from private companies.

Three types of corruption are focused upon: underpricing on inputs bought from the government, overpricing of outputs sold to the government and the perversion of attempts to subsidize positive externality-producing behavior. The first two types of corruption are quite obvious and simple to describe.

Overpricing of Outputs

There is no more straightforward means of raiding a public treasury than overpaying for inputs with government money. Typically either a politician himself or a confederate contracts with the government to provide some type of service. The politician's influence ensures that the contract will go to the corrupt contractor, and not the lowest bidder (if indeed bids were even taken). The contractor then shares the proceeds with the politician.

A typical example is described by the muckraking journalist Lincoln Steffens in *The Shame of the Cities*: in Pittsburgh, 'one firm [Flinn's] received practically all the asphalt-paving contracts at prices ranging from $1 to $1.80 per square yard higher than the average price paid in neighboring cities' (Steffens, 1904, p.145). Steffens goes on to show that 99 per cent of the business over a nine-year period went to this single firm. He describes a situation where a less-connected rival who offered to provide higher-quality granite for two-thirds of the price of the Flinn firm was rebuffed. It should be no surprise that Flinn was himself a politician and one of the bosses of the city.

This type of story is repeated throughout Steffens' volume. In Philadelphia, Boss Martin's firm 'Filbert and Porter got all the public contracts they could handle, and the rest went to other contractors friendly to them and the ring' (ibid.). In St. Louis, 'A member of the Assembly . . . succeeded in having his bid for city supplies accepted although the figures were in excess of his competitors' (ibid., p.24). In New York, 'There are public works for Tammany contracts . . . Low bids and short deliveries, generally speaking (and that is the only way I can speak here), is the method' (ibid. p.209). The term 'short deliveries' means that, in New York, underpaying for inputs took the form of giving the contract to the Tammany-backed low bidder, who would then raise the price per unit delivered by lowering the number of units delivered.

This sophisticated form of corruption represents an evolution from the days of the Tweed ring, where New York led the nation in this form of corruption. Under Tweed, 'Plunder of the city treasury, especially in the form of jobbing contracts, was no new thing in New York, but it had never before reached such colossal dimensions' (Bryce, 1914). The ultimate highlight of this form of corruption was the Tweed courthouse. As Ellis (1966) writes:

> Under the new Tweed charter the new board of audit consisted of Tweed, Hall and Connolly. At one of the board's first meetings, on May 5, 1870, the trio authorized the payment of an additional $6,300,000 for the new courthouse they were building. Nearly 90 percent of this sum was padding, and they pocketed the extra $5,500,000.

But this is only the most famous example of Tweed's corruption through overpaying for privately provided services. For example, Tweed centralized street cleaning and gave the contract to a single company. 'The successful bidder was paid $279,000 for a year's work – and immediately 'kicked back' $40,000 from his fee' (Glaab and Brown, 1967, p.204). This type of corruption seems to have been particularly simple to implement and enormously profitable.

This type of corruption is relevant for several of the major public services. For example, public provision of gas and light was often motivated by high prices charged by private providers for these services. In 1895, Detroit started to run a public electric plant to provide power for streetlights. As Judd and Swanstrom (1994) write, the reforming mayor of Detroit, Hazen Pingree's 'main argument against the private control of electricity was that it cost too much . . . Corruption became the issue that tipped the scales in his favor'. Street cleaning and maintenance is another area where the legacy of corruption led to direct public provision. For example, in 1895, George E. Waring, Jr led the reorganization of street cleaning in New York and moved cleaning from private contractors to a public department.

Underpricing of Inputs

A second, primary form of corruption that is intimately related with the move to public ownership is the underpricing of publicly owned inputs that are then sold to private firms. Again the chief method of this type of corruption is that a powerful politician, or his private allies, would buy some government asset for a fraction of its price. The spoils from this transaction would then be shared with the government agent responsible for running the sale. In Steffens' words, 'The riffraff, catching the smell of corruption, rushed in the Municipal Assembly, drove out the remaining respectable men, and sold the city – its streets, its wharves, its markets, and all that it had – to the now greedy business men and bribers.'

Again Steffens' chronicle of corruption stretches across all of America. In St. Louis, 'Municipal legislators sold rights, privileges and public franchises for their own individual profit and at regular schedule rates.' Steffens relates the 1898 Central Traction deal in that city where Robert Snyder handed out $250000 in bribes to get a traction (public transit) franchise from the government (nothing was formally paid for the franchise) that he immediately resold for $1250000. In Pittsburgh, Boss Magee used his power 'turning the streets to his uses, delivering to himself franchises, and building and running railroads'. These franchises represented the right to run trolleys on city streets, often for 999 years, with no payment to the city.

In New York, 'just as other cities share their corrupt dealings with railways and their terminals, so New York's great terminal business is with steamships and docks. These docks should pay the city handsomely. Mr. Murphy [the Boss of Tammany Hall] says they shouldn't'.

Free use of public land and facilities, such as docks, were the primary forms of underpayment by private firms for inputs, but there were other less frequent examples. George Washington Plunkitt describes how he used his political influence to buy 250000 fine granite paving stones from the government for $2.50. He promptly resold them. City governments depositing their funds with banks at no interest, in exchange for kickbacks, can also be seen as an example of this phenomenon.

As the previous examples have already suggested, the corrupt underpricing of inputs was probably most important in the transport industry. As roads are generally public, if private transport companies were to use roads for their operations they would have to buy this right from the public government. Public governments would grant the right to use particular roads in the form of franchises. These franchises might just allow the private transport firm use of the existing road space, as in the case of bus lines.

Alternatively, rail transport (whether horse-drawn, steam-powered or electric) required alterations to the existing road structure. These alterations are socially costly both to create and to maintain (such as with delays due to lost road use), but they also in a sense permanently reduce the space in the road that was available for public traffic. Economic efficiency would generally dictate that the transport firms should pay for the social costs of these roads, but they generally did not (except through bribes). Franchises were generally free or priced at far below market values.

One way to think about the corruption involved is that the government owns land that it is renting at far below market prices to corrupt firms. An even more extreme example in the rail industry was the construction of the transcontinental railroad. Josephson (1934) writes, 'the railroads, especially in the West, were "land companies" which acquired their principal raw material through pure grants in return for their promise to build, and whose directors, combined with friendly statesmen, such as Douglas, did a rushing land business in farm lands and town sites at rising prices'. There is perhaps an argument that there are externalities associated with rail that justify these grants. However this argument still must face the fact that these land grants were paid for by massive bribes to local and national politicians (see Josephson, 1934, for details). Often politicians were themselves massive shareholders of the railroads, as they were in the case of the *Crédit Mobilier* scandal.

But transportation is not the only industry that used public land as a major input. All of the public utilities, including water supply, sewers and the power and light industries, make use of land. In all of these industries, corrupt government officials handed over use of public property and state privileges in exchange for private bribes. Aaron Burr's Manhattan Water Company managed to get 'substantial rights of eminent domain over lands, river and streams', through the political strength of its owner. It did not hurt that the Council of Revision which gave the final approval to the bill included the largest shareholder of the company (see Koeppel, 2000). Electricity franchises for putting up wire poles, or for burying wires beneath the ground, were also generally given out free.

Did this underpricing of public inputs motivate public ownership? The great advocate of municipal ownership, Hazen Pingree, the Mayor of Detroit, 'first concerned himself with the gas problem in 1891, when he became annoyed at the excavation of the pavements and streets by the companies' (Holli, 1969, p.87). The movement for public ownership of transportation in Chicago seems to have been galvanized by a proposal to give Charles Yerkes a 99-year extension of his franchise at quite favorable rates, which was being considered by a city council that was supposedly bribed by Yerkes. Cudahy (1990) writes that 'an angry mob of citizens armed with clubs and carrying flaming torches . . . surrounded City Hall during the deliberations and demanded, successfully, that Yerkes be repudiated. Yerkes had marshaled all the usual arguments about socialism and government inefficiency and what he felt was the inherent superiority of the private sector for accomplishing just about any task, but the idea of public ownership and operation continued to gather momentum in Chicago'.

Perversion of Subsidization

The third type of corruption, the perversion of subsidization, is far less obvious than the other two types. Throughout history, city governments have recognized that there were a variety of services where private provision would fail to meet social goals. In particular there are certain services that are either public goods or that have very large-scale externalities. Most basically the justice system, sanitation and fire prevention have long been thought of as services worthy of profound government involvement. In the 19th century, clean water was another good that was clearly very important for public health. The great plagues of central cities were thought, from the beginning of the 1900s, to have some connection with the water supply. Economists are still unsure as to whether there are large positive externalities associated with transportation. For example, in 1828, Daniel Webster urged public subsidization of canals because of the general benefit to the United States. Of course, schooling was also thought to have a widespread general benefit.

The traditional economics approach to these types of economics might predict that the government would use money to subsidize directly the private firms providing water and transport. However this very rarely occurred. Perhaps direct subsidization of private firms was understood to have been too much of a temptation to boodlers. Instead the subsidization came primarily through land grants and tax abatements. I have already given examples of what I see as the corruption that was involved in property gifts to railroads, buses and even private water suppliers. The evidence for corrupt underpricing of public inputs is, in a sense, also evidence for corruption of the practice of subsidizing certain businesses.

Tax subsidies were also determined by corrupt bargains between firms and politicians. As Glaab and Brown (1967) write:

> In many places, part of the [cities'] debt was due to lavish encouragement to railroads, which stemmed from local rivalries during the booster years; city and country obligations of this kind were conservatively estimated at $185,000,000 in 1870. Inefficiency and corruption explained some part of the cities' skyrocketing obligations – how much cannot be estimated realistically.

For example, as of 1891, Detroit railroads were exempted from taxation by the state legislature. While I do not have direct evidence that this privilege came about as the result of bribery, it seems likely. After all, the Detroit railway company offered Pingree himself $75000 to cease his fight against them (Judd and Swanstrom, 1994). The Detroit Transportation Company, another tax avoider, was owned by the powerful Senator MacMillan.

I cannot prove that subsidies to railroads were themselves inefficient. However an efficient subsidy scheme would presumably not lead to massive profits for politically well connected firms. Furthermore an efficient subsidy scheme would be more likely to direct payments on the basis of efficiency considerations than on the basis of bribes and political connections.

A SERIES OF SIMPLE MODELS

This section presents three simple models which formalize the corruption problems discussed above. The models are meant to illustrate the impact that municipal ownership would have on consumer welfare and the trade-offs involved in publicly owned firms. The first model deals with underpricing inputs. This type of corruption is addressed first since it is the most important phenomenon in the industries that were eventually made public. The second model addresses overpricing outputs, and the third model addresses the perversion of subsidization.

Underpricing Inputs

In this case, there is a fixed quantity constraint on producing the good, denoted Q, and the price of the good, which is sold on the free market, is P. For each unit of the good that is made, the producer requires ϕ_L units of labor and ϕ_P units of a public good. The free market cost of labor is w. The social cost of the public good is c_P. To keep social analysis simple, we will assume that, if the firm pays for the social cost of its inputs, it will receive zero profits, that is, $P = \phi_L w + \phi_P c_P$.

We assume that the government has ruled that the firm should be charged the true social cost, c_P, for each unit of the public good. In this case, other prices would be non-distortionary. However this social cost seems like a reasonable benchmark. A reasonable alternative is that the government will act like a monopolist. I denote the price paid to the government as $\tilde{c}_P$.

In this and the following models, I make the assumption that voters are able to write down clear rules limiting the ways in which the government can transfer funds to private entities and individuals. Until I discuss subsidies explicitly (in the third model), I will assume that the people are able to craft a bright line rule that ensures that the government can only pay money in exchange for services rendered. The price for these services may well be overinflated, but this assumption strongly limits the forms which corruption might take.

The sale of the public good is handled by an individual, who must approve a sale. Throughout this model, I assume a detection technology which is an increasing function of the difference between the price that the government is paid for something and the true social cost of the good: $\delta(c_P - \tilde{c}_P)$. This function is continuously increasing, as long as $\tilde{c}_P < c_P$, and continuously differentiable. I also assume that it is convex, so that, as the underpayment becomes more and more flagrant, the marginal effect of lowering the price further will be greater. When $c_P = \tilde{c}_P$, the probability of detection equals zero, and the derivative also goes to zero. If the government official is caught taking a bribe, he goes to jail and pays a penalty of K, which includes lost salary, jail time and so on. The official also receives a baseline utility level that is independent of bribes and being caught. The net gains to the official from bribery equals $b - \delta(c_P - \tilde{c}_P)K$.

The company's net gain from bribery will equal $(c_P - \tilde{c}_P)\phi_P \bar{Q}$ minus the cost of bribery, b. As such, the total gain to the two actors from bribery equals $(c_P - \tilde{c}_P)\phi_P \bar{Q} - \delta(c_P - \tilde{c}_P)K$. We assume that this surplus is split between the firm and the government official, according to some bargaining. Any deal must maximize just surplus, which implies the first-order condition: $\delta'(c_P - \tilde{c}_P) = \phi_P \bar{Q}/K$. The convexity of $\delta(c_P - \tilde{c}_P)$ ensures that the problem satisfies second-order conditions. Differences in bargaining power will not change the level of the bribe. Differentiating this condition produces proposition 1 (proofs of all propositions are in the Appendix):

Proposition 1: the firm will pay less for the public good if (1) the firm is larger, (2) the firm buys a greater share of its inputs from the government, (3) the penalty associated with being caught taking a bribe is lower. If the detection technology $\delta(c_P - \tilde{c}_P) = d_0{}^{*}d(c_P - \tilde{c}_P)$, then the firm will pay more for the good as d_0 rises.

Proposition 1 helps us to understand the conditions under which we should expect to see bribery and underpricing of government inputs. Larger firms will be more likely to bribe the government. This actually creates an incentive for mergers, and some of the merger wave of the 19th century can be understood as a means of getting advantages of scale in subverting the government. This chapter follows Glaeser and Shleifer (2001) in emphasizing the existence of scale economies in the subversion of justice and government. In the earlier publication, we argued that the increased scale of business explains why corruption appears to have increased in the late 19th century.

Firms that purchase a large amount of their inputs from the government will also be likely to engage in more bribery. Public utilities and transportation are a classic example of firms with large government inputs. In public utilities, pipes and wires must be laid underground. Installing and repairing these pipes requires the use of government property – the roads. Public transportation also uses the roads or land below the streets. Frequently public utilities and transportation seem to have underpaid, or not paid at all, for the privilege of using these government inputs.

The penalty result is unsurprising and suggests that we should expect more bribery in governments that pay less or that have fewer penalties for being caught taking bribes. Indeed one of the ideas of civil service reform was that through this reform corruption would be eliminated as workers became better paid and more professional. The detection result is also unsurprising, but it also means that, as police and journalism technology improved over the 20th century, the level of bribery decreased.

Of course, in this simple model, there are no distortions from this bribery – it just leads to a redistribution of wealth from the city to the firm. However, we will consider the problem from the point of view of the taxpayers who want to maximize overall government revenue. Thus the underpayment for inputs represents pure social loss. In a more complex model, mispricing of the inputs will lead to overuse of them as well, which will create a true social loss. Indeed it is debatable whether we should include the bribe payments as part of the social gains. If the government offset higher bribes with lower wages, for example, it might be appropriate to include this bribery amount. However we will restrict our analysis of costs and benefits to the losses from underpayment. In that case, the social loss from private ownership (relative to the first best) is $(c_P - \tilde{c}_P)\phi_P\bar{Q}$.

An alternative assumption is that there is no detection, but that instead the government is just not allowed to pay private firms anything (except when buying goods). In that case, there is just a non-negativity constraint on the price for the input and the equilibrium price will be zero. The loss to the public is then $c_P\phi_P\bar{Q}$.

We now consider the alternative possibility that the firm is run by a public entrepreneur. In the spirit of Hart *et al.* (1997), public ownership changes the objective function of the firm. In this case, the manager's salary is assumed to be fixed and independent of firm profits. Thus, if the public official faces any penalty from bribing someone else, he will not himself engage in bribery to get the public input for a lower price. Since his compensation is not tied to firm profits, there is no reason why he would risk jail to increase profits by bribing an input supplier.

However, in this model the government official will overpay his employees and receive kickbacks from these workers for their higher wages. In principle, it is also possible that the government official will underprice the output and receive kickbacks for these lower prices. I assume away the second possibility by assuming that the consumer base for the good is just too widespread for this to occur. In the cases of water supply or public transportation, this assumption is likely to be met. It would be very difficult to have extralegal arrangements with millions of subway passengers where they got a price below the market price.

However it is possible for the government official to collaborate with the workers, overpaying them and then getting a kickback. Indeed the turn-of-the-century Tammany Hall Satchem warmly applauded municipal ownership because of the opportunities for patronage: 'It's a grand idea – the city ownin' the railroads, the gas works and all that. Just see how many thousands of new places there would be for the workers in Tammany!' (Riordan, 1995, p.54).

This quotation perfectly captures the structure of the model. Under municipal ownership, the government raises wages to above competitive levels, and jobs go to cronies. As Leonard Darwin wrote in 1907, 'And as regards wages, here also it must be remembered that [under municipal ownership] the civic authorities would always remain under the temptation of buying the votes of the municipal workmen by raising their wages or shortening their hours of work.'

Since the wage is now endogenous, we denote this as $\tilde{w}$. The gap between $\tilde{w}$ and w will be shared between the public official and the workers. Historically it is certainly true that in many cases direct kickbacks for lucrative public jobs certainly did occur. However, in many cases, the kickback would represent payment in kind. For example, it was particularly typical for highly paid government workers to reward their patrons with effort during election campaigns. As George Washington Plunkitt said, 'Parties can't hold together if their workers don't get the offices when they win' (Riordan, 1995, p.13). Even more obviously Plunkitt says that 'A Supreme Court Judge in New York City gets $17,500 a year, and he's expected, when nominated, to help along the good cause [Tammany Hall] with a year's salary' (ibid., p.74).

There continues to be a probability of detection equal to the difference between the paid price and the market price, or, in this case, the market wage and the true wage. Thus the public official faces a probability of detection equal to $\delta(\tilde{w} - w)$, which is an increasing and convex function, just as before. The joint surplus between the workers and the government official will again be split by some bargaining rule, and they will act in such a way as to maximize their joint surplus.

A key question is whether the payment to each worker should be treated as a separate bribe, for the purposes of the detection technology, or whether the entire wage bill should be considered one bribe. Is it true that each time you bribe a worker you run a risk, or is the bribe to the union of workers as a whole? The truth is surely between these two extremes. To capture this we assume that, if there are N workers taking bribes, the probability of detection equals $N^{\alpha}\delta(\tilde{w} - w)$, where α is a parameter between zero and one.[4] When α is close to one, bribing workers is quite hard and represents individual bargains with them. When α is close to zero, bribing workers becomes much easier.

In this case, the joint surplus will equal $\phi_L\bar{Q}(\tilde{w} - w) - (\phi_L\bar{Q})^{\alpha}\delta(\tilde{w} - w)K$; that is, the excess wages paid to the workers minus the cost to the government employee of getting caught. The first-order condition is $\delta'(\tilde{w} - w) = (\phi_L\bar{Q})^{1-\alpha}/K$. We assume $\phi_L\bar{Q} > 1$. In this case, it is obvious that the amount of bribery will be rising with the size of the firm, declining with K and increasing the extent to which the firm uses labor. Furthermore the amount of bribery will be declining with the value of α. This parameter partially captures the extent to which the workers are organized, and thus more organization will lead to more bribery. This leads us to proposition 2: corruption leads private firms to earn excess profits and public firms to earn losses.

This model predicts that public firms will overpay their workers and earn losses.[5] As Plunkitt said, 'If the city owned the railroads, etc., salaries would be sure to go up. Higher salaries is the cryin' need of the day.' The model also explains why unions would lobby heavily for government ownership. As long as the workers get some benefit from the firm, they will prefer the case of public firms, where they are being paid above market wages, to the case of private firms where they are being paid market wages. If politicians could actually increase the employment of the firm, this analysis predicts that they would do so.[6]

Despite these profits and losses, it is still not clear whether the public or private firms are better at maximizing taxpayer's welfare. The taxpayer's losses from the public firm equals $(\tilde{w}-w)\phi_L\bar{Q}$ or $\phi_L\bar{Q}\delta'^{-1}((\phi_L\bar{Q})^{1-\alpha}/K$ and this must be compared with the losses from the public firm, which are equal to $(c_P-\tilde{c}_P)\phi_P\bar{Q}$ or $\phi_P\bar{Q}\delta'^{-1}(\phi_P\bar{Q}/K)$. The following proposition discusses the conditions under which public ownership dominates private ownership from the taxpayer's perspective.

Proposition 3: there exists a value of ϕ_P, denoted $\phi_P{}^*$, where the losses to taxpayers from public and private ownership are equal. For values of ϕ_P above $\phi_P{}^*$, public ownership dominates private ownership, and for values of ϕ_P below $\phi_P{}^*$, private ownership dominates public ownership. The value of $\phi_P{}^*$ is rising with ϕ_L and falling with α.

This proposition gives us one main result. First, firms that purchase a great deal of their inputs from the government are more likely candidates for public ownership. This is certainly part of the story for both public transportation and the utilities. Furthermore firms that use a lot of labor are somewhat less attractive to make public. The intuition of this result is clear, since public ownership leads to overpayment of workers, firms that are labor-intensive will be a particularly poor choice for public ownership. In this sense, I mirror Boyko *et al.* (1996) who argue that a primary cost of public ownership is overemployment.

The next result tells us that public ownership becomes more attractive when it is harder to bribe large numbers of actors. Indeed, when α is sufficiently high (and the number of workers is high) there is almost no overpayment at all. An advantage of publicly owned firms is that their natural form of corruption (overpayment of workers) is hard if there are large numbers of workers.

Of course, if there were other inputs of the firm that were supplied privately, this would create another problem. The input suppliers would bribe the manager of the government firm. We will address overpaying by the government for inputs in the next section, but we note here that, in some cases, public ownership of a firm simply pushes the corruption upstream.

I have assumed symmetry between public inputs and labor inputs. If corrupting many workers turned out to be fairly difficult, this would make public ownership more appealing. If the workers' welfare entered into the social welfare calculation, this would also make public ownership more appealing.[7] If there were other effort-related choices that the firm needed to make, this would make public ownership less appealing, since the weaker incentives would be harmful.

These caveats to the model are certainly important, but they do not eliminate the basic message: public ownership embodies a tradeoff where private companies will corrupt the city government and underpay for public inputs, while public companies will overpay their workers.

In some cases, regulation, particularly limiting profits, may solve the corruption problem more effectively than government ownership. What will be the impact of regulation where the firm's profits are regulated by the government? In principle, regulated profits will act to reduce the benefits from bribing the government and can achieve positive effects. The firm itself will have little to gain from bribing its workers either. Consequently regulation may offer a more attractive course of action than pure public ownership. Indeed it is not surprising that progressives often supported regulation instead of wholesale government ownership.

However regulation still has its own problems. Like public ownership, it will sap the incentives to innovate or put out high levels of effort. This cost has been well discussed in the literature, and certainly does not create a case for public ownership relative to regulation. A second problem with regulation is that the regulated firm may coerce (capture?) its regulator (as in Stigler, 1971). Through direct or indirect bribery, the firm may get the regulator to increase its profit levels or overlook indirect profit taking. Thus regulation may end up being quite ineffective.

A final problem with regulation may occur if the firm managers figure out ways to get profits out of the firm indirectly. For example, the private utility may purchase from a co-owned private supplier. If that supplier is not itself regulated, the firm can overpay for its inputs and thereby get its profits indirectly. If the firm still has an incentive to make profits, it will still have an incentive to bribe officials. An extreme example of this will occur if the managers personally steal from the firm. The managers can overpay for their inputs, such as labor, and pocket the proceeds. Thus regulation is a reasonable alternative to public ownership, but it brings its own problems.

Overpricing Outputs

A natural extension of the model eliminates the government input, and focuses on the role of government as consumer. This is particularly relevant for government services such as sanitation or highway construction and maintenance. In these cases, government demand is relatively fixed and the key issue is how much the government pays for its services. We will again use the notation of $\bar{Q}$ to denote the government's demand for the good.

In this case, the problem will be that the government's purchasing agent may be bribed by his supplier. Here, to simplify, we assume that the only input is labor, and again ϕ_L units of labor are needed to produce the good.

If the good is priced at marginal price the cost should be $w\phi_L$, and an honest official will pay $w\phi_L$ for the good. We will let $\tilde{P}$ denote the agreed-upon price for the good. In this case, the probability of detection will be $\delta(\tilde{P}-w\phi_L)$, which is again increasing and convex. The cost of being caught is again K.

Again we assume that the supplier and the government official share in the rents and maximize their joint surplus. The total surplus for the supplier and the government official to split is $(\tilde{P}-w\phi_L)\bar{Q}-\delta(\tilde{P}-w\phi_L)K$, which has first-order condition $\delta'(\tilde{P}-w\phi_L)=\bar{Q}/K$. Overpayment will tend to be bigger if the firm is larger, or if the penalty is higher. The structure of this extension has not changed from the previous model. In the case of private ownership, the lost revenues to the taxpayer will equal $(P-w\phi_L)\bar{Q}$.

In the case of public ownership, the situation is the same as above. The cost of public ownership is overpayment of the workers, and the level of overpayment will again satisfy $\delta'(\tilde{w}-w)=(\phi_L\bar{Q})^{1-\alpha}/K$. The total losses to the taxpayer will equal $(\tilde{w}-w)\phi_L\bar{Q})$. Which policy leads to greater losses? Again higher values of ϕ_L and α make public ownership less appealing. Large labor consumption acts to exacerbate the cost of public ownership: padded payrolls. Higher values of α make the bribing of workers easier to accomplish.

The Perversion of Subsidies

In this final variant on the model, I discuss situations where the government is neither buyer nor seller, but wants to subsidize the provision of the good. A natural example might be sanitation or clean water. Both of these goods have large externalities working through disease. Classical economic analysis has tended to imply that all of the benefits of public provision in the presence of externalities can be created through subsidies. If there is bribery, this claim may no longer be true. The private firms may bribe the government to oversubsidize the commodity, and the result may be corruption. In practice, private firms have also tended to bribe the government to overlook the poor quality of their product.

I continue to assume that total fixed demand for the product is $\bar{Q}$, but we assume that there is now a quality margin. The firm can either produce high-quality goods, which again are made using ϕ_L units of labor, which is again purchased at a cost w, or low-quality goods which are made using $\lambda\phi_L$, where $\lambda<1$. The high-quality good costs $\phi_L w$ to produce and the low-quality good costs $\lambda\phi_L w$ to make. The low-quality good produces private benefits B_1, and the high-quality good provides private benefits of B_2. In addition the high-quality good produces social benefits of B_s. These added social benefits from quality represent the health advantages, perhaps, to the entire community of having clean water.

I assume that there is one producer who is a monopolist. The monopolist faces a demand curve that allows him to sell $\bar{Q}$ units of either good at a price of B_1 or lower, but nothing at any price above that. Just as before, though, we will assume that $B_1 = \lambda\phi_L w$, so, if the producer makes the low-quality good and sells it, it earns no profits.

I assume that $B_s + B_2 > \phi_L w > B_2 > B_1 = \lambda\phi_L w$. This tells us that, in the absence of government subsidies, consumers would not pay for the high-quality good, at its production cost, but that socially they should. The externality leads to underconsumption of quality relative to the free market. The social welfare to consumers (who are assumed to be the taxpayers) from complete non-intervention is therefore zero (which is also the monopolists' profit level).

In the case of public ownership, the firm will be instructed to produce the high-quality good and sell it for B_2. In this case, the consumers will all buy the high-quality good and social benefits equal to $\bar{Q}(B_s + B_2)$. However, in this case, the firm will, as before, overpay their workers and receive kickbacks. The level of overpayment will once again satisfy $\delta'(\tilde{w} - w) = (\phi_L \bar{Q})^{1-\alpha}/K$. Total social welfare will equal $\bar{Q}(B_s + B_2 - \phi_L \tilde{w})$. The comparison between the public and private ownership is described by proposition 4: there exists a value of B_s, denoted $B_s{}^*$, where consumers are indifferent between completely private provision and public provision. For values of B_s above $B_s{}^*$, consumers will strictly prefer public ownership and, for values of B_s below $B_s{}^*$, consumers will strictly prefer private ownership. The value of $B_s{}^*$ is rising with ϕ_L, rising with $\bar{Q}$, falling with K, and rising with α.

The intuition of this is straightforward. Public ownership is more desirable, relative to the complete free market, when there are large externalities from consumption. Public ownership becomes less attractive when the public official is harder to punish, or when the scale of the enterprise is larger, or uses more labor.

We now move on to consider the case of subsidized private provision. In principle, standard economics would tell us that the first best could be achieved if the government pays each firm $\phi_L w - B_2$ for each unit of high-quality good that is sold. In that case, the firm will earn as much by producing the high quality good and selling it at B_2, the highest price that the market will bear, as by producing the low-quality good. Critically I assume that the quality of the good is perfectly observable to all actors involved.

In a situation like this there are many opportunities for corruption, all of which would have been exploited by men like William Marcy Tweed. The producer can shirk on quality and bribe the government to overlook the low-quality product and still give the subsidy. The producer can bribe the government official to certify that he has sold a falsely high amount of the product. Finally the government can bribe the government official to increase the level of the subsidy.

The third type of bribery is most in line with the previous model. In this case we can again assume that the probability of detection for the official is increasing in the distance between the optimal subsidy and the paid subsidy, that is, $\delta(S-(\phi_L w - B_2))$, where S denotes the post-bribe subsidy. In this case, the combined surplus of the industry and the government official will equal $\bar{Q}(S+B_2-\phi_L w)-\delta(S-(\phi_L w-B_2))K$, which has first-order condition $\bar{Q}=\delta'(S-(\phi_L w-B_2))K$. Taxpayer welfare under this situation equals $\bar{Q}(B_s+B_2-S-\phi_L w)$. For high enough levels of B_s this will also dominate private provision without a subsidy.

More interesting for our purposes is the comparison of this situation and welfare under public ownership. Public ownership will dominate subsidy and private provision if $S>\phi_L(\tilde{w}-w)$. This will be less likely to hold if ϕ_L is high or if α is high; this will be less likely to hold if B_2 is high.

PUBLIC OWNERSHIP AND CONTROL IN NEW YORK CITY

This section gives thumbnail sketches of the history of municipal ownership of a variety of services in New York, with reference to some other cities. The goal is to highlight the factors that seem to be most important in the decision to have the government own and manage these services. In particular we will look at the importance of three theories of government ownership: first, the corruption theories outlined above; second, the classic economic theory of natural monopoly, which argues that government ownership is necessary to keep prices away from monopoly levels; third, the quality-shirking model of Hart *et al.* (1997). This model argues that private provision will lead to undersupply of quality, when quality is non-contractible. Private agents will reduce quality to cut costs. Because the government manager faces softer incentives, he may not engage in cost-cutting, quality-reducing innovations. Finally we will discuss cases that seem to be motivated by purely selfish politicians trying to extend their reach.

The focus is on the water supply, sanitation, roads, power and light, and public transportation. After five longer sections on these services, we discuss three other areas of local government expenditure: the justice system, fire safety and schools.

Water Supply and Sewers[8]

Government involvement in New York's water supply dates back to 1666, two years after the Dutch surrender, when the English governor sunk the first public well. Apparently water, fire and sanitation were the primary responsibilities of the earliest government of New York, the Common Council (Koeppel, 2000), which established a public well system. This stands in contrast to the Dutch, who had private wells (most of the water seems to have been turned into beer). It is not obvious whether the English preference for public wells came about because of a greater belief in the positive externalities associated with water or (more likely in my opinion) because wells are large resources that can easily be shared. Presumably the price of water would have been so low at this time that the time involved for a retailer actually to manage the operations of a well would not have been worth it.

In any case, early public wells certainly did not engender much corruption. After all, the expenditures were so low that there was really no opportunity for bribery. They did, however, deteriorate. Again I am unsure whether the depreciation of the public wells came about naturally, as a result of rising population levels, or the public status of the wells meant that no private individuals had a stake in maintaining them. In any case, by the 18th century New York's public wells no longer produced good water.

To substitute for the breakdown in the public system, a more sophisticated private system developed. Private wells, set at a distance from the main population center, became the norm. The size of the city, and the rising price of water, now justified a distribution system that involved bringing water down from private wells. Public wells were still important, but they served primarily as an input into fire safety. As Koeppel (2000) writes, 'As the laws protecting the public wells and pumps make clear, the greatest interest was in having plenty of water to douse fires.' Thus there was a two-tiered water supply system. Cheap public water from wells in high-density areas served to stop fires, and residents (at least wealthy ones) drank from more distant private wells.

Eventually the quality of the private wells appears to have deteriorated as well. This may have had an aspect of the Hart *et al.* (1997) shirking on quality, but it can also be easily attributed, again, to rising density levels. Since waste was deposited on the ground, high-density levels naturally led to poisoned water. New York also had outbreaks of yellow fever which were linked by some to poor water quality. Government re-entered the water supply market in a significant way with Christopher Colles' project to pipe water from further uptown. This project would have used a large well and a steam engine. It seems that the externalities involved in water supply in combination with the large scale of the project made it seem appropriate for government involvement. Eventually this project was abandoned when the British occupied New York during the American Revolution.

After the revolution, the city tried a private water project. In 1798, New York had a significant yellow fever outbreak and public interest in cleaner water increased. However, instead of pure public funding, in this case they opted for a subsidized private scheme. Aaron Burr and Alexander Hamilton collaborated on the project, which would involve a private company with some public funding. The company claimed that it would bring water in from the Bronx. It received two substantial rights in exchange for bringing water. First, it was entitled to rights of eminent domain and, second, it was allowed to use its surplus capital in any way that the directors of the company saw fit. This was a substantial right: at this time, limited liability companies were generally extremely restricted in their operation. The substantial political clout of the company's founders overcame initial opposition to these aspects of the company.

As it happened the company did almost nothing with water: it used its surplus capital clause to engage in various more lucrative aspects and skipped the much harder task of bringing in water. In fact, the Manhattan Water Company is the direct ancestor of the Chase Manhattan Bank. While public interest in water came about because of health and safety, the problems with private provision had already become obvious 200 years ago. Political clout led to substantial gifts to the company, with no recompense.

Meanwhile Philadelphia had begun to move ahead with its pathbreaking water works. There are two aspects of Philadelphia which make it radically different from New York. First, it is swampier and even more innately disease-prone. In 1793, approximately 8 per cent of the population died from yellow fever. Second, it is bordered by fresh, not salt, water rivers. As as result, large water works were both more necessary and easier to build. Philadelphia had tried a prior experiment in private, large-scale water works with the Delaware and Schuylkill Canal Company. Like the Manhattan Water Company, this private company also failed to deliver water to the city, despite substantial government subsidization. Under Benjamin Latrobe's leadership, Philadelphia began a large-scale public water works system that was eventually quite successful in delivering water. However, despite high charges for some subscribers, it regularly ran at a loss.

New York moved more slowly. It was not until the cholera epidemic of 1832 that the city seriously focused on large-scale public water supply. The Croton Aqueduct was built over a seven-year period, starting in 1835, and its $11.5 million cost represented a massive investment of government funds. Like Latrobe's works, it eventually delivered clean water efficiently, but it took 30 years more until annual revenues from the water works exceeded expenses (including debt on the fixed costs of construction). Since this period, New York has never experimented with private provision of water systematically.

The first public sewer in New York was built in 1703, but large-scale sewers ultimately followed the Croton Aqueduct. They were built by the Aqueduct authority, and were essentially always public. Sewers and water supply appear to be complementary enough, if water is to be provided by a public company, for it to be sensible for that company also to handle the sewer system.

The provision of water in other cities eventually followed. Boston built its Cochituate system over a nine-year period, starting in 1846. All of these water supply systems were massively expensive. For example, by 1900, municipal spending on water in the USA was significantly greater than all US federal government spending excluding the Armed Forces and the Postal Services.

The corruption story seems to play only a minor role in municipal water works. The main problem seems to be that consumers were unwilling to pay the actual costs of expensive clean water piped in from outside the big cities. As a result, private companies either went bankrupt (like the Delaware Canal Company) or avoided water production entirely (like the Manhattan Company). Public spending was necessary if clean water was to be provided to stop disease, but that does not explain why public subsidies of private companies were not successful.

A first possibility is that people were afraid of the natural monopoly that would be created by large-scale water works. There is certainly some truth to that, and the privately subsidized schemes generally had to agree to some limits on their prices. However, given that it seems that there was nowhere near enough demand to pay for construction, this fear does seem a little misplaced, at least during the early time period.

A second possibility is that people were afraid that the private company would shirk on quality. This may have been an issue at some point, but fears about quality levels do not surround the private companies. At this point, knowledge of water quality was limited, and both government and private providers would have judged the water to be high-quality if it came from a clean source far from the city. This would have been quite contractible and observable. A third possibility is the corruption theory. There clearly was something like corruption in the Manhattan Company.

Ultimately the answer in New York's case is probably that no private company could have been trusted with the levels of subsidy needed to build large-scale water works. After the experience of Aaron Burr, what sensible politician would have voted to trust a private entrepreneur with the $11.5 million needed to build the Croton? The problem with privately provided, publicly funded, water works was not shirking on the quality of water. More likely, it was just stealing the money, probably in some semi-legitimate manner. Consequently, the softer incentives of government ownership seem to have been the only possibility.

Sanitation

Early government involvement in sanitation took the form of regulating private behavior, not public provision. The Dutch had strong street cleaning regulations which compelled private citizens to clean the streets near their homes and forbad dumping certain types of waste into the street. The English later adopted these regulations. While private citizens frequently ignored public regulations, it is clear that the government always saw clean streets as public responsibility. In 1670, the city created a system where the cartmen's monopoly (a quasi-guild of transport professionals) was obliged to carry away refuse to keep their monopoly. Essentially this was private provision with public (indirect) subsidy. This arrangement seems to have persisted until the early 19th century.

In the 19th century, direct public subcontracting appears to have replaced this subsidy system. There were two primary problems with subcontracting. First, as discussed above, subcontractors would frequently bribe public officials to overpay for their services. Boss Tweed's $40 000 kickback is a classic example. More importantly, corruption led to underprovision of quality. When the machine was required to take competitive bids, it could still dispense favors by overlooking low-quality provision. Firms were able to bribe officials to overlook the fact that they underdelivered on their street cleaning obligations. As the sanitation reformer George Soper wrote in 1909, 'The contractor is often suspected of wielding, or being subservient to, political influence.' The resulting poor quality of sanitation led to a public outcry for reform and indeed for public street cleaning. The Department of Street Cleaning was established in 1881, but there seems to have been little real innovation until Tammany was ousted, albeit briefly, in the 1890s.

In 1895, the Waring era began. In response to public outcry, the reform administration of William Strong brought in the sanitation expert Colonel George Waring to run the city's street cleaning department. Waring was a visionary reformer who dressed his street cleaners in white and created a quasi-military operation. He seems to have created a remarkably efficient, honest system at least for his period in office. While he did not outlast the reform administration, public street cleaning was firmly established.

Tammany Hall was unlikely to lose this attractive source of political patronage.

The case for public involvement in street cleaning is based on the massive externalities associated with filth. In principle, street cleaning could be handled by subcontracting cleaning to private providers. Indeed, within the USA, as Lopes-de-Silanes *et al.* (1997) show, private contracting is quite common. However private contracting creates the problem of bribery, overpayment and underprovision. Public provision was seen as a means of fighting these problems and, at least briefly, it was successful.

Streets and Roads

While private roads have certainly existed, streets and roads have generally been public responsibilities. This presumably occurs because the administrative costs of tolls have usually been too high to have a functioning private road system in most cases. In New York City, the government has always taken responsibility for roads. New York's famous grid system was laid out by the government. I have already discussed street cleaning and I will discuss street lighting shortly. Here I briefly discuss road construction, that is paving.

As in the case of street cleaning, colonial governments originally tried to handle paving through regulation. In 1684, New York's common council ruled that streets be paved by adjacent property owners. This regulatory era was generally marked by enforcement problems, as private owners often disregarded the relatively weak powers of municipal government. The parallel with street cleaning is close. Eventually the state began paving streets itself. This public involvement would continue up to our day.

The primary public/private distinction in road building has therefore been the issue of subcontracting. Progressive era reformers frequently complained about street paving contracts; the 1911 Mayor's Committee on Pavements reported, 'there can be no doubt that much of the trouble with our pavements has been due to long-term maintenance contracts'. The subcontractors were seen as shirking on quality, and public provision was put forward as a remedy. It is possible that the desire for public provision came from true contracting difficulties. However it is relatively easy to write a contract with quality provisions in this area. It is more difficult to enforce the contract, if city officials are subject to bribery. As the street paving interests were certainly well connected politically, I certainly suspect that the bulk of the quality problems came more from corruption than from standard contracting problems.

Mass Transit

According to legend (Cudahy, 1990), mass transit began in New York city in the 1740s as ox carts carried passengers up and down Broadway. True fixed-route transit lines, however, did not begin until 100 years later. In 1827, Abraham Brower pioneered mass transit in the Americas with a stagecoach that ran from the Battery to Bleeker Street along Broadway (1.75 mile). By 1831, Brower had three vehicles and the largest of them was referred to as an omnibus (the term was borrowed from Paris). These buses just used city streets, like any other vehicle.

In 1832, the New York and Harlem Railroad pioneered these buses' main competitors, the street railroad. These railroads were horse-drawn carriages that used rails set in city streets. In the cobblestone era of street paving, this represented a massive advance over buses. Cars with metal wheels moving along rails were much more comfortable and much easier to move than buses. While eventually these rails would use electricity and steam, for the first 50 years street railways were horse-drawn. Still the New York mayor in 1832 thought that the recently-patented street railways represented such an improvement over other technologies that 'this event [the first street railways] will go in history of our country as the greatest achievement of man' (Cudahy, 1990).

While both omnibuses and street railways used city streets, street railways actually physically altered the streets by covering them with rail. The rail itself, even when not in use, posed a barrier to other forms of transportation. The rails blocked both wheels and sleighs and were clearly something of an impediment to other forms of travel. Cudahy (1990) describes ferocious conflicts between private citizens who were used to using sleighs in the winter and street railway companies. Since the railroad companies had to clear the snow around their rails, the sleigh-users were blocked from using these roads. While the rail beds themselves were an inconvenience to others, railways were also legally given rights-of-way on their rail beds. Thus the use of rail imposed costs on citizens who were walking or using horses.

In principle, of course, the market is supposed to allocate resources efficiently between two consumers with competing claims. The city governments could have made some attempt to charge the railway companies appropriately for the costs that they imposed on the public as a whole. As described earlier, the traction magnates were given the use of city streets for usually nominal fees. They received long franchises (including perpetual or thousand-year franchises) to use city streets at little official cost. Of course, unofficially, they would end up paying significantly in bribes to government officials. In almost every major city in the country, there appears to have been at least some bribery associated with street railways franchises.

Eventually horses were replaced by other technologies. First, cable cars were used. In this technology, cars were pulled along tracks by cables, which were in turn pulled by steam engines. Second, electricity revolutionized the industry between 1890 and 1902. These innovations required other publicly supplied inputs. Electricity was run using either overhead current or third rails. The poles that provided the current clearly also imposed some public costs (visual externalities, perhaps). Both technologies led occasionally to socially costly accidents, for which the traction companies were only rarely fined.

The transit industry in the street railway era was fairly decentralized. At the turn of the century there were 415 firms in the street railway association (ibid.). Eventually, individual cities moved toward concentration, mainly as entrepreneurs tried to seize monopoly profits. Overall, though, there seems to have been little natural monopoly at this stage in the transit industry. Indeed, even when the city began the 25-year process of moving from private to public transportation between 1934 and 1960, the New York City streetcar and bus industry had a large number of independent firms. It is also clear that the Hart *et al.* (1997) theory of public ownership had little relevance in this market. Quality in street transport is observable and firms competed regularly on ride quality.

Of course, in the 19th century, public transit began using more than just the streets. In the 1860s, New York began using elevated railways. Later, subways would begin playing a bigger role in America's larger cities. In these situations, the possibility of true natural monopoly seems to have been more important. However corrupt sale of railway franchises also seems to have been extremely important. After all, New York began its elevated railways in the days of William Marcy Tweed.

New York's first elevated railway was built by Charles Harvey in 1867–70. Harvey's company used cable technology and failed, but the tracks were taken over by the New York Elevated Railroad Company which used steam. In the 1870s, a competing elevated railway company, the Gilbert Elevated Railway, began operating on Second and Sixth Avenues. Eventually these railways consolidated, and Jay Gould ended up running a large elevated railway consortium in New York City. Competition would continue in this industry, but there is no question that the elevated networks had greater returns to scale than the streetcar lines.

In general the elevated rails paid nothing in New York for running lines over city streets, despite the fact that they imposed large social costs on the properties that abutted their lines. Indeed, eventually, LaGuardia would tear down elevated rails to increase property values in the area. There was some attempt to limit rail fares as a means of extracting some rents to compensate for the use of previously public airspace. However most of the attempts to reduce fares were defeated by the politically powerful rails.

This situation of free airspace can be contrasted with the case of Chicago, where statute required that a majority of abutting property owners would have to agree to the building of elevated railways. This policy explains why Chicago's elevated railways were generally built on alleys rather than on main thoroughfares. Pricing space seems in this case to have led to less socially costly elevated rails.

The final major type of mass transit is the subway. The first New York subway was built in 1870 by Alfred Beach. However attempts to expand the small pneumatic tube were blocked by Boss Tweed, who saw this as a threat to his interests in surface transit. At this time, a free 100-year franchise for a tunnel railway was given to Cornelius Vanderbilt. Again public rights were given away to an entrepreneur for nothing. However New York's first subway was not built in 1900. This construction was financed jointly by public and private funds. Essentially the public sector paid for the large costs of building the tunnel which was then leased to the private company for far less than its cost. Again bribery appears to have been rampant.

Again there were a limited number of subway companies in New York (relative to streetcar companies). At the time when Mayor John 'Red Mike' Hylan tried to move to municipal rail, there were two dominant companies (the IRT and the BMT). The returns to scale were again much larger. Hylan implemented his own public rail system by building the Independent Subway System (IND). Eventually restrictions on fares, union wages and competition from the public sector would push the private subways into financial difficulties. In 1940, the city bought both of the subway companies and ended private subways in New York.[9]

There were clearly several things that led to public ownership of transit in New York, and the USA as a whole. There was certainly some truth to the argument that rail is a natural monopoly and public ownership can eliminate monopoly pricing and profits. Hylan was also clearly an empire builder, and state ownership may have much to do with his desire to expand the size of government. However there is no doubt that the sentiment for public ownership in transit had much to do with corruption in the industry. Transport companies received a tremendous amount of public inputs at below cost. They received the use of the streets in the case of streetcars and elevated rail. In the case of subways, the government actually paid for the construction of the tunnels. In all of these cases there was at least the appearance that corruption led to underpaying for these inputs, and this fueled the popular desire for public ownership.

Power and Light

Large-scale utility companies in New York began in 1823, when the New York Gas Light Company won a 30-year franchise to lay gas pipes underground. A number of gas companies soon followed. These companies interacted with the city in two important ways. First, they used city resources, as their pipes went under city streets. As usual, 'the gas companies have usually obtained their franchises for the asking, and practically no revenue has been derived from this source' (Bemis, 1904). Second, they sold gas to the city for use in street lamps (and public buildings). It seems that, in this case, the city both underpriced its inputs and overpaid for the companies' output.

In the 1880s, electricity began to replace gaslight. The city granted perpetual franchises to the electricity companies, generally for nothing. Again there were initially a large number of companies competing in the provision of this commodity. Eventually consolidation in the industry occurred, and now Con Edison provides almost all of the electricity in the city. The combination of scale economies and standard gains from monopoly clearly motivated this trend.

Other cities began to operate public utilities themselves. This public provision generally began as a means of providing power for street lamps and other public purposes. Reformers, such as Pingree, thought that private provision led to overcharging, mainly because of political corruption. Indeed Detroit's public electric plant lowered costs significantly to both public and private customers. In New York, regulation rather than public ownership was the norm. This regulation was regularly aimed at reducing prices and refunding 'excess' profits by the utilities to the public in the form of lower prices. As usual, political influence limited the extent to which lower prices ever materialized. As Plunkitt writes, 'Since the eighty-cent gas bill was defeated in Albany, everybody's talkin' about senators bein' bribed' (Riordan, 1995).

Why did New York never move to public ownership of the utilities? As Wilcox (1910) wrote, 'The only interesting thing about the electric light and power franchises of New York City is the magnitude of the privileges involved and the absence of any appreciable restrictions upon the companies for the protection of the public interest.' One might think that the size of New York City might have made competition more possible, and thus public ownership less necessary, but, while competition certainly was possible (it existed during an earlier era), it did not exist. My best explanation of this fact is that Con Edison was just too powerful to touch. In the early years it was controlled by Rockefeller interests and it would have been very difficult to fight. Of course, the perceived (and quite true) costs of public ownership also must have dissuaded reformers from public provision of these utilities.

Other Services: Justice, Fire Safety, Charity and Schools

The justice system has always had an overwhelming public component, although private protection is also common. Since the dawn of recorded history, rulers have tried to maintain their control of the justice system. There is a clear public good aspect to protecting property right. Private police forces will have a tendency to exploit their physical power. Indeed the market system often depends on the existence of disinterested courts. Consequently police and courts have always been run by the government in New York and elsewhere. Of course corruption has also been rampant in these areas, but there really is no feasible private alternative.

In the USA, fire safety began with volunteer regiments. These groups would be subsidized by the state. For example, volunteers were often exempted from jury duty and their equipment was paid for by the state. Corruption was a problem in volunteer fire departments, as money meant for equipment got spent elsewhere. William Marcy Tweed got his start as a volunteer fireman. As New York grew, and as the gains from having a specialized fire department increased, volunteers were replaced by professional departments. The government's interest in fire safety is natural: there are massive externalities associated with fire. Indeed history is full of great cities being demolished by rampant flames (as in the great Chicago fire of 1873, the New York fire of 1835).

The government must therefore at least subsidize fire prevention. In principle subcontracting to private providers is a possibility, but here the analysis of Hart *et al.* (1997) seems apt. Given the difficulties that would be related to contracting on quality, private providers would be likely to shirk. Low quality is observable only when a true disaster strikes and limited liability may mean that private providers are comfortable taking the risk of their low quality being exposed in rare events. Public provision was necessary to keep quality up.

Larger cities have often spent a considerable amount on charity. For example, Boston in 1825 spent 25 per cent of its budget on poor relief. More recently redistribution to the poor has often taken the form of public housing and public hospitals. Often public redistribution was motivated by a desire to eliminate social problems associated with extreme poverty. Of course public charity is also often an appeal to poorer voters. Redistribution is not really a service, and therefore one cannot really view public redistribution through the same lens as the other services. This is not really a service, but rather conventional redistribution, and public provision does not really have much to do with any one of the three models.

Finally there is the question of public provision of education. City governments have provided public schools since the nation's beginning. The case for government subsidy of education has always been based on the claim that it creates positive externalities of one sort or another. The case for government ownership and control has always been less clear. Schools do not seem to be a natural monopoly. The Hart *et al.* (1997) model does not seem to apply, as it is hard to argue that public ownership and control improves school quality. Of course, if quality is defined as adherence to the government's ideal curriculum, perhaps this might have some importance. It is conceivable that the difficulties with governmental subsidization, highlighted above, may have played some role in public provision: perhaps it was hard for early Americans to subsidize education effectively without directly providing it, because of the openings for corruption. Ultimately it is hard to understand why schooling has long been such a big part of local government budgets. I hope future work in this area will clear up my confusion.

CONCLUSION

This chapter has argued that corruption was a major force leading to support for municipal ownership in the United States. When private firms buy or sell from the government, there are large opportunities for corruption, and the government will often overpay for privately provided goods or undercharge for publicly provided inputs. Public ownership provided one means of fighting this problem. Of course public ownership creates its own problems. On top of the incentive problems that are usually discussed, corruption will lead publicly owned firms to overpay for their own inputs, especially labor.

Can this analysis help us to think about the appropriate level of public ownership today throughout the world? Within the USA and most of the developed world, the weapons against corruption are much stronger today than they were in 1900. Few public governments could engage in the kind of practices that were the norm during the Gilded Age. Consequently the corruption-eliminating advantages of public ownership have diminished steadily within the USA and anywhere else where corruption is limited.

However, in the developing world, it may be that the 19th-century USA still provides valuable lessons. In countries such as the transition economies, or much of Latin America, corruption is still more the norm than the exception. The justice systems are weak, and there is often no independent press to rake the muck. In these places municipal ownership may still have some value as a means of reducing corruption. However, even in these areas, it must always be recognized that there are serious costs, including corruption, as well as benefits associated with public ownership.

NOTES

1. This paper was written for a festschrift volume dedicated to Dick Netzer. The NSF (National Service Foundation) provided financial assistance. Emily Oster was an excellent research assistant. This paper is part of a current research project that is joint with Andrei Shleifer, and this paper embodies thoughts that are his as well as mine.
2. Lopes-de-Silanes *et al.* (1997) provide a careful description of public services in the US today.
3. At the dawn of the public era, Wilcox (1910) wrote, 'the manufacture and distribution of electricity is inherently the least monopolistic of public service utilities'.
4. Thus, for bribes to consumers, we are effectively assuming that N is infinite.
5. The lack of profitability of public firms is one of the main stylized facts in the public/private debate; see, for example, Pashigian (1976).
6. In this way, the model provides a justification for the pro-labor preferences of politicians assumed in Shleifer and Vishny (1994).
7. Indeed it is often argued that machines were socially productive because they redistributed to the poor, often through public patronage.
8. Koeppel (2000) provides an extremely useful history of New York's water, on which this discussion is based.
9. Other public transit facilities also owed their existence to public buyouts of private companies. For example, Boston bought its ferries in the 1840s when they were in financial trouble. In this case, the buyout can be seen as a transfer to the private companies as a result of their political influence.

REFERENCES

Atkinson, A. and J. Stiglitz (1980), *Lectures on Public Economics*, London: McGraw-Hill.

Bemis, E. (1904), *Municipal Monopolies*, New York: Thomas Cromwell.

Boyko, M., A. Shleifer and R. Vishny (1996), 'A Theory of Privatization', *Economic Journal*, **106**, 309–19.

Bryce, J. (1914), *The American Commonwealth*, New York: Macmillan.

Cudahy, B. (1990), *Cash, Tokens and Transfers: A History of Urban Mass Transit in America*, New York: Fordham University Press.

Darwin, L. (1907), *Municipal Ownership*, New York: E.F. Dutton.

Ellis, E. (1966), *The Epic of New York City: A Narrative History*, New York: Kodansha.

Glaab, C. and A. Brown (1967), *A History of Urban America*, London: Macmillan.

Glaeser, E. and A. Shleifer (2001), 'The Rise of the Regulatory State', Harvard University mimeograph, Cambridge, MA.

Hart, O., A. Shleifer and R. Vishny (1997), 'The Proper Scope of Governance', *Quarterly Journal of Economics*, **112** (4), 1127–62.

Holli, M. (1969), *Reform in Detroit*, Westport: Greenwood.

Josephson, M. (1934), *The Robber Barons*, New York: Harcourt.

Judd, D. and T. Swanstrom (1994), *City Politics*, New York: Harper Collins.
Koeppel, G. (2000), *Water for Gotham: A History*, Princeton, NJ: Princeton University Press.
Lopes-de-Silanes, F., A. Shleifer and R. Vishny (1997) 'Privatization in the United States', *Rand Journal of Economics*, **28** (3), 447–71.
Pashigian, P. (1976), 'Public Ownership of Urban Transit Facilities', *Journal of Political Economy*, **84** (6), 1239–59.
Riordan, W. (1995), *Plunkitt of Tammany Hall*, New York: Signet.
Shleifer, A. and R. Vishny (1994), 'Politicians and Firms', *Quarterly Journal of Economics*, **109**, 995–1025.
Soper, G. (1909), *Modern Methods of Street Cleaning*, New York: The Engineering News Publishing Company.
Stigler, G. (1971), 'The Economic Theory of Regulation', *Bell Journal of Economics*, **2**, 3–21.
Steffens, L. (1904), *The Shame of the Cities*, New York: McClure, Phillips.
Wilcox, D. (1910), *Municipal Franchises*, Rochester, NY: Gervaise.

APPENDIX: PROOFS OF PROPOSITIONS

Proof of proposition 1 Differentiation and using the convexity of $\delta(c_P - \tilde{c}_P)$ yields:

$$\frac{\partial \tilde{c}_P}{\partial \phi_P} = -\frac{\overline{Q}}{K\delta''(c_P - \tilde{c}_P)} < 0, \frac{\partial \tilde{c}_P}{\partial \overline{Q}} = -\frac{\phi_P}{K\delta''(c_P - \tilde{c}_P)} < 0 \text{ and } \frac{\partial \tilde{c}_P}{\partial K} =$$

$$\frac{\phi_K \overline{Q}}{K^2\delta''(c_K - \tilde{c}_K)} > 0.$$

If we let $\delta(c_P - \tilde{c}_P) = d_0 {}^* d(c_P - \tilde{c}_P)$ and differentiate with respect to d_0 we get:

$$\frac{\partial \tilde{c}_P}{\partial d_0} = \frac{d'(c_P - \tilde{c}_P)}{d_0 d''(c_P - \tilde{c}_P)} > 0.$$

Proof of proposition 2 Since $\delta'(0) = 0$, and $\delta''(x) > 0$, for $x < 0$, there will be positive levels of corruption in both public and private firms. In the case of private firms, corruption leads to underpaying for inputs, which leads to positive profits. In the case of public firms, corruptions leads to overpaying for output, which leads to negative profits.

Proof of proposition 3 First, the derivative of $(c_P - \tilde{c}_P)\phi_P\bar{Q}$ with respect to ϕ_P equals $(c_P - \tilde{c}_P)\overline{Q} - \phi_P\overline{Q}\frac{\partial \tilde{c}_P}{\partial \phi_P} > 0$, since $\frac{\partial \tilde{c}_P}{\partial \phi_P} < 0$. When ϕ_P equals zero, the social costs from private ownership are zero. When $\phi_P = \phi_L + (\phi_L\bar{Q})^{1-\alpha}$, social losses from public ownership are less than the losses from private ownership because $\phi_P\bar{Q}\delta'^{-1}(\phi_P\bar{Q}/K) = (\phi_L + (\phi_L\bar{Q})^{1-\alpha})\bar{Q}\delta'^{-1}((\phi_L + (\phi_L\bar{Q})^{1-\alpha})\bar{Q}/K) > \phi_L\bar{Q}\delta'^{-1}((\phi_L\bar{Q})^{1-\alpha}/K)$.

The last inequality follows because $\frac{d\delta'^{-1}(x)}{dx} = \frac{1}{\delta''(\delta'^{-1}(x))} > 0$. As social losses from public ownership are above those of private ownership when ϕ_P equals zero and below those of private ownership when ϕ_P is sufficiently high, and social losses from private ownership are monotonically increasing in ϕ_P, then continuity ensures that there exists a value of ϕ_P such that the losses from private and public ownership are equal. At the point where the social losses are equal, $\phi_P{}^*\delta'^{-1}(\phi_P{}^*\bar{Q}/K) = \phi_L\delta'^{-1}((\phi_L\bar{Q})^{1-\alpha}/K)$. The right hand side of this equation is increasing in ϕ_L and the left-hand side is increasing in $\phi_P{}^*$, so if ϕ_L rises, then $\phi_P{}^*$ must rise as well. Higher levels of α will cause $(\phi_L\bar{Q})^{1-\alpha}/K$ to fall, so $\phi_P{}^*$ will fall as well.

Proof of proposition 4 It is clear that $\bar{Q}(B_s + B_2 - \phi_{?L}\tilde{w})$ is strictly increasing in $B_s{}^*$ and that, for high enough values of B_2, this level of welfare is strictly positive. When $B_s = \phi_L w - B_2 + \varepsilon$, then the social welfare under public provision equals $\bar{Q}(\varepsilon - \phi_{?L}(\tilde{w} - w))$, and for ε arbitrarily small, this quantity must be strictly negative, and thus lower than social welfare under private provision. Therefore, by continuity, there must exist a value of B_s where the two welfare levels are equal. As the value of $B_s{}^*$ satisfies $B_s{}^* = \phi_{?L}\tilde{w} - B_2$, simple differentiation tells us that $B_s{}^*$ is rising with $\phi_{?L}$, rising with $\bar{Q}$, falling with K, falling with B_2 and rising with α.

COMMENT

Robert M. Solow

This is a neat chapter. It is interesting both for its own train of thought and because it illustrates the modern trend to political economy, what Assar Lindbeck called 'economics with endogenous politicians'. It is an appropriate tribute to an early master of political economy like Dick Netzer.

I will begin by reminding you what is in the chapter. These days business firms never stop talking about sticking to their 'core competences', and the tendency is to outsource more and more peripheral functions. But municipal governments continue to engage in many activities that could in principle be outsourced. Obvious examples include schools, sanitation, at least some transportation, and – with more difficulty – even certain police and fire services. The question is, why does this tendency persist?

The commonest textbook answer is that these functions are natural monopolies. This explanation could cover some, but not all, cases. It would not apply very well to sanitation, for instance. (At one point Glaeser suggests that even the New York subway system once had three independent lines. No; I go back to that period, and I do not believe that the BMT, the IRT and the 8th Avenue (IND) systems could have been regarded as competing for traffic.) Even where the natural monopoly argument applies, why is municipal ownership and operation usually preferred to regulation in these cases? Glaeser wants to explore the possibility that the dominant reason may be fear of corruption. A private operator has a strong motive to swindle the city government and bribe municipal officials to look the other way. There are easy examples of how this might be done: overcharging for services, or underpaying for private use of municipal property, especially land, as an input to production. More subtle, but very interesting, is what Glaeser calls perversion of subsidies. Where social benefit exceeds private benefit, privatization will lead to underprovision; so there is reason to subsidize the producer, who pockets the subsidy and continues to underproduce, protected by corruption. As Glaeser shows, the muckrakers had no trouble finding egregious examples. Where is Lincoln Steffens when we need him?

So the idea is that municipal ownership and operation will provide more net utility because salaried government officials do not collect profits dollar for dollar. They have a much weaker incentive to steal.

On the other hand, Glaeser argues that municipal enterprise has some avenues of corruption that are not available or not profitable in the case of privatization. The main one is overpayment of wages to municipal employees, the idea being that this recruits political strength for the incumbent political group. This happens pretty obviously in some notorious instances, but I do not know if there is systematic empirical study, or what it shows. There is another aspect that I will discuss briefly in a moment: overpayment of wages is a transfer from taxpayers to municipal employees, who are also taxpayers. We need to know if there is much deadweight loss.

Glaeser tries to make simple models of these two alternatives, and then calculate what characteristics of the situation make one of the alternatives socially superior to the other. (He apologizes for the ad hoc character of the models. That is not necessary: what else should they be 'ad'?) There are no surprises in his results. If detection of corruption is difficult, this favors municipal operation. The same thing follows if the cost of being found out is small. Usually larger firms are more likely to bribe government officials, because bribes are not usually *ad valorem*. Labor-intensive production is better outsourced. Production using a lot of public property is better government-operated, because scope for underpayment and bribery is larger.

The models treat the cost of being found out – fines, jail time, loss of reputation, and so on – as a given constant. One might experiment with allowing that cost to increase with the size of the bribe. That might make a difference. The trouble is, as it often is, that this introduces another unknown and unresearchable element into the model.

These are commonsense results. They serve the purpose, however, of reminding serious people what to think about when trendy privatization, or the reverse, gets to be fashionable; and it does, it does.

I want to make three constructive comments about this kind of reasoning. First, you can describe much of economic theory as an exhaustive study of the implications of greed and rationality. That is exactly what Glaeser does here, in this slightly unusual context. Offering and accepting bribes are treated exactly like any other economic transaction, to be engaged in precisely to the extent that marginal private pecuniary benefit exceeds marginal private pecuniary cost to the participants. It will not do to be moralistic about this. There is no doubt that, if successful corruption becomes easier, or if its rewards increase, there will be more corruption But I also think that this kind of modeling has limits.

Glaeser makes a lot of use of the example of Boss Tweed. He is entitled to do that. But I would call attention to the fact that Tweed was Irish, and most of the beneficiaries of his corrupt activities were Irish contractors and Irish hod-carriers. The activity was to some significant extent redistributive, with the Irish making up for institutionalized discrimination against them, no doubt with a deadweight loss. You will not fully understand what was going on without taking this into account.

Sixty years ago I was a 17-year-old sophomore in Ed Glaeser's university. Every day I walked a couple of blocks from where I lived, in Dunster House, to the Yard where classes took place. In those days, now long gone, those blocks had brownstones housing working-class Irish families, and even a couple of vacant lots where kids pitched horseshoes. In those days, James Michael Curley (our Boss Tweed, who had been mayor of Boston and had been elected to Congress) was languishing in jail. One afternoon I stopped, as I sometimes did, to pitch horseshoes with some of the kids. With my own ears I heard one of them say to another: 'That Curley, he's just like Robin Hood: takes from the rich and gives to the poor.' It matters.

For similar reasons, the case of public education is more subtle than the models allow, though they must capture part of the truth. The public schools were intended, and actually served, as producers of citizenship as well as book-learning. Exposing all, or nearly all, children to the same curriculum, and to each other, was part of the socialization process. In olden times, it actually worked. A system of regulated private schools would not perform that function unless the regulation turned into something like management, and then the schools would be private only in name.

Here is a second methodological point. Glaeser treats the whole problem in static terms, one-shot: either private operation and corruption or public operation and excess wages is socially better. I think you could make a case that the repetitive character of the activity might be important. It is not clear in which direction that works, however. Repeated corruption might become intolerable to voters, in which case a private operator faces a trade-off between amount and duration of corruption. Or voters might become habituated to corruption, in which case there may be an optimal time-path, starting with minor corruption and building up to something bigger as routine gets established. You might also see big-time corruption in the last year of a politician's term.

Third, the 'detection technology' plays an important part in Glaeser's models. But it is not really a technology, more a matter of institutional design. Outsourcing should become more common, in his framework, if institutions can be designed that will discover and discourage bribery and corruption. This suggests the importance of watchdogs, yardsticks, benchmarks and other such institutions. Of course they can be corrupted too. OK, nothing is perfect. There is bribery in private industry too. These institutional mechanisms may be an interesting topic for research.

7. The nonprofit sector in K-12 education

Charles T. Clotfelter[1]

INTRODUCTION

This chapter incorporates at least two of the broad topics to which Dick Netzer has devoted his attention, the nonprofit sector and the economics of local government.[2] The nonprofit sector, the vast and variegated group of organizations that operate under the beneficial blanket of favorable tax treatment, includes as one of its most prominent subsectors some 27 400 private and parochial schools (1997–8; U.S. Department of Education 2000, Table 5, p.14). The nonprofit sector manifests itself in K-12 (Kindergarten through to 12th grade) education in other ways as well, ranging across extensive volunteer work in both public and private schools, parental support organizations, organizations providing after-school and other services to students and voluntary membership organizations within the schools. To be sure, private schools by any measure are the most important example of nonprofit activity in K-12 education, and for that reason they receive the bulk of attention in the current chapter.

In 1999, private schools enrolled some 5.4 million students, representing 17 per cent of all kindergarten students, 11 per cent of all elementary students and 8 per cent of secondary school students. Private schools thus offer an important alternative to the nation's public schools, one that is available in every metropolitan area and many non-metropolitan communities. Compared to some other subsectors of the nonprofit sector that can be seen as supplementary or complementary to their corresponding public services – such as programs that help the poor and disabled, museums and other cultural organizations, university and medical research, as well as the nonprofit organizations providing after-school services (discussed below), private schools are decidedly a substitute rather than a supplement to the corresponding public service, the public schools: enrolling in private school means not being enrolled in public school. As argued below, this either/or nature of participation in private schools increases the significance of heterogeneity in demand for this group of nonprofit organizations.

Private schools have received an increasing amount of scholarly attention in recent years. This seems justified, for at least four reasons. First, private schools offer an alternative model (more exactly, alternative models) for K-12 education, one that is divorced from the bureaucratic, intensely political and often large-scale organizations that operate public schools. They are most clearly distinct in the extent to which they emphasize religious and other moral instruction not available in public schools. They are also, according to a number of recent studies, more successful than their public counterparts in educating their students.[3] Not only do the private schools exist as a model that can be copied, their existence has been viewed as allowing market-type forces to work, offering the benefits typically associated with competition.[4]

Second, private schools are important because they affect the mix of students in the public schools. To the extent that they attract as students those who systematically differ from those enrolled in public schools in economic, demographic or other personal characteristics, their existence will necessarily change public schools. And, to the extent that peer effects differ by type of student or diversity of student bodies is an important aspect of K-12 education, such spillovers will have real effects (both efficiency and distributive) on public education. One obvious difference is racial composition: because private schools tend to enroll nonwhites at lower rates than whites, public schools have a higher percentage of nonwhite students (38.0 per cent in 1999, nationwide) than the percentage in the school-age population (36.3 per cent) (U.S. Bureau of the Census, 1999, Table 6.5).

A third reason to pay attention to private schools complements the first two: owing to their tax-exempt status, private schools enjoy public subsidies, principally at the local level. Their exemption from property and sales taxes is certainly worth something, though I have seen no estimates of its size. However these subsidies pale in comparison to those that would be involved if voucher programs were widely adopted that would allow families to pay for private schooling with publicly financed vouchers. The adoption of such a payment system would heighten the policy significance of both the efficiency and distributional issues surrounding private schools.

A fourth reason to examine private schools is for what they might reveal about the value of the nonprofit sector itself. Does the raison d'être that scholars have attributed to nonprofit organizations in general hold for this particular subsector? Observers dating back to Alexis de Tocqueville have explained voluntarism and nonprofit organization in terms of decentralized responses to diversity of tastes, yielding social benefits by facilitating pluralism within a democracy. The possibility seems well worth considering that some nonprofit organizations, among them private schools, may also have deleterious effects, offsetting the happy implications of the

Tocquevillian vision. On the other hand, private schools may have beneficial effects on residential segregation by income level. Those steeped in the Tiebout model (Tiebout, 1956) will recognize in many nonprofit organizations, including private schools, an alternative to local jurisdictions for meeting households' diverse demands for local public goods. Thus, to the extent that nonprofit organizations rather than local governments meet diverse needs, geographic segregation by taste may well be reduced.

The purpose of this chapter is to consider the role of the nonprofit sector in K-12 education, with particular emphasis on private schools. It asks how well private schools conform to the theories advanced and the judgments made by scholars of nonprofit organizations. It pays special attention to the consequences of the differential appeals of private schools for the patterns of association among school-age individuals. The next section of the chapter begins by viewing nonprofit organizations from the perspective of public economics, relating this perspective to existing research on the nonprofit sector, and noting a darker side to the diversity that is a hallmark of the nonprofit sector. The third section discusses ways in which K-12 private schools are distinct from public schools and how they differ from one another. The fourth section describes overall patterns and trends in private school enrollment and reviews empirical studies of the forces that affect the demand for private schooling. The fifth section addresses a little-discussed drawback of nonprofit organizations, their potentially divisive effect, for the case of K-12 private schools, while the sixth section notes other manifestations of the nonprofit sector in K-12 schools, both public and private. A final section concludes.

PUBLIC ECONOMICS AND THE NONPROFIT SECTOR

To see the significance of the nonprofit sector for public economics, it is very useful to begin by considering the process by which households satisfy their demand for services. From this perspective, nonprofit organizations turn out to be merely one of several means by which household demand can be met. What significance household choices have will depend on characteristics of the alternative chosen.

The Centrality of Household Production

As Bradford *et al.* (1969) argue, the outputs arising from public expenditures (for example, number of police patrols, miles of streets) can be distinguished from the aspects valued by households (for example, safety, accessibility). The insight contained in their article can be generalized by viewing households as satisfying their wants by engaging in a process of 'home production', using as inputs their own time and effort, goods and services purchased in the market, services provided by government and services produced by nonprofit organizations.[5] What combination of these inputs a household decides to utilize will depend on the household's income and preferences, the cost and effectiveness of the available inputs, and the household's own 'production' skills. While it turns out to be most effective for households to buy many of its inputs, from groceries to galoshes, in the private market, some services are most economically purchased from government or nonprofit providers.

Consider the important case of K-12 schools. While many parents would consider themselves competent to 'home-school' their children, for most people the necessary skills are lacking or the opportunity cost is simply too great. Most households therefore choose to send their children to public or private schools. Because most families live in communities that offer more than one school district, households can choose their district by way of their location decision. Such voting-with-feet emphasized in Tiebout's (1956) famous article can be seen as a special case of household production. If the type of services that K-12 schools produce were unidimensional, straightforward indifference curve analysis implies that any given household would be more likely to choose private schools over public school the lower the public school's output of services, the higher the household's income (assuming education is a normal good) or the more emphatically the household's preferences are oriented toward education. (Obviously education is not unidimensional, so the analysis necessarily becomes more complex.) Our household also has the option of using its own time and effort to influence the level of the intermediate good received from schools, either public or private; these include participation in local politics, volunteering at school or attempting to influence teachers or administrators (the 'voice' option).

From this perspective, nonprofit organizations such as private schools are simply one of several institutional alternatives open to households. How many households choose the nonprofit option will depend on the costs, effectiveness and distinctive aspects of each alternative. The attractiveness of private schools will be influenced in part by aspects of public schools such as the extent of interracial contact or the opportunities available for religious observation. If it becomes impossible for one's children to pray in school, for example, some families will prefer private schools that offer religious training.[6] Similarly, tracking of students in public schools may make public schools more attractive to parents who would like their children to be in classes with students similar to them.

As a general matter, a household's decision to opt for a nonprofit alternative over a public service may have more or less policy significance depending on the nature of the activity in question. Services provided by nonprofit organizations may be supplementary to those provided by government, or they may be exclusive. K-12 education is decidedly in the latter, either/or category. If, in addition, the service has participation or peer effects, individual household choices will have spillover effects. In this case, use of nonprofit services will have both efficiency and distributional implications in the same way spillovers generally do. In this case, any subsidies accorded to nonprofit activities would be subject to the usual criteria of applied welfare economics.

The Role of the Nonprofit Sector

Scholars of nonprofit organizations are familiar with Alexis de Tocqueville's celebration of what he saw as Americans' singular tendency to form voluntary associations. He wrote:

> The Americans make associations to give entertainments, to found seminaries, to build inns, to construct churches, to diffuse books, to send missionaries to the antipodes; in this manner they found hospitals, prisons, and schools. If it is proposed to inculcate some truth or to foster some feeling by the encouragement of a great example, they form a society. (Tocqueville, 1840; 1998, p.150)

Among the many things this 19th-century observer admired about America was the way voluntary associations complemented democracy, especially by giving voice to diverse interests and opinions. This celebratory theme carries through to much current writing about the sector, the idea being that the tendency and opportunity to form voluntary associations allows pluralism in economy and polity to thrive, effectively allowing for differences to be voiced and acted upon without necessarily spilling over to form deeply divided political factions. According to Douglas (1987), the sector's contribution to pluralism lies in the capacity it provides to meet a wider variety of wants in society than is possible through government alone. The sector has perhaps its most distinctive role in performing functions in the religious sphere, allowing tax-subsidized religious organizations to perform functions that would otherwise be strictly prohibited by the constitutional separation of church and state.

The economic parallel to this political function is best described by Weisbrod (1988), who sees nonprofit organizations as filling in gaps in the demand for 'collective-type' goods left over after government is done with responding to the median voter. Those who are not satisfied with the amount or nature of services provided by government, he argues, always have the option of buying private goods to supplement or substitute for public services. The major drawback to this course of action is that the cost of such private goods is often prohibitive. For some services, such as education, economies of scale are such that service is much more economical when provided collectively.[7] This is where nonprofit organizations come in. Nonprofit organizations such as private schools stand ready to perform the economic function of meeting diverse demands while also cultivating the pluralism so highly valued in the political realm.

Not only may private schools offer some features (such as religious instruction) not available in public schools, their organizational structure, in one view, makes them inherently superior to most public schools. In the case they make for 'school choice', Chubb and Moe (1990) argue that private schools, by virtue of institutional arrangements quite different from those in public schools, are able to provide schooling that is on average superior to that offered in public schools. Public schools, they argue, are hamstrung by a bureaucratic structure developed decades ago by Progressive reformers to protect the schools from interference by political machines and special interest groups. In addition, they argue, public schools have accumulated a vast array of objectives, resulting in a loss of clear mission. In such a system, principals and teachers have little autonomy, but rather are forced to behave as bureaucratic functionaries. By contrast, Chubb and Moe assert, private schools have the luxury of needing to appeal only to a narrow segment of the population and thus act according to a much clearer mission. And, without the shackles of a large bureaucracy, the argument goes, their heads can use the autonomy their independent status gives them to exert leadership and to give their teachers the freedom to act more like professionals than mere employees.

From Pluralism to Segregation

While scholars have justifiably emphasized the role of nonprofit organizations (including private schools) in serving pluralism and diversity in demand, less attention has been paid to the flip side of that diversity coin: segregation. As social scientists use the term, segregation refers to the non-uniform bunching of individuals by some, usually identifiable, trait, such as income, race or religious affiliation. To the extent that birds of a feather join in pursuing common aims through the nonprofit sector, patterns of association will necessarily be non-uniform. Whether this non-uniformity results in a form of segregation worthy of concern depends, however, on the nature of the service or activity being provided. For services that do not entail an either/or choice by participants – and this includes a wide variety of nonprofit organizations, including museums, research institutes, environmental organizations, advocacy groups and human service organizations – the non-uniform pattern of support and participation does not produce anything one would call 'segregation'. But for those nonprofit services that do entail an either/or choice (religious congregations and private schools are prime examples) segregation appears to be a rather necessary consequence of the differentiated demand that the nonprofit sector invites.

Whether this segregation is important depends on one's assessment of the benefit or harm that arises from it. In the case of religious congregations, for example, few would think that the separation of Quakers from Muslims and Catholics threatens any important social principle. Indeed the freedom of religious observation established so clearly in the Constitution would appear to be served by this separation. At the same time, the degree of racial segregation evident among religious congregations, evident in popular references to eleven o'clock on Sunday mornings as the most segregated hour in the week,[8] does appear to be a source of concern on the part of at least some observers, presumably because that racial segregation stands in contrast to public policies favoring racial integration. By the same token, segregation arising from private school enrollment would also appear to raise concerns from the standpoint of public policy. It would stand in contrast to the public policy in place since 1954 stating that school segregation in the public schools is unconstitutional (*Brown* v. *Board of Education*, 347 U.S. 483 (1954)), although no one would argue that public–private racial disparities are unconstitutional. Similar concerns arise in connection with socioeconomic disparities between public and private schools. Not only are economic disparities an issue that touches many public policy debates, such disparities in the public schools have risen to the level of constitutional challenge in many states to conventional systems of financing schools. In sum, segregation by race or income that arises from or is exacerbated by private schools is a subject of legitimate policy attention. As a consequence, this flip-side of pluralism is a characteristic of at least some parts of the nonprofit sector that is worthy of serious consideration. The fifth section of this chapter examines the role of private enrollment in racial and economic segregation.

HOW ARE NONPROFIT SCHOOLS DISTINCTIVE?

Private schools may act as a substitute for public schools, but they are by no means a perfect substitute. In fact their differences constitute a principal reason for their attractiveness. Their distinctiveness can be discussed in at least four ways: how they perceive themselves to be different, how other people perceive them to be different, how their clientele differs from that of public schools, and whether they have effects on students that are different from those brought about by the public schools.

Their Professed Differences

Private schools differentiate themselves not only from public schools but also from each other. At the grossest level of categorization, they differ in academic orientation or in religious orientation. Table 7.1 gives a breakdown by orientation of the close to 26000 private schools operating in the

Table 7.1 K-12 private schools, by type, 1995–6

Type	Number of schools	Percentage of total	Number of students	Percentage of total
Regular	20096	77.6	4287300	93.5
Montessori	1833	7.1	71604	1.6
Special program emphasis				
Military	29	0.1	10584	0.2
Bilingual	49	0.2	8357	0.2
Other	431	1.7	70155	1.5
Special education	137	0.5	7923	0.2
Vocational/technical	10	0.0	1248	0.0
Early childhood/daycare	1864	7.2	30774	0.7
Alternative				
Home schooling	255	1.0	19295	0.4
Other	1201	4.6	75754	1.6
All	25905	100.0	4601744	100.0

Note: Enrollment figures cover K12 students only. Percentages may not add up to 100 owing to rounding.

Source: US Department of Education, National Center for Education Statistics (1997), *Private School University Survey*, 1995–6.

fall of 1995. While most of them offered academic programs similar to those in public schools, almost a quarter of them offered a distinctive academic program. Among these were Montessori schools, military academies, early childhood and daycare schools, and schools specializing in the support of parents 'home schooling' their children. In scale, the military schools were the largest, with an average enrollment of 365, compared to the 213 average for regular schools.

But it is in religious orientation that private schools are most distinct from public schools. As shown in Table 7.2, over 85 per cent of private

Table 7.2 Private schools, by religious affiliation or other orientation, 1995–6

	Number of schools	Total enrollment	Percentage of all private enrollment	Number of states represented[a]	Region with highest concentration[b]
Roman Catholic	8050	2432871	52.8	51	Midwest
Greek Orthodox	24	4388	0.0	7	Northeast
Protestant					
Baptist	1811	261279	5.7	51	South
Lutheran	1665	215351	4.7	46	Midwest
Episcopal, Presbyterian, Methodist	742	130944	2.8	45	South
Seventh Day Adventist	991	62586	1.4	51	South
Assembly of God	469	64860	1.4	50	South
Pentecostal	383	24992	0.5	46	South
Other Conservative Christian	3073	433447	9.4	51	South
Jewish	670	147078	3.2	37	Northeast
Islamic	87	8632	0.2	27	Northeast
Other religious	1659	180222	3.9	51	
Non-religious					
Montessori	1661	63036	1.4	51	Midwest
Other	4620	572058	12.4	51	West
Total	25905	4601744	100.0		

Notes:
[a] Includes Washington DC.
[b] Region in which category has the highest percentage of region's private students. For region definitions, see text.

Source: See Table 7.1.

schools had some religious affiliation or orientation. Catholic schools claimed by far the biggest share, accounting for over half of all private students. It is instructive to note that enrollments in Catholic schools as a proportion of all enrollments in religiously-oriented schools are much greater than the share of Catholics among all those affiliated with religious faiths and denominations (61 versus 37 per cent).[9] By contrast, Baptists were underrepresented in private school enrollment (7 versus 22 per cent), as were Methodists, Presbyterians and Episcopalians (3 versus 13 per cent).[10] Not surprisingly, the geographical distribution of religiously-oriented private schools tends to mirror the importance of the various churches, with Catholic schools most heavily represented in the Midwest, Protestant schools in the South and Jewish schools in the Northeast.

The differences in orientation between public and private schools go deeper than a label or religious affiliation. In contrast to public schools, private schools appear to lay heavier emphasis on the inculcation of values. In a survey of principals of private schools conducted in 1977, 95 per cent of those responding thought that 'developing high moral standards and citizenship' was very important; and a comparison of responses by public and private school principals revealed that private school principals were more likely to say that the development of moral standards was a very important goal (Abramowitz and Stackhouse, 1981, p.45). In a full-page advertisement in the *New York Times* in 2001, the Archdiocese of New York made this explicit statement about its schools' emphasis on values: 'In addition to a well-rounded education, our schools teach such virtues as self-discipline, diligence, honesty, courage and compassion' (Inner-City Scholarship Fund, 2001).

Perceived Distinctive Aspects of Private Schools

Beyond the high proportion of them that have religious orientations, private schools enjoy generally favorable perceptions regarding their attention to discipline and success in academic preparation. In a Gallup Poll taken in 2001, for example, adults who were asked where they would prefer to send a child to school if cost were not a factor were more likely to say private school than public school.[11] In surveys of parents of public school students only, private schools consistently were named as having higher academic standards.[12]

Private schools are also widely believed to be characterized by better discipline. Supporting this perception are results from the national High School and Beyond survey of high school students. When asked to rate the effectiveness of discipline in their schools, seniors in private high schools were most likely to rate it highly: 72 per cent in Catholic schools and 58 per cent in other private schools rated it as 'excellent' or 'good', compared to just 42 per cent in public schools (Coleman *et al.*, 1982, p.99). At the same time, seniors in private schools thought their teachers were more interested in them than did public school seniors: the percentage who rated as 'excellent' their teachers' interest in them was 25 per cent in Catholic, 34 per cent in other private, but only 9 per cent in public schools (ibid., p.100).

Differences in who attends

While they naturally differ among themselves, students in private schools on average clearly differ from those in public schools by residence, socioeconomic status, racial composition and religious orientation. Table 7.3 summarizes rates of private enrollment by grade level, metropolitan status and racial and ethnic group. Rates of private enrollment are higher in metropolitan areas than outside them. Among major racial and ethnic groups, whites enroll at the highest rates, followed generally by Asian and Pacific

Table 7.3 Percentage of elementary and secondary school students in private school, by race and Hispanic origin and metropolitan status, October 2000

	Metropolitan Area			
	Central city	Outside central city	Nonmetropolitan	All
All races				
Elementary K-8	11.5	10.9	8.9	10.7
High school	9.5	8.7	5.8	8.4
White non-Hispanic				
Elementary K-8	21.4	12.8	10.4	13.8
High school	15.7	9.6	7.0	10.0
Black non-Hispanic				
Elementary K-8	6.1	8.3	2.0	6.3
High school	4.7	8.8	1.0	5.8
Hispanic				
Elementary K-8	4.8	3.8	1.7	4.1
High school	5.2	4.1	1.1	4.4
Asian & Pacific Islander				
Elementary K-8	5.8	6.5	16.5	6.9
High school	8.0	4.8	8.3	6.5

Source: US Bureau of the Census (2001), *School Enrollment, October 2000*, www.census.gov/population/www/socdemo/school/ppl-148.html, accessed 1 June. Table 5. Level of Enrollment Below College for People 3 to 24 Years Old, By Control of School, Sex, Metropolitan Status, Race and Hispanic Origin, October 2000.

Table 7.4 Private school enrollment, by family income and grade level, 1998

	Percentage enrolled in private school		
Family income ($)	Kindergarten	Grades 1–8	Grade 9–12
Less than 10000	5.1	5.3	3.8
10000 to under 15000	4.8	2.7	1.6
15000 to under 20000	11.7	5.1	2.3
20000 to under 25000	19.6	6.8	5.6
25000 to under 30000	8.4	6.7	7.0
30000 to under 35000	17.9	8.2	7.9
35000 to under 40000	20.9	11.5	7.1
40000 to under 50000	16.8	8.5	7.7
50000 to under 75000	23.3	14.3	9.6
75000 and over	36.5	19.6	14.7
Not reported	21.3	11.4	7.0
Total	18.6	10.8	8.5

Source: U.S. Bureau of the Census, *Current Population Reports*, series P-20, no. 521; *School Enrollment – Social and Economic Characteristics of Students, October 1998* (Washington, DC, GPO September 1999), Table 6.

Islanders. Rates tend to be the lowest among blacks and Hispanics. Table 7.4 shows the very strong correlation with income, with the percentage of elementary children in private school rising from less than 6 per cent among families with incomes below $20000 to 19.6 per cent for families in the highest income class ($75000 and over). At the high school level, private school enrollment rises from less than 4 per cent below $20000 to 14.7 per cent in the highest income class.

Effects of attendance

Perhaps the question about private schools that has done the most to emphasize their social importance is whether such schools are actually more effective than public schools in educating students. Coleman *et al.* (1982) sparked a lively scholarly debate with their claim that Catholic schools were more effective than public schools in raising the academic achievement of their students, as measured by standardized achievement tests. Critics of the study argued that it dealt inadequately with the sample selection problem, the bias that would result if those students attending Catholic schools systematically differed in unmeasured ways from those who did not. Subsequent studies, dealing with this selection problem in different ways and focusing on attainment (high school completion, college enrollment) rather than test scores, have tended to support the superior performance of Catholic schools.[13] Neal (1997) and Grogger and Neal (2000) find that Catholic schools are especially effective in raising the graduation rates for urban minorities, arguing that for these groups the differences between the available public and private schools are especially large.

Private schooling is associated with non-academic benefits as well. Figlio and Ludwig (2000), for example, find that students in private religious schools report less sexual activity, fewer arrests and lower rates of cocaine use; the authors use differences in transportation costs to deal with the selection problem. In another study looking at non-academic effects, Greene *et al.* (1999) argue that Latino students who attend private schools have higher levels of political participation, tolerance and social capital; however selection issues receive little attention in this study.

DEMAND FOR PRIVATE SCHOOLING

Enrollment Patterns and Trends

Table 7.5 presents an overview of K-12 enrollment trends, showing the share in private schools from 1960 to 1999. Private schools have historically claimed their highest percentage of students in kindergarten, with the share declining in elementary grades and then again in high school. From 1960 to 1990, the proportion of students in private schools declined at each level, after which they rose again during the 1990s. Underlying these trends has been a marked decline in the importance of Catholic schools. As a share of all private school enrollment, Catholic enrollments fell from more than 85 per cent in 1960 to less than half by 1999. The shrinking of Catholic schooling has been most pronounced in large cities, as indicated by Grogger and Neal's (2000) tracking of the supply of Catholic high schools by city size. Whereas the number of Catholic high schools in the country declined by 28 per cent in the 25 years ending in 1999, those in the largest cities declined by 36 per cent. As the authors note, however, most of these declines were completed by 1994. On the basis of Grogger and Neal's figures, the number of Catholic high schools fell at an annual rate of 1.6 per cent from 1974 to 1994 but by only 0.1 per cent after 1994. By 1999, Catholic schools still represented an important segment of private enrollment, but nothing like the dominant share they constituted in 1960. Masked by the decline in Catholic schools has been growth over time in the proportion of students attending non-Catholic private schools, especially in the 1990s. Between 1960 and 1999, the percentage of all students attending non-Catholic private schools more than doubled.

Table 7.5 US enrollment, by type of school, fall 1960, 1970, 1980, 1990, 1999 (thousands)

	1960	1970	1980	1990	1999
Kindergarten					
Public	1691	2647	2690	3322	3167
Private	401	536	486	567	658
Total	2092	3183	3176	3899	3825
Elementary (1–8)					
Public	25814	30001	24398	26591	29253
Private	4535	3949	3051	2674	3609
Total	30349	33950	27449	29265	32863
Secondary (9–12)					
Public	9215	13332	13242	11818	14559
Private	1033	1311	1339	903	1271
Total	10248	14643	14581	12721	15830
Total private, K-12	5969	5796	4876	4144	5538
Private as % of total					
Kindergarten	19.2	16.8	15.3	14.5	17.2
Elementary	14.9	11.6	11.1	9.1	11.0
Secondary	10.1	9.0	9.2	7.1	8.0
Total, K-12	14.0	11.2	10.8	9.0	10.5
Catholic as % of all private					
Kindergarten and elementary	88.6	74.8	64.2	58.1	44.0
Secondary	85.2	76.9	62.5	65.5	49.0
Non-Catholic private as % of all enrollment					
Kindergarten and elementary	1.7	3.0	4.1	4.1	6.5
Secondary	1.5	2.1	3.4	2.4	4.1

Sources: U.S. Bureau of the Census, *Current Population Reports*, P-20; *School Enrollment – Social and Economic Characteristics of Students, October 2000* (Washington: Government Printing Office, 1 June 2001) Table A-1, at www.census.gov/population/www/socdemo/school.html, historical tables, 7/2/01; U.S. Department of Education, *Digest of Education Statistics 2000*, Tables 45 and 63.

Owing in large part to differences in religious affiliation, patterns of private school enrollment differ markedly by region. These differences, and changes in them, are well illustrated by comparable data by region for high schools. Table 7.6 gives the percentage of students in Catholic and non-Catholic high schools for 1980 and 1995, based on the High School and Beyond survey for 1980 and the Common Core of Data and the Private School Universe Survey for 1995–6. While the share of students in Catholic schools declined in all regions over this period, sizeable differences by

Table 7.6 Percentage of students in private schools, grade 9–12, by region, 1980 and 1995

Division	1980[a]			1995[b]		
	Total	Catholic	Non-Catholic	Total	Catholic	Non-Catholic
United States total	9.1	6.1	3.0	8.1	4.6	3.5
New England	13.8	8.1	5.7	13.8	6.7	7.1
Middle Atlantic	13.0	10.3	2.7	13.2	9.0	4.2
South Atlantic	8.1	3.3	4.8	7.2	2.5	4.7
East South Central	8.1	2.8	5.3	7.5	2.3	5.2
West South Central	5.4	3.5	1.9	5.2	2.8	2.4
East North Central	9.3	7.4	1.9	8.9	6.3	2.6
West North Central	8.9	6.9	2.0	7.3	5.1	2.2
Mountain	4.4	2.3	2.1	3.8	1.7	1.9
Pacific	7.6	4.7	2.9	7.8	4.2	3.6

Notes: States in each Census division are: New England: CT, ME, MA, NH, RI, VT; Middle Atlantic: NJ, NY, PA; South Atlantic: DE, DC, FL, GA, MD, NC, SC, VA, WV; East South Central: AL, KY, MS, TN; West South Central: AR, LA. OK, TX; East North Central: IL, IN, MI, WI; West North Central: IA, KS, MN, MO, NE, ND, SD; Mountain: AZ, CO, ID, MT, NV, NM, UT, WY; Pacific: AK, CA, HI, OR, WA.

[a] Estimates based on High School and Beyond (Coleman *et al.*, 1982, Table 2-2).

[b] *Source:* US Department of Education, National Center for Education Statistics, *Common Core of Data, Public School Universe: 1995–1996* and *Private School Universe Survey: 1995–1996*.

region remained, with rates in New England and the Middle Atlantic states being over twice as large as those in the West South Central and Mountain states. Meanwhile the proportion attending non-Catholic schools increased over the period in most regions and in the nation as a whole.

Explaining Demand

To understand the enrollment choices that underlie the measurable differences between public and private school students, it is useful to turn to research that seeks to explain the demand for private schools. Increasingly using micro data on the enrollment decisions of individual students and their families, economic studies of demand have examined a variety of possible factors. Of the factors examined, perhaps income is the most consistent distinguishing feature of those who choose private schools. Illustrating the quantitative importance of income and socioeconomic status in determining private enrollment, Betts and Fairlie (2001) estimated models attempting to explain the observed differences in private enrollment rates by race and immigration status. They found that family income explains about 30 per cent of the observed difference in elementary private enrollment between native whites and all other groups and 36 per cent of the difference in private secondary enrollment. Differences in parental education explain an even greater share. Whether it is measured on a current or a permanent basis, then, income is an important predictor of private enrollment.[14]

Not surprisingly, demand for private schools is associated with other personal characteristics, among them religious affiliation. Interestingly, Figlio and Stone (2001, Table 1) also found that private enrollment is higher among families that are active participants in religious congregations.

Other research on demand suggests strongly that families seek private enrollment as a way of avoiding characteristics or problems associated with the public schools. Most notably, private enrollment tends to be higher where the public schools have higher proportions of minority students. Clotfelter (1976) and Conlon and Kimenyi (1991) found this for private schools in Mississippi, a state whose public schools feature some of the highest nonwhite shares in the nation. But qualitatively similar effects have been observed outside the South as well. Lankford *et al.* (1995) and Fairlie and Resch (2000), for example, found that the choice of private schools was significantly associated with the racial composition of public schools. Betts and Fairlie (2000) looked specifically at enrollment changes associated with immigration, much of which involves students who are members of minority groups. In secondary schools (but not in elementary schools) they find strong evidence of flight by native whites out of public schools in response to immigration: one white native student goes to private school for every four new immigrants entering the public schools.

Private schools also appear to be viewed as a means of escape from crime and low quality public instruction. Lankford *et al.* (1995) and Figlio and Stone (2001) found that private enrollment was positively associated with crime rates. The latter study found an association with the student–teacher ratio in local schools and with the degree of concentration in local schools (signifying lack of choice among districts).

SEGREGATIVE EFFECTS OF PRIVATE SCHOOLS

Because private schools enroll whites at higher rates than nonwhites and students from high-income families at higher rates than those from less affluent families, it might seem obvious that the existence of private schools must necessarily increase the overall degree of racial and economic segregation in schools. As Coleman *et al.* (1982) point out, however, public/private disparities in racial composition are only one of two factors determining the effect of private schools on overall segregation. The other depends on the extent of segregation *within* the private sector. It would be possible for the existence of private schools to decrease overall racial segregation, for instance, if private schools were less segregated than public schools and if this difference were large enough to offset the racial disparity in enrollment rates. This section examines the contribution made by private schools to overall segregation in schools, by race and by income. Ultimately, determining the effect of private schools on overall segregation involves a counterfactual comparison between actual segregation and the degree of segregation that would hypothetically be achieved were there no private schools.

Racial Segregation

Coleman *et al.* (1982) address this question using data on 1015 public and private high schools from the High School and Beyond survey. They conclude that, with regard to racial segregation, at the high school level, private schools had little impact on overall racial segregation in 1982. They base this conclusion on a comparison of two segregation indices: the actual segregation index (incorporating private schools in the calculation) and the segregation index in public schools alone. They argue that the segregation index of public schools is the same index that would be achieved if all private schools were closed and the private schools' students enrolled in public schools in proportion to the numbers of blacks and whites already attending public schools. This assertion turns out to be almost, but not quite, correct.[15] More problematical is their calculation of segregation indices using national racial compositions to calculate gaps between actual and potential interracial exposure. Although this approach was necessitated by their reliance on a relatively small sample of schools and students, the resulting segregation indices do not incorporate the kinds of gaps that are involved in segregation as it is normally thought of. To the degree that different regions of the country have different racial compositions, a significant amount of 'segregation' would show up even if every metropolitan area were to balance its schools racially. For this reason, calculations of segregation indices made at the local level contain a more realistic implicit benchmark than those calculated at the national, or even regional, level.

I therefore turned to racial compositions at the local level to define segregation, making calculations using detailed data on all public and private schools in 1995–6. Table 7.7 summarizes these calculations by region. As previous research on public schools alone has shown (see Clotfelter, 1999,

Table 7.7 *Enrollment, racial composition and segregation in K-12 schools, by region, 1995*

	South	Border	Northeast	Midwest	West	USA
K-12 enrollment (000s)	13900.8	4216.1	8780.5	10277.1	10602.2	47776.6
Percent nonwhite	41.0	24.7	28.5	19.7	44.7	33.5
Percent in private school	7.3	9.7	13.4	11.0	8.1	9.6
Overall segregation index	0.265	0.268	0.372	0.310	0.236	0.288
Benchmark segregation index	0.246	0.261	0.360	0.310	0.229	0.278

Note: Benchmark segregation in public schools is the calculated segregation index calculated for the hypothetical distribution in public schools if private school students were returned to public schools in proportion to their public school enrollments. For definition of segregation index and components of segregation, see text.

Source: US Department of Education, National Center for Education Statistics, *Common Core of Data, Public School Universe Data*, 1995–6; *Private School Universe Study*, 1995–6; author's calculations.

for example), overall segregation is highest in the Northeast and lowest in the West. In every region the benchmark segregation index, indicating the hypothetical segregation rate in public schools if private schools were closed, is lower. While necessarily speculative, this comparison indicates that existing patterns of private school enrollment have the effect of increasing measured racial segregation in K-12 schools, in contrast to the conclusion of Coleman *et al.* (1982).

It should be remembered that such comparisons remain speculative to the extent that they depend on indices comparing actual enrollment patterns with hypothetical patterns. To the extent that those hypothetical patterns are unrealistic, the comparisons are not useful. In the hypothetical closing of private schools, whites and nonwhites are assumed to return to public schools in proportion to the actual public enrollments by race. If, perhaps because of their greater average affluence, private school students were disproportionately likely to enroll in public schools with lower minority percentages (manifested in more Tiebout sorting), the benchmark segregation would understate the segregation that would obtain under the realistic counterfactual, thus making it less likely that private schools actually increase overall segregation.

Segregation by Income

Using their sample of high school students in 1980, Coleman *et al.* applied their methodology to segregation by income.[16] While acknowledging the higher incomes of families using private schools, they show that the exposure of low-income students to upper-income students was greater in the private sector and that economic segregation there was less, as compared to public schools. Still the effect of private schools was to increase economic segregation; whereas thc segregation index by income was 0.21 in the public sector alone, it was 0.23 overall (Coleman *et al.*, 1982, p.41).

The more recent private school data used above do not contain information on student income levels, so it is impossible to replicate these calculations for the more recent period. It is possible, and useful, however, to examine trends in enrollment by income level for the nation. Using data from the October Current Population Survey, one can calculate private school enrollment rates for each of the major racial ethnic groups, for those above and below the median income for each group. Graphs showing these enrollment rates (based on a three-year rolling average) are shown in Figure 7.1. Not surprisingly, those above the median are more likely to attend private school than those below. A general downward drift is evident for both sets of Hispanic students. There is, however, no discernible trend in the ratio of higher to lower income groups in any of the racial groups.

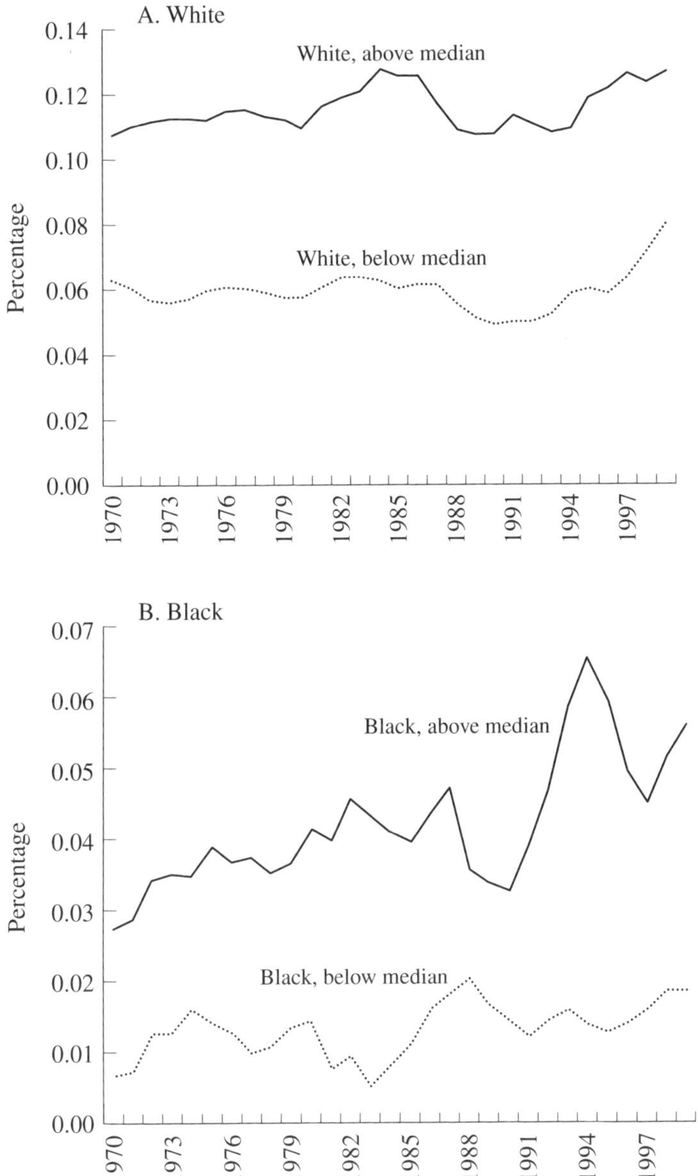

Notes: Yearly percentages are three-year rolling averages; Hispanic percentage data not available before 1971.

Figure 7.1 Private school enrollment percentage, 1970–99, in relation to median income, by race

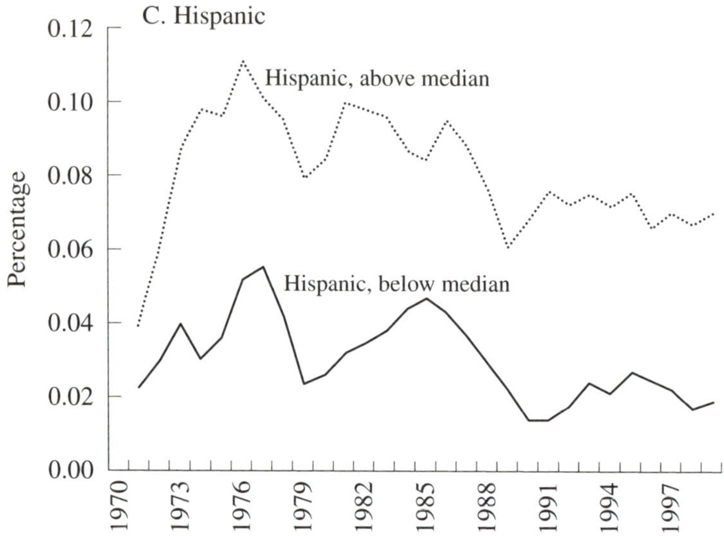

Figure 7.1 (*continued*)

Despite the increasing inequality in income and the decline in Catholic schooling, two trends that might conceivably affect economic segregation in private schools, these figures offer no evidence that economic segregation is increasing over time.

OTHER NONPROFIT ORGANIZATIONS IN K-12 EDUCATION

Although they are less important than private schools, other nonprofit organizations play influential roles in K-12 education. This section discusses two broad groups of organizations. The first group contains organizations designed to supplement the education offered by schools, both public and private. The second includes the clubs and other membership organizations for students within schools, particularly high schools.

Supplemental Service Organizations

Thousands of nonprofit organizations exist to serve, support or enhance the efforts of individual schools. The ubiquitous parent–teacher associations (PTA) and booster clubs are noteworthy because of their broad reach and the legions of parents who volunteer through them on behalf of schools.[17] Through them, parents not only join together to provide volunteer work and financial support for activities deemed to be insufficiently funded, but also probably hope to influence the decisions of school administrators.[18]

A variety of other nonprofit organizations provide services explicitly designed to supplement the offerings of K-12 schools, particularly public schools. Through after-school programs, summer camps, mentorships and other programs involving students, these organizations often utilize volunteers, museums and other local nonprofit organizations, and local businesses. Dick Netzer's New York offers several noteworthy examples which serve to illustrate some of the ways nonprofits are involved in K-12 education. The Children's Aid Society, older than the PTA, provides school children with after-school programs, including arts and recreation and summer day camps, in addition to an array of social services, directed particularly at low-income children. Another nonprofit, the Albert G. Oliver Program, recruits promising black and Latino students in New York, aids their enrollment in private schools, and provides them with support designed to enable them to enroll and graduate from college. A third New York nonprofit, this one more explicitly intended as a supplement to the offerings of the public schools, is the Center for Arts Education. Founded to counteract the effects of cutbacks in arts education in the public schools, this organization works with individual schools and collaborates with local arts organizations to provide programs on the arts.[19]

Surely one of the most ambitious of the nonprofits engaged in K-12 education is the After-School Corporation. Supported by a large matching grant from the Open Society Institute, it boldly aims to provide programs operating from 3 to 6 pm each weekday afternoon throughout New York City, New York State and, eventually, across the nation. It has operated since 1998 by involving in its cooperative programs the public schools, other public agencies and many corporations, foundations and individual donors. Using community organizations as local contractors to staff and operate the after-school programs, the organization involves parents, local volunteers and AmeriCorps members, as well as paid staff. It has established guidelines for operating these programs, including the standard of a 10:1 student-to-adult ratio. These four examples from New York illustrate the variety and scope of the supplemental programs initiated by nonprofit organizations. What their effects will be cannot yet be judged.[20]

Membership Organizations for Students

Another class of nonprofit organization in high schools includes the clubs and other voluntary organizations that are an unmistakeable component of the high school landscape. High schools, both public and private, offer an array of membership organizations. Although they are not usually thought of when the nonprofit sector is discussed, these organizations look and act a great deal like nonprofit organizations outside high schools: they have members, they perform activities and they are voluntary. In recent years religious organizations have been front and center in the battleground over religion in the schools, as noted above. Out of a sample of 194 high schools whose yearbooks for 1997–8 were examined, 188 offered a total of 4418 different organizations (not counting sports teams). These organizations included some activities actively sponsored by the schools, such as newspapers and choral groups, as well as others that probably received only minimal support. Among the organizations were some whose names suggested they were explicitly aimed at minority students, but, interestingly, there were fewer whose names suggested they were aimed at majority students.[21]

Whether these organizations are 'segregative' depends on one's point of view. Like nonprofit organizations in the rest of society, a sizeable number of the high school organizations studied were racially homogenous. Counting both sports teams and clubs in 101 high schools with racial compositions between 10 and 90 per cent nonwhite, 19 per cent of all organizations were all-white and 3.6 per cent were all-nonwhite. Examples show that many organizations composed exclusively of nonwhite students appear explicitly to appeal to minority students. All-white organizations rarely appear to be designed exclusively for whites, a contrast that surely has roots in the majority status of whites.[22] Do such clubs, racially distinct as many of them are, actually promote overall segregation among students? If one compares the exposure rates available in high school clubs with that which would result from voluntary association through friendships, it may well be that these clubs, despite their failure to mirror the racial composition of their schools, provide opportunities for students in different groups to associate with one another. Because they are (unlike private schools) non-exclusive, they appear to offer as many opportunities for togetherness as for separation.

CONCLUSION

This chapter examines the nonprofit sector in K-12 schools. Although nonprofit and voluntary activity in the schools includes high school membership organizations, parent organizations such as the PTA and other nonprofit organizations providing supplementary services for students, private schools constitute the bulk of the nonprofit presence in K-12 education. Like other nonprofit organizations, private schools provide services that respond to the diversity of household demand, offering the economies of collective action without the necessity of government sanction. Thus they provide an outlet for diversity in household demand, accommodating, for example, the desires of many families for religious content in their children's schooling. One aspect of this accommodation to diversity in tastes that has received little attention in research on the nonprofit sector (one that is important for services that require an either/or choice between public and nonprofit services) is the potential it holds to induce segregation. In the case of K-12 private schools, this segregation takes the form of non-uniform attendance patterns by race, income or taste. Analysis of attendance patterns for 1995–6 suggests that the existence of private schools increased the degree of racial segregation in K-12 schools. Judging from the large differences in average family income between public and private school students, similar effects on economic segregation are also likely, although there is no evidence that economic separation has intensified in recent years.

Effects on segregation such as these need to be considered in judging public policies affecting nonprofit organizations. An appealing economic justification for providing tax subsidies for nonprofit organizations in general is that such organizations produce external benefits. In the case of private schools, however, such external benefits are reduced if not nullified as a result of the spillovers arising from segregation. By drawing away students from the public schools on a decidedly nonrandom basis, private schools deny those students remaining in the public schools any peer effects their presence would have produced. While those remaining public school students have no 'right' to these peer effects, this loss certainly undermines the case for government subsidies to private schools.

NOTES

1. I am grateful to Jason DeRousie, Robert Malme, Meghan Poe and Jasmina Radeva for research assistance and to Angela Covert, Katherine O'Regan and Amy Ellen Schwartz for helpful discussions and comments on an earlier draft of the chapter.
2. In particular, see Netzer (1978, 1992).
3. Research on this issue is discussed below (pp.175–6).
4. This argument, made most prominently by Chubb and Moe (1990), is discussed below (pp.171).
5. For a more extensive exposition of this perspective and its implications for public economics, see Clotfelter (1993).
6. Indeed, the constitutionality of prayer in public schools has been a highly visible issue in recent court cases. See, for example, *Good News Club* v. *Milford Central School* (121 S.Ct. 2093 (2001)), in which the Supreme Court ruled that a school could allow a Christian club to use its facilities after hours.

7. Economists have discussed the advantages of collective action outside government in the literature on clubs. For a review of this literature, see Sandler and Tschirhart (1980).
8. See, for example, Kraushaar (1972, pp.253–4).
9. Catholic school enrollments in Table 7.2 are 61 per cent of all religiously-oriented school enrollments. According to estimates in Wright (1997, pp.418–19), Catholics accounted for 37 per cent of all members of religious faiths or denominations in the USA, based on 1995 figures.
10. Students in Baptist-related private schools were 7 per cent of all religiously-oriented school enrollment. Calculations based on figures in Wright (1997, pp.418–19).
11. Roper Center (2001), Gallup survey, January 2001, accession number 0376454, question 015.
12. Roper Center (1998, 1999, 2001), Public Agenda Foundation survey, September–October 1997, October–November 1998, November–December 2000, access (and question) numbers 0293717(005), 0324823(005), and 0379239(001).
13. See, for example, Evans and Schwab (1995).
14. Long and Toma (1988) suggest that income became less important during the 1970s, but I know no other studies to examine changes over time in the importance of income. For another study examining the importance of income, see Buddin *et al.* (1998).
15. For example, the segregation index for Athens, Georgia was 0.309, whereas the calculated index for the hypothetical scenario described in the text was 0.304. In general, the corresponding indices differ by small but variable amounts.
16. Specifically they based calculations on enrollment of students with family incomes above $20000 and those under $12000. Note that the use of national comparisons is not nearly so problematic with income as it is with race, owing to the considerably greater homogeneity of income distributions across regions.
17. The national PTA reports total membership of 6.5 million (www.pta.org, 2/14/02). This is to be compared to total K-12 enrollment in 2000 of some 53.3 million (U.S. Department of Education, 2001, p.11).
18. It is interesting to note that parents of higher socioeconomic status are more likely to attend PTA meetings, volunteer in the schools, or contact their children's schools to discuss academic matters (Horn and West, 1992).
19. Web sites describing these organizations are www.childrensaidsociety.org, visited 30 January 2002; www.albertgoliver.com, 4 February 2002; and www.cae-nyc.org, 30 January 2002.
20. Three other organizations providing similar services outside New York are Posse (www.possefoundation.org) 4 February 2002, and A Better Chance (http://abetterchance.org) 14 February 2002, which recruit and prepare minority students with the aim of enrolling them in selective colleges, and Citizen Schools (www.google.com/search?q=cache:kRI2J7sr-6UC:www.onechoice.com/citizenschools/) 4 February 2002, which joins small groups of students aged 9–14 with adult volunteers in practically oriented learning projects.
21. For a description of this sample, see Clotfelter (2002).
22. Examples of all-white organizations other than sports teams were: Fitness Club, Gaelic Club, Interact Club, Fellowship of Christian Athletes, Astronomy Club and Thespian Society. Examples of all-nonwhite organizations were: Black Action Student Association, La Nación Latina, Latino-American Club, Asian-American Club, Aframhis Club, Movimiento Estudiantil Chicano De Azlan, Hispanic Youth Leadership, Southeastern Consortium of Minority Engineers and Vocational Industrial Clubs of America.

REFERENCES

Abramowitz, Susan and E. Ann Stackhouse (1981), *The Private High School Today*, Washington, DC: National Institute of Education.

Betts, Julian R. and Robert W. Fairlie (2000), 'Does immigration induce "native flight" from public schools into private schools?', Public Policy Institute of California working paper, May.
Betts, Julian R. and Robert W. Fairlie (2001), 'Explaining ethnic, racial, and immigrant differences in private school attendance', *Journal of Urban Economics*, **50**, 26–51.
Bradford, David F., R.A. Malt and Wallace E. Oates (1969), 'The rising cost of local public services: some evidence and reflections', *National Tax Journal*, **22** (June), 185–202.
Buddin, Richard J., Joseph J. Cordes and Sheila Nataraj Kirby (1998), 'School choice in California: who chooses private schools?', *Journal of Urban Economics*, **44**, 110–34.
Chubb, John E. and Terry M. Moe (1990), *Politics, Markets, and America's Schools*, Washington, DC: Brookings Institution.
Clotfelter, Charles T. (1976), 'School desegregation, "tipping", and private school enrollment', *Journal of Human Resources*, **22** (Winter), 29–50.
Clotfelter, Charles T. (1993), 'The private life of public economics', *Southern Economic Journal*, **59** (April), 579–96.
Clotfelter, Charles T. (1999), 'Public school segregation in metropolitan areas', *Land Economics*, **75** (November), 487–504.
Clotfelter, Charles T. (2002), 'Interracial contact in high school extracurricular activities', *Urban Review*, **34** (March), 25–46.
Coleman, James S., Thomas Hoffer and Sally Kilgore (1982), *High School Achievement: Public, Catholic and Private Schools Compared*, New York: Basic Books.
Conlon, John R. and Mwangi S. Kimenyi (1991), 'Attitudes towards race and poverty in the demand for private education: the case of Mississippi', *Review of Black Political Economy*, **20**, 5–22.
Douglas, James (1987), 'Political theories of nonprofit organization', in Walter W. Powell (ed.), *The Nonprofit Sector*, New Haven: Yale University Press.
Evans, William and Robert Schwab (1995), 'Finishing high school and starting college: do Catholic schools make a difference?', *Quarterly Journal of Economics*, **110** (4), 941–74.
Fairlie, Robert W. and Alexandra M. Resch (2000), 'Is there "white flight" into private schools? Evidence from the National Educational Longitudinal Survey', unpublished paper, November.
Figlio, David and Jens Ludwig (2000), 'Sex, drugs and Catholic schools: private schooling and non-market adolescent behaviors', National Bureau of Economic Research working paper 7990, November.
Figlio, David N. and Joe A. Stone (2001), 'Can public policy affect private school cream skimming?', *Journal of Urban Economics*, **49**, 240–66.
Greene, Jay P., Joseph Giammo and Nicole Mellow (1999), 'The effect of private education on political participation, social capital and tolerance: an examination of the Latino National Political Survey', *Georgetown Public Policy Review*, **53** (Fall).
Grogger, Jeffrey and Derek Neal (2000), 'Further evidence on the effects of Catholic secondary schooling', in William G. Gale and Janet Rothenberg Pack (eds), *Brookings-Wharton Papers on Urban Affairs 2000*, Washington: Brookings Institution Press.
Horn, Laura and Jerry West (1992), 'A Profile of Parents of Eighth Graders', Department of Education, Washington, July.

Inner-City Scholarship Fund (2001), Advertisement in *New York Times*, 26 June, 2001, p.A9.

Kraushaar, Otto F. (1972), *American Nonpublic Schools: Patterns of Diversity*, Baltimore: Johns Hopkins University Press.

Lankford, Hamilton, E.S. Lee and James Wyckoff (1995), 'An analysis of elementary and secondary school choice', *Journal of Urban Economics*, **38**, 236–51.

Long, James E. and Eugenia F. Toma (1988), 'The determinants of private school attendance, 1970–1980', *Review of Economics and Statistics*, **70** (May), 351–7.

Neal, Derek (1997), 'The effects of Catholic secondary schooling on educational achievement', *Journal of Labor Economics*, **15** (1), 98–123.

Netzer, Dick (1978), *The Subsidized Muse*, New York: Cambridge University Press.

Netzer, Dick (1992), 'Arts and culture', in Charles T. Clotfelter (ed.), *Who Benefits from the Nonprofit Sector?*, Chicago: University of Chicago Press.

Sandler, Todd and John T. Tschirhart (1980), 'The economic theory of clubs: an evaluative survey', *Journal of Economic Literature*, **18** (December), 1481–521.

Tiebout, Charles (1956), 'A pure theory of local expenditures', *Journal of Political Economy*, **64** (1956), 416–24.

Tocqueville, Alexis de (1840), 'Of the use which Americans make of public associations in civil life' from *Democracy in America*, reprinted in David C. Hammack (ed.) (1998), *Making the Nonprofit Sector in the United States*, Bloomington: Indiana University Press.

U.S. Bureau of the Census (1999), 'School enrollment – social and economic characteristics of students, October 1998', *Current Population Reports*, Series P-20, no. 521, September, Washington: U.S. Government Printing Office.

U.S. Department of Education, National Center for Education Statistics (2000), *Digest of Education Statistics, 1999*, Washington: Government Printing Office.

U.S. Department of Education, National Center for Education Statistics (2001), *Digest of Education Statistics 2000*, Washington: Government Printing Office.

Weisbrod, Burton A. (1988), *The Nonprofit Economy*, Cambridge, MA: Harvard University Press.

Wright, John W. (ed.) (1997), *The New York Times Almanac*, 1998, New York: Penguin Putnam.

COMMENT

Katherine O'Regan

This chapter provides a very nice summary of a variety of literatures, each of which feeds into a particular aspect of the nonprofit sector in K-12 education. It is essentially a primer for anyone wishing to think seriously about the sector differences within education. The author takes his charge to be a broad one, considering not only the role of private schools, but also the implications of the existence of the range of voluntary activities and associations linked to schools.

Rather than summarize the entire chapter, I am going to focus on a final point made in the conclusion, one which is somewhat provocative. The author suggests that the negative effects on segregation associated with the existence of private schools be taken into account when assessing the case for tax subsidies of nonprofits. This is an interesting argument. It made me grapple much more seriously with the overall effects of private provision of education on the ability of local governments to provide services, an area in which Dick Netzer has worked extensively. A key contribution of the Clotfelter piece is the manner in which it connects and quickly reviews the distinct literatures needed to consider this issue.

To begin, I review the key themes in the chapter that lay the foundation for the author's point. Then I attempt to push the point a bit further to suggest some additional implications.

Private Schools and Public Education

The role of the sectors

Clotfelter does a nice job explicating the roles of the sectors. Several of the chapters in this volume consider the role of the public sector, whether and which services it should provide, including whether it should provide education. Here, the same issues are applied to the nonprofit sector.

The author summarizes a view of the nonprofit sector as a gap-filler (*à la* Weisbrod, 1988), one where the nonprofit sector allows pluralism to thrive. This arises from its capacity to meet a wider variety of wants in society than is possible through government alone. Nonprofit organizations fill the gaps in the demand for collective-type services, left over after the government responds to the median voter. 'Nonprofits such as private schools stand ready to perform the economic function of meeting diverse demands while also cultivating the pluralism so highly valued in the political realm' (Weisbrod, 1988, page 9).

A key point from this is that, by meeting these distinct 'niche' needs, nonprofits can aid in the functioning of society. Rather than depicting nonprofits as competing with government, their existence enhances the government's role.

Nature of the benefit

Much of the empirical work in the chapter can be seen as clarifying (and assessing) the most commonly cited benefits of private education. These potential benefits arise from the distinctiveness of the sector/schools in:

- the way they provide education (that is, religious nature, focus on discipline);
- who they serve, populations that look distinct, suggesting these are groups not otherwise served well by public provision;
- how well they serve; private schools certainly appear to be providing their students with benefits of equal if not greater size than public schools (although many weaknesses in the evidence are cited).

In some sense, this is really documenting whether there is evidence that private schools may be playing the supportive role discussed previously, and (while not stated as explicitly as this) if so, whether these benefits might be the source of justification for tax benefits.

Sorting

For these benefits to be realized requires sorting. Groups with similar desires must associate and get these common desires served – this is, by its nature, 'sorting'. By meeting the needs of distinct subgroups, the nonprofits provide diversity in the provision of goods, much as with the Tiebout mechanism, the benefits of which are experienced through sorting.

Segregation

The implications of sorting depend in part on the nature of the good. In the case of nonprofit provision of the arts (see Ladd, this volume), the sorting occurred over a good which supplements public provision, rather than replaces it. In essence, the existence of the supplementary good permitted individuals with different tastes to consume the same level of public provision and yet have their tastes met. Part of the policy significance in education comes from the exclusive nature of the consumption: students attend either public or private schools. And because the service has peer effects, individual decisions to use nonprofits will have efficiency and distributional implications, specifically related to the nonuniform nature of the sorting, from segregation.

This is the effect of nonprofits that leads to the author's comment in his conclusion concerning tax benefits. But he also notes a potentially ameliorative effect of private schools, on residential segregation. And it is these two forces on which I would like to focus, connecting them to the rest of the volume, thinking about housing choices, government provision of services and taxation.

Private Schools and Local Government

There seem to be three main avenues through which we would expect the use of nonprofit schools to clearly have an impact on local government provision of education. These are now addressed in turn.

Costs associated with 'flight'

The first avenue arises from households removing their children from the public school system and sending them to private schools. This is discussed at length in the paper, in terms of its affect on both racial and income segregation in schools. We need also to consider that this may affect the cost of providing public education, which in turn influences the ability of local government to provide a key public service. Given the existence of peer effects, and possible cost differentials, this directly affects the public school system in terms of performance. To the extent that parents play a role in supporting schools through their participation, it is also possible that there is a loss at the parent level.

But if households who are unhappy with the local public school system, or just their neighborhood's, 'opt out' through private schools, they may not 'opt out' of the jurisdiction, through moving. Here is where Clotfelter noted the potentially positive impact on residential segregation through private schools. By virtue of disentangling the composition of the school from the composition of the neighborhood, a potentially critical motivator in neighborhood segregation could be, if not removed, decreased.

In Gerald Gamm's *Urban Exodus* a very similar argument is developed, considering the connection between neighborhood-based institutions and population mobility. Gamm was examining the role of religious institutions, contrasting the Jewish synagogue (which is not neighborhood-based) to the Catholic church, where membership in a parish, including the ability to get married in a church and be buried in its cemetery, is determined by neighborhood residence. This difference was posited to play a role in the stability (possibly rigidity and segregation) of Irish Catholic neighborhoods in Boston, compared to its Jewish neighborhoods.

By disconnecting the composition of a key institution from the composition of a neighborhood, some of the motivation for residential segregation was removed. This is essentially the point made in Clotfelter, with respect to schools. Given the great importance of schools for families when choosing neighborhoods, the decreased motivation for segregation could be large.

Disconnecting residential location from school choice

This would be a second avenue through which private schools could affect local government. If their existence affects the sorting of households within one jurisdiction, or even across jurisdictions, households need not flee a city, for example, to acquire the type of education found in some suburban locations.

To think rather more systematically about this, I actually reviewed Dick Netzer's 1968 piece, on the roles of the various government sectors, in *Issues in Urban Economics*. A theme of that piece is that the fiscal fragmentation of metropolitan areas leads to suboptimal location and restricts the output of public services. In that context, an institutional arrangement that permits households to select a different educational package without moving appears to ease income and perhaps racial segregation pressure. Across jurisdictions, this may improve the ability of local governments to provide services.

However, thinking more about the mechanism that led to the spending and tax differentials discussed by Netzer, it seems to me that this second avenue would only *potentially* decrease residential segregation.

Residential choice and local fiscal packages

What disconnecting residence from schools certainly does is change the nature of housing and residential choices and, through that, has implications for local government spending and taxation, a third avenue. If a household's children are in private schools, this presumably lessens the effect of school quality and spending differentials on their choice of neighborhoods and jurisdiction. However it also likely changes such households' preferred spending package as regards school education and alters their tax sensitivity. The households who have been 'retained' will operate differently than they would have if their children were in the public school system. They are now picking neighborhoods and jurisdictions on the basis of different criteria. And they may well choose to live in a low-tax jurisdiction, not in the city.

Obviously how matters develop will depend on the nature of the options and the preferences, but the disentangling of schools from neighborhoods will not necessarily lead to a decrease in residential segregation – not if the schools are private and a household's consumption of education is independent of the jurisdiction's public school system. A priori, it is unclear in which direction the forces might operate.

But the existence of private schools has multiple avenues of influence when it disconnects the link between neighborhoods and schools. This is an area in which more systemic work is needed in the field. This may be particularly important when contrasting private schools with some of the other existing choice options, such as public choice systems and charter schools. For each of these alternatives, while choice of neighborhood residence could be disentangled from choice of school, the public financing connection between type of school attended and how residents vote remains. These options are not limited to whether funding is kept in the public school system, but for how residents make choices about neighborhoods, jurisdictions and voting.

REFERENCES

Gamm, Gerald (1999), *Urban Exodus: why the Jews left Boston and the Catholics stayed*, Cambridge, MA: Harvard University Press.

Netzer, Dick (1968), 'Federal, State and Local Finance in a Metropolitan Context', in Harvey Perloff and Lowdon Wingo (eds), *Issues in Urban Economics*, Baltimore, MD: The Johns Hopkins Press.

Weisbrod, Burton (1988), *The Nonprofit Economy*, Cambridge, MA: Harvard University Press.

8. The partially subsidized muse: estimating the value and incidence of public support received by nonprofit arts organizations

Joseph J. Cordes

INTRODUCTION

Publication of *The Subsidized Muse* in 1978 marked an important milestone in the application of economic analysis in several respects. It provided one of the first comprehensive treatments, not only of the economic magnitude of public support of the arts in the United States, but also of the policy issues raised by such support. Moreover, because nonprofit organizations play a major part in the production and distribution of artistic goods and services, the book was also among the first to offer a detailed economic analysis of one of the most visible and important parts of the nonprofit economy.[1]

A hallmark of the economist's approach to studying the arts is to remind (even unwilling) listeners of the marketplace's role in guiding the allocation of resources and talents to artistic endeavors generally, as well as among different types of artistic activity. It is thus fitting to note that the marketplace offers one tangible acknowledgment of the intellectual importance of Dick Netzer's contribution. Today, more than 20 years after its first release, the interested reader can order a newly reprinted copy of *The Subsidized Muse* which, like a well-loved musical performance or literary work, has been re-released as a 'classic' in public finance.[2]

Much has happened to public support of the arts since the late 1970s. Direct public support of the arts, which showed signs of becoming more generous when the *Muse* was written, has become embroiled in continual, often heated, public controversy about what control, if any, the state should wield over the content of publicly subsidized art. Budgetary and political pressures (in part related to public controversies) have caused the trajectory of direct public support to become less generous than one might have expected in the 1970s. Lastly, a series of changes in tax policy has affected the value of indirect tax subsidies for the arts, as may the recently enacted rollback of the estate tax, should it become permanent.

Enough has happened in the arts to warrant someone undertaking to write a sequel to *The Subsidized Muse*. This chapter has the considerably more modest objective of attempting to estimate the value of both direct and indirect subsidies received by nonprofit arts organizations, which, along with individual artists, are the heart of what most would regard as the arts sector in the USA.

To set the context for examining public subsidies to the arts, we first describe the economic scope of all enterprises (for-profit as well as not-for-profit) that produce artistic and/or entertainment goods and services. The focus then narrows to enterprises within this broad category that are engaged in the visual, performing and creative arts, and, within this group of arts providers, still further to nonprofit arts organizations.

We then summarize the main types of public subsidy that are received by nonprofit organizations, and discuss issues that arise in estimating the value of these subsidies to their recipients. Data on the financial characteristics of nonprofit arts organizations are then used to estimate the economic value and incidence of direct and indirect public subsidies received by nonprofit arts organizations. The chapter concludes with a brief discussion of the policy implications of the estimates.

ARTS PROVIDERS AND THE ROLE OF NONPROFIT ORGANIZATIONS

Figures 8.1 to 8.3 present estimates from the 1997 Economic Census of the relative economic importance of establishments engaged in providing arts among establishments generally engaged in providing arts, entertainment or recreation goods and services. Following Netzer, the definition of arts providers is broadened to include not only establishments included in the arts and entertainment North American Industrial Classification System (NAICS) category but also certain artistic activities in the information sector, which include 'cultural products . . . that directly express . . . artistic creativity . . . [including] popular, mass-produced, products as well as cultural products that normally have a more limited audience, such as poetry books, literary magazines, or classical records'.[3] Activities classified by NAICS as being in the information goods and services sector, that are treated as arts organizations, include production of motion pictures and phonograph records and tapes, as well as an estimate of the artistic share of production in sectors such as broadcasting, and book publishing and related literary activities.

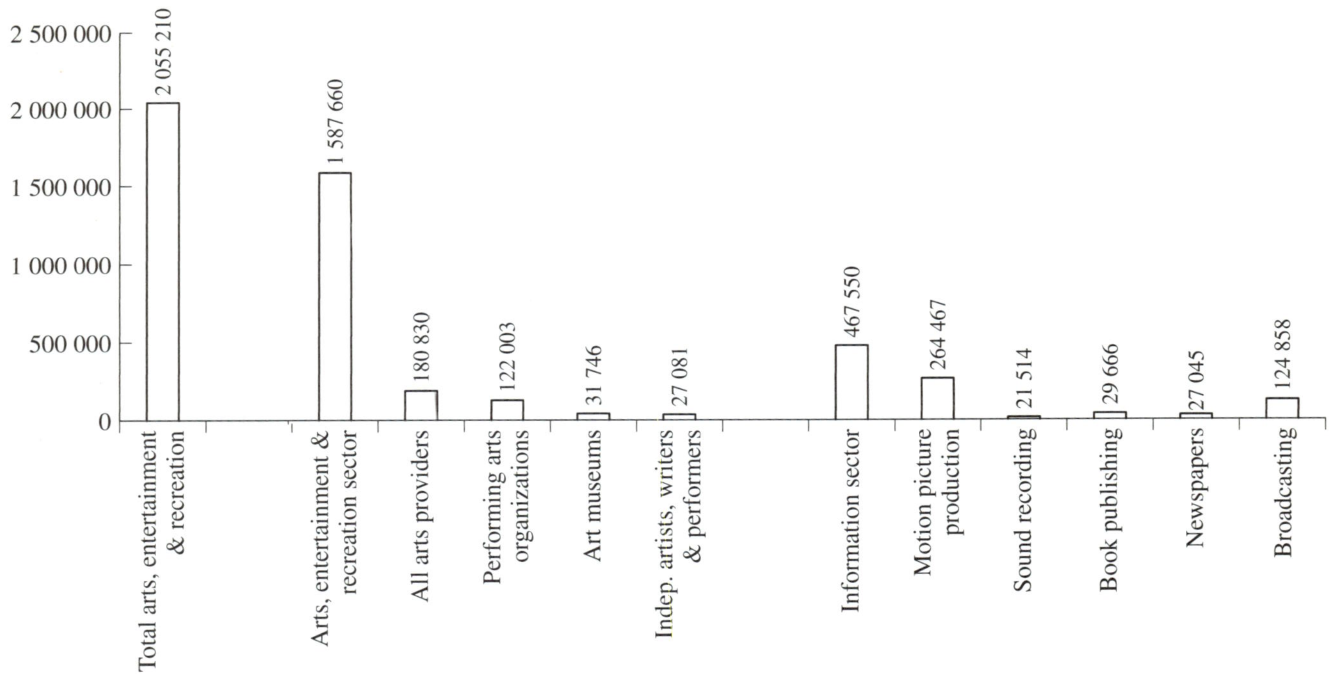

Figure 8.1 *Employment in arts, entertainment and recreation*

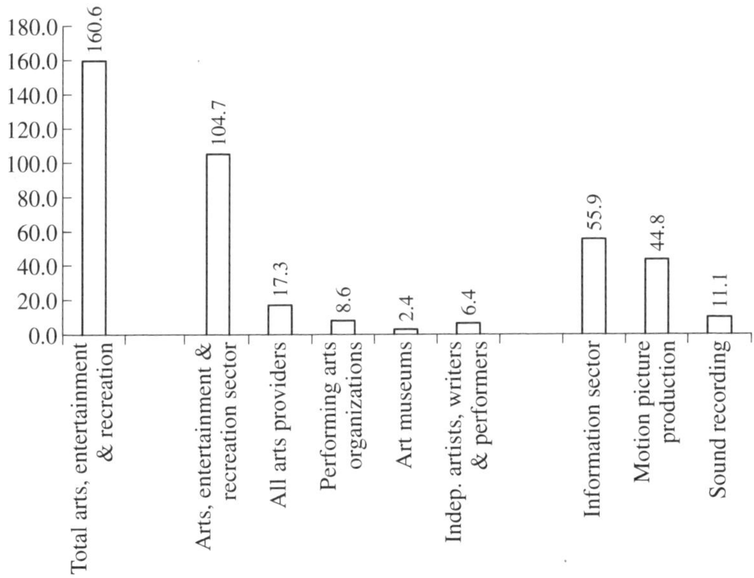

Figure 8.2 Receipts in arts, entertainment and recreation ($billion)

As may be seen from Figures 8.1 and 8.2, in 1997 establishments engaged in the production of arts, entertainment or recreation services employed just over 2 million workers and generated just over $160 billion in revenues. Establishments engaged in providing artistic goods and services in the arts, entertainment and recreations sectors (NAICS Code 71) or in the information sector (NAICS Code 51) together employed almost 650000 workers, and generated almost $75 billion in total revenue. Producers of what might be termed 'media-related' artistic goods and services accounted for the lion's share of both employment (467 thousand) and receipts ($56 billion) among arts providers generally, while those artistic activities that might traditionally be defined as 'high culture', such as drama, music and the visual arts (excluding motion picture production), account for considerably more modest shares of employment (180 thousand) and economic activity ($17 billion).

Figure 8.3 presents census data on the relative importance of nonprofit organizations in the various artistic pursuits, as measured by the share of establishments, employment, receipts and payroll. In this regard, it is noteworthy that the Census Bureau provides separate tabulations of tax-exempt and for-profit producers engaged in the production of the nonmedia-related arts, but not for artistic activities that are grouped in the information sector. This reflects the fact that nonprofit organizations play either a very small role in production (motion pictures, printing and publishing)[4] or no role (recording).

Nonprofit organizations do, however, play a significant role in the production of nonmedia-based arts. Overall, tax-exempt arts providers account for about a fifth of providers, employment, receipts and payroll among all arts providers. Moreover nonprofit providers dominate some forms of artistic endeavors such as arts museums and the musical performing arts, where tax-exempt providers account for between 70 per cent and almost 100 per cent of establishments, employment, receipts and payroll, and to a lesser extent theater companies where nonprofit providers account for over one-half of establishments and employment, and roughly two-fifths of receipts and payroll.

By and large, it is the group of organizations listed in Figure 8.3 that is eligible to receive either direct support from federal, state and local government, indirect support in the form of tax-deductible gifts from individuals or businesses, or that benefit from a variety of tax preferences given to organizations that are tax-exempt. These organizations, along with individual artists who may receive publicly financed grants, make up the 'subsidized Muses' in America today.

DIRECT PUBLIC SUPPORT

An enduring 'stylized fact' about government support of the arts in the United States is the paucity of direct government funding of the arts, in comparison with other developed economies. When *The Subsidized Muse* was published in 1978, the rapid growth in appropriations for the National Endowment of Arts seemed to indicate that perhaps the USA would move somewhat closer to funding patterns for the arts observed in other countries. Indeed, in the introductory chapter to *The Subsidized Muse*, Netzer observes:

> For a good many years, cosmopolitan Americans viewed as evidence of cultural barbarism the failure of the United States to provide as much public support of the arts and cultural institutions as a number of much poorer European countries. . . . From this perspective, we have joined the ranks of the civilized nations only in the last ten years or so.[5]

At the same time, Netzer also observed that, despite the substantial increase in direct public support that had occurred in the 1970s, the total amount of public arts subsidies, which was roughly $300 million in 1975, was an amount that 'most people in the world of the arts [would] agree [was] a very small – even scandalously small – amount'.

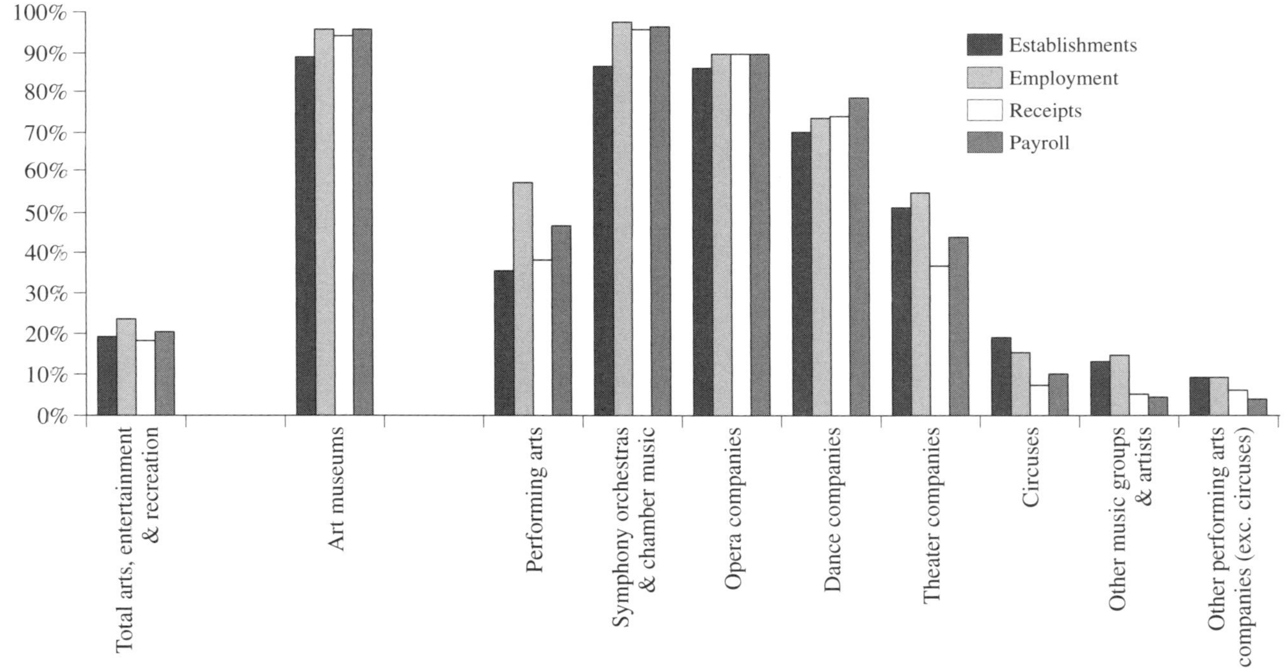

Figure 8.3 Role of nonprofit organizations in arts provision

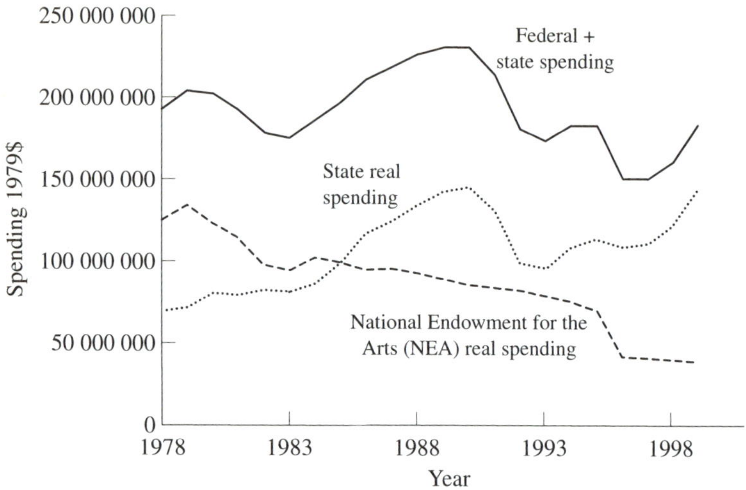

Figure 8.4 Real federal and state arts spending

Federal and state funding

Figures 8.4 and 8.5, which are based on data compiled by the National Assembly of State Arts Agencies, show that, if the amount of direct public subsidy was regarded as small by advocates of more direct government support for the arts, it would be regarded as still austere today (National Assembly of State Arts Agencies, 2001). Since the increase in federal arts funding in the 1970s, real federal spending on the arts has fallen steadily since 1980 to a point where federal spending on the arts in 1999 is (roughly) comparable in real terms to what it was in the early 1970s.

State arts funding fared somewhat better than federal arts funding, and since the mid-1980s has exceeded federal arts support. Despite increases in state arts funding from the mid-1980s to the mid-1990s, however, combined federal and state funding for the arts had fallen in real terms by just under $10 billion in the 20-year period from 1978 to 1999.

Local Funding

As Netzer has noted, federal and state spending does not include local government funding of arts organizations. Unfortunately, however, although data on federal and state arts funding are much more readily available than in 1979, systematic data on local government spending for the arts remain hard to come by. It is, therefore, not possible to discern directly any trends

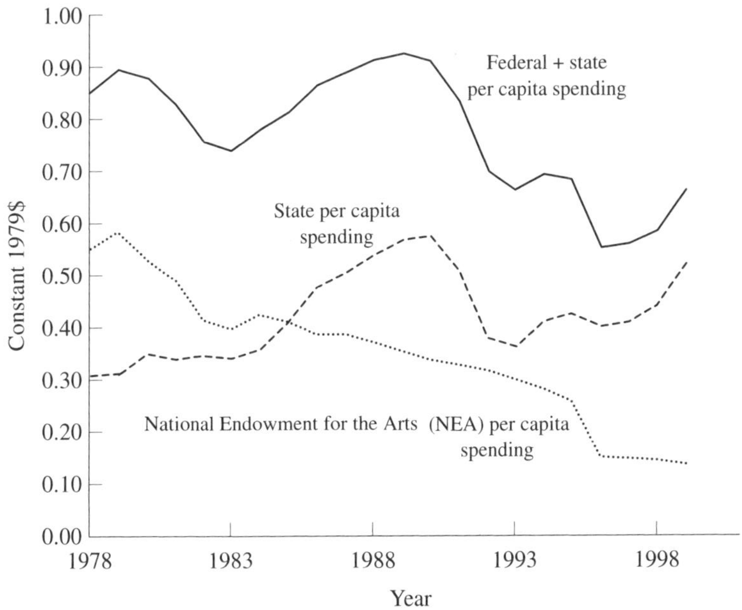

Figure 8.5 Real per capita government arts spending

over time in local arts funding. There is, however, indirect evidence that this component of government arts funding has increased over time.

Nezter's estimate of local arts spending in *The Subsidized Muse* indicated that, in the 1970s, local arts spending was roughly comparable in magnitude to total state spending on the arts. More recent estimates in *Giving USA* (AAFRC Trust for Philanthropy, 2000), however, suggest that local arts spending in 1999 may be as much as two to three times as large as state spending. If one uses these more recent ratios to estimate the local component of arts spending in 1999, total direct public subsidies to the arts would equal some $500 million in 1979 dollars, a 40 per cent increase in the estimated total figure of $300 million in direct government arts spending reported by Netzer in *The Subsidized Muse* for the year 1975. Most of the increase would appear to be due to greater local and, to a lesser extent, state funding for the arts. These estimates are consistent with Throsby's observation that government arts spending has shifted away from the center (Throsby, 1994).

The Importance of Direct Public Support to Arts Organizations

The data shown in Figures 8.4 and 8.5 reflect the budgetary cost of arts subsidies, but do not measure the financial importance of direct public subsidies to individual arts organizations. Constructing such a measure requires that one have estimates of the amounts of direct financial support received by arts organizations.

THE NCCS GUIDESTAR DATABASE OF IRS FORM 990 TAX RETURNS

New data, complied by the Urban Institute's National Center on Charitable Statistics (NCCS), in collaboration with the Internal Revenue Service (IRS), and Philanthropic Research Institute Guidestar (PRI) make it possible to obtain such estimates. It is worth digressing briefly to discuss the source and general reliability of these data because they are used to estimate the value, not only of direct, but also indirect, arts subsidies.

Each year, all nonprofit organizations with gross revenues of at least $25 000 are required to file the IRS Form 990 which is an information tax return. Organizations that file the 990 return are required to report total amounts and sources of revenue and expense. For the purposes of this study, sources of revenue that are reported include (1) direct contributions received from government sources, (2) charitable contributions received from private individuals, businesses and foundations, and (3) income earned from investments and the conduct of commercial activities.

NCCS, working with the IRS and PRI, has created an electronic file of all IRS 990 returns filed for the tax year 1999. This file, hereafter referred to as the NCCS/PRI file, includes 990 returns filed by over 7000 arts organizations, and has the potential to provide comprehensive data on different sources of revenue, including those which provide either direct or indirect subsidies to nonprofit arts organizations.

Some scholars, however, have raised concerns about the reliability of information reported on the 990 return because, unlike tax returns filed by for-profit enterprises, items reported on the IRS 990 have no financial consequences for an organization. The general reliability of data from the IRS 990 return is examined by Froelich, Knoepfle and Pollak, who compare information reported by a sample of 350 nonprofits on their IRS 990 returns with financial information reported by these same organizations on their audited financial statements (Froelich *et al.*, 2001).

The overall conclusion of the analysis by Froelich *et al.* is that amounts reported for items such as total revenue and total expenses reported on the IRS 990 return are highly consistent with those reported on the audited financial statements. Amounts reported on the IRS 990 for items such as total contributions are somewhat less (but still reasonably) consistent with amounts for the same item reported on the audited financial statement.

Froelich *et al.* did, however, find more discrepancies between information reported on the IRS 990 and audited financial statement among arts organizations than among all nonprofits. Even in this case, however, in 1994, over half of arts organizations in the sample reported total contributions on the IRS 990 that were within 10 per cent of contributions reported on their audited financial statements, and three-quarters reported amounts that differed by 25 per cent or less.

On one hand, these numbers suggest that amounts reported on the IRS 990 by some arts organizations may be measured with error. On the other hand, given the large numbers of organizations included in the NCCS/PRI file, it seems likely that such errors would average out, producing unbiased estimates of average amounts of direct and indirect subsidy. Moreover, measurement errors aside, the fact that arts providers are required to report contributions received from all sources, including federal, state and local governments, as well as private contributions, combined with the size and scope of the NCCS/PRI file, provides a hitherto unavailable opportunity to gauge the combined impact of direct and indirect government subsidies received by a wide swath of arts providers engaged in a broad range of artistic activities.

Estimates of Direct Public Support

Table 8.1 provides tabulations of government contributions and grants received from all levels of government, reported by more than 7000 nonprofit arts organizations in the NCCS/PRI file for the year 1999. A description of the types of arts organizations included in the analysis is provided in the appendix to this chapter. Overall these organizations reported receiving just over $1 billion in government contributions and grants aid in 1999 dollars, or about $450 million in 1979 dollars, which is close to the estimate of total government arts spending presented above.

On one hand, the data in Table 8.1 suggest that the overall level of financial support received by arts organizations from government ranges from nonexistent to modest: more than half of all arts organizations reported receiving no government contributions or grants; three out of four arts organizations reported receiving amounts of less than $30 000 in government funding and, for three out of four arts organizations, government contributions and grants accounted for 8 per cent or less of revenue from all sources. On the other hand, the data also indicate that the distribution and financial importance of public support for the arts varies with the type of artistic activity. For example, government support does account for 9 per cent or more of all revenue received by nonprofit film and/or television producers, art museums, visual arts and performing arts organizations. In

Table 8.1 Amount and relative importance of direct government support of the arts

	Number of organizations	Percentage reporting government grants	Amount of government grants reported on IRS Form 990 ($)				Government grants as percentage of total revenue			
			Mean	Median	Upper quartile	Upper decile	Mean	Median	Upper quartile	Upper decile
All organizations	7342	46.0	141738	0	28170	143519	7.9	0.0	7.9	24.7
Media and communications	281	21.7	1107689	0	0	190189	6.5	0.0	0.0	22.4
Film & TV	520	43.1	239920	0	135861	661450	15.8	0.0	20.3	64.9
Publishing	488	15.6	32265	0	0	31060	4.5	0.0	0.0	11.8
Radio	233	30.9	179759	0	27810	163552	8.8	0.0	7.9	28.3
Visual arts	185	45.9	29341	0	29962	97071	9.2	0.0	10.9	28.4
Museums (multipurpose)	845	36.8	100699	0	26370	151725	10.2	0.0	8.8	43.0
Art museums	387	62.0	416603	14600	139021	439650	9.3	2.6	11.8	31.0
Performing arts	703	51.4	127167	1570	38111	134324	9.2	0.5	10.2	30.1
Dance companies	486	58.4	54686	7700	32575	133026	8.0	2.5	10.0	23.3
Theaters	1381	52.9	63605	2000	30480	120830	7.3	1.0	8.4	22.2
Music not elsewhere classified	408	42.4	44480	0	12894	41400	5.2	0.0	6.9	15.6
Orchestras	553	60.6	82502	7616	32700	118567	5.7	2.5	6.7	14.2
Opera companies	203	57.6	76070	7500	60213	220156	5.2	2.1	6.2	14.5
Choral groups	281	44.8	13056	0	9418	26426	4.3	0.0	5.5	11.7
Bands not elsewhere classified	142	35.9	17028	0	7500	36500	5.0	0.0	4.6	14.9
Music schools	204	37.7	17131	0	16625	60400	4.2	0.0	2.7	14.5
Arts not elsewhere classified	42	52.4	62598	7529	18850	54743	11.9	1.1	17.7	35.2

Source: NCCS/PRI digitized database of IRS Form 990 returns.

addition, one out of ten nonprofit arts organizations reported government contributions and grants that represented a quarter or more of all revenue received.

Table 8.2 shows how direct government support is distributed among arts organizations by their age and size. The patterns are somewhat mixed. New arts organizations are less likely to receive any form of government support than are more established organizations, but, among organizations that receive government support, direct government support is significantly more important among organizations that are five years or younger. The likelihood of receiving public support also increases with organization size, but, among organizations that receive government funding, the importance of such funding does not seem to vary systematically with size. (The results of descriptive regressions not reported here indicate that the general relationships shown in Table 8.2 persist after one has controlled for the type of arts organization.)

Indirect Public Support

A majority of arts organizations receive little or no direct government support, but almost all benefit from a range of tax policies that have the effect of increasing the financial resources available to nonprofit arts providers. Indeed substantial reliance on indirect government support for the arts through a variety of tax incentives and exemptions, instead of direct support, is seen to be one of the defining features of 'American-style', as distinguished from 'European-style', arts policy.[6]

Tax Deductions for Charitable Gifts

The most visible forms of indirect support for the arts are provisions in the individual and corporate income tax that allow private donors to deduct contributions made to charitable nonprofit organizations, including those engaged in providing arts and culture. The federal estate tax also allows bequests made to charities to be deducted against estate tax liabilities, although the value of the estate tax deduction is scheduled to decline steadily over the next ten years, and to disappear altogether if the estate tax is repealed, as currently contemplated in the Economic Growth and Tax Relief Reconciliation Act of 2001.

Price Incentives to Give

Allowing charitable contributions to be deducted effectively reduces the out-of-pocket cost of supporting nonprofit organizations by an amount

Table 8.2 *Amount and relative importance of direct government support of the arts, by age and size*

	Number of organizations	Percentage reporting government grants	Amount of government grants reported on IRS Form 990 ($)				Government grants as percentage of total revenue			
			Mean	Median	Upper quartile	Upper decile	Mean	Median	Upper quartile	Upper decile
All organizations										
Organization age										
Five years or less	856	30.4	70 197	0	5 860	57 863	8.2	0.0	4.1	29.7
More than five years	6486	47.6	171 408	0	34 019	163 552	7.9	0.0	8.3	24.5
Organization size ($assets)										
Less than or equal 100 000	2 749	42.4	14 040	0	12 000	37 815	8.2	0.0	8.8	25.9
100 000 to 500 000	2 261	42.7	30 839	0	23 400	82 731	7.9	0.0	7.5	23.9
500 000 to 1 000 000	695	42.2	55 528	0	41 795	160 214	7.9	0.0	6.6	26.3
1 000 000 to 5 000 000	981	51.8	166 967	5 000	108 361	416 655	8.3	0.5	8.7	27.6
More than 5 000 000	656	62.7	1 113 852	73 953	420 207	1 536 389	6.7	1.6	6.9	20.6
Organizations with govt grants										
Organization age										
Five years or less	260	N.A.	231 110	27 390	99 874	294 038	27.1	16.6	41.6	77.7
More than five years	3085	N.A.	317 846	35 448	123 002	398 838	16.6	9.0	20.8	43.4
Organization size ($assets)										
Less than or equal 100 000	1 166	N.A.	33 101	16 000	35 600	785 871	19.3	11.0	24.5	49.0
100 000 to 500 000	966	N.A.	72 181	31 625	96 975	167 438	18.4	9.5	22.7	49.5
500 000 to 1 000 000	293	N.A.	131 714	58 857	152 600	340 026	18.7	9.1	22.5	52.5
1 000 000 to 5 000 000	509	N.A.	320 313	99 748	292 650	775 000	16.0	8.2	20.6	45.0
More than 5 000 000	411	N.A.	1 777 827	291 328	798 260	2 427 691	10.9	4.9	12.2	28.7

Source: NCCS/PRI digitized database of IRS Form 990 returns.

that depends on the donor's tax rate. For example, in the case of cash gifts made to a charity, if the donor's tax rate was 25 per cent, allowing a tax deduction for the gift cuts the net cost of contributing from one dollar to 75 cents, because the taxpayer receives a tax deduction that saves 25 cents in tax for every dollar contributed.[7] Similarly, if the estate tax rate was 50 per cent, allowing charitable bequests to be deducted means that to bequeath a dollar to a charity comes at a cost of only 50 cents to other beneficiaries (that is, family and other heirs of the estate).[8]

If the gift takes the form of appreciated property instead of cash, the out-of-pocket costs of giving will be reduced not only by the income tax deduction of the (full) value of the property but also by the capital gains tax that would otherwise have been paid had the donated property instead been sold. As a result, a donor facing a 25 per cent tax rate on income, and a 20 per cent tax rate on capital gains, could find the after-tax cost of giving one dollar of appreciated property cut to as little as 55 cents.[9]

Budgetary Cost of Tax-deductible Contributions

What is the economic significance of tax incentives for giving to arts organizations? Each year, the Joint Committee on Taxation estimates the cost to the Treasury, in terms of forgone tax revenue, of allowing individuals and corporations to make tax-deductible charitable contributions. The estimated value of tax expenditures in 1999 for charitable contributions other than for 'education and health' – the broad category that includes charitable deductions for corporate and individual contributions to the arts – was just under $21 billion. Using data published in *Giving USA* (2000), one can infer that contributions to arts organizations comprise on the order of 5 per cent of all individual and corporate contributions. If this percentage is applied to the aggregate tax expenditure estimate of $21 billion, the estimated federal budgetary cost tax for tax incentives for giving to the arts would be on the order of $1 billion.

In addition, tabulations of estate tax returns filed in 1995 indicate that arts and culture organizations were the recipients of $272 million in bequests.[10] Data on the distribution of these bequests by the size of the taxable estate imply that, had these gifts been taxed, they would have been subject to an estate tax rate of roughly 40 per cent, implying an additional federal budgetary cost of just under $110 billion.

Thus the federal budgetary cost in 1999 of tax incentives for giving to the arts is estimated to have been roughly $1.1 billion. Since state governments generally also allow individuals and corporations to claim deductions for charitable contributions, the total budgetary cost of charitable tax incentives would be greater than this amount. A very crude estimate is that the total state budgetary cost of tax incentives for giving to the arts might be perhaps 17 per cent of the total federal cost. Applying this factor to the total estimated federal budgetary cost results in a total estimated budgetary cost of $1.3 billion.[11]

Economic Importance of Tax Incentives to Arts Organizations

From the perspective of nonprofit arts organizations, what matters, however, is not the budgetary cost of tax incentives for charitable deductions, but rather the importance of charitable contributions as a financial resource, and how much additional giving is encouraged by these tax incentives.

Of particular importance is the amount of added giving that is stimulated by the charitable deduction which may or may not equal the budgetary cost of tax incentives for giving. The key factor is the *price elasticity of giving to the arts*. Broadly speaking, if this price elasticity is 1.0 or higher (in absolute value) the effective subsidy received by arts organizations from tax-deductible contributions would equal or exceed the actual budgetary cost of the subsidy. If the price elasticity of arts giving is lower, however, the budgetary cost would overstate the effective subsidy received by arts organizations.

Price elasticity of individual giving[12]

There is general agreement among researchers who have examined charitable giving that people will give more when the cost of giving falls. Indeed, until the 1990s, there also seemed to be an empirical consensus that charitable giving was rather sensitive to price. This earlier consensus, however, was challenged, both by the response of taxpayers to tax reform, which had the effect of increasing the cost of giving, and by the results of new empirical research that was able to draw on better data on variation in individual tax rates.

The first generation of statistical studies of private giving, conducted in the 1970s, generally found that the price elasticity of giving was equal to or greater than one (in absolute value), in some cases significantly so. The implication was that giving was fairly sensitive to the after-tax cost of giving and that changes in tax rates that raised or lowered the cost of giving could significantly affect the amount of charitable contributions.

Yet tax rate cuts enacted in the 1980s raised questions about the magnitude of these estimates. The Tax Reform Act of 1986 increased the after-tax cost of giving, often significantly. There were concerns that, if private giving was as sensitive to cost as implied by the existing research, lower tax rates – which meant higher after-tax costs of giving – would cause private giving to fall by an appreciable amount. The predicted drop in giving, however, did not materialize. With the exception of taxpayers in the highest income tax brackets, charitable giving remained quite stable. The implication was that giving may not be as sensitive to price incentives as indicated by some econometric models.

What might account for the discrepancy between the observed response of taxpayers and the predictions of statistical models? One explanation is that early studies were prone to overstate the 'long-run' price responsiveness of giving because these studies were forced to use data that reflected responses to temporary as well as permanent changes in the after-tax cost of giving. For example, a taxpayer who faces a higher than usual tax rate in a particular year might also be prompted to give more than the usual amount in that year (indeed, he or she could be advised to do so by a tax planner) because the cost of giving was temporarily low. A taxpayer's income in such a year is also likely to be higher than usual, which would further encourage giving. The implication is that the observed reaction of a taxpayer to a temporary drop in the cost of giving might overstate the change that would be prompted by a more permanent drop in the cost of giving. An opposite pattern of responses would be expected in a year in which a taxpayer's income and tax rate were lower than usual. In any given year, a sample of tax returns will likely include a number of taxpayers whose observed tax rates are temporarily higher or lower than usual.

In the 1980s and 1990s, improved data have made it possible to distinguish better between temporary and permanent changes in the cost of giving. As expected, researchers using these data have generally found that annual giving is less responsive to permanent than to temporary tax changes. Indeed the results of several recent studies suggest that the overall 'average' price elasticity of giving, among all taxpayers and all types of giving, may be less than one, perhaps closer to −0.40.

Price elasticity of individual giving to the arts

The above results could be interpreted to mean that the price elasticity of giving to the arts is less than unity, with the implication that the effective subsidy received by arts organizations from the ability to receive tax deductible contributions is less than the budgetary cost to federal and state governments. A good case can be made, however, that even if the overall price elasticity of charitable contributions is less than unity, the price elasticity of charitable giving to the arts may nonetheless be large enough for the budgetary cost to be a good approximation of the effective subsidy value to arts organizations.

The case rests on several considerations. One is that researchers have found that the price sensitivity of giving varies with the type of giving, and that the price sensitivity of giving to arts organizations is likely to be higher than for other forms of charity (Clotfelter, 1991). For example, the discussion in Fullerton implies that the price elasticity of giving to the arts could plausibly be assumed to be higher than 2.0 (Fullerton, 1991).

Researchers have also found that the price sensitivity of giving increases with the income level of the giver, and there is evidence that charitable contributions to the arts tend to be concentrated among higher income taxpayers. For example, data from the *Statistics of Income Bulletin*, combined with simulations presented in Fullerton, suggest that, in 1998, the average dollar of contributions to the arts was deducted at a weighted average marginal tax rate of 33 per cent, rather than at 28 per cent or 15 per cent (Eller, 1999; Fullerton, 1991). Thus, donors to arts organizations face a somewhat stronger financial incentive to give than do donors to other forms of charity; estimates in Clotfelter and Steuerle imply that the price sensitivity varies with the taxpayer's marginal tax rate, and that it was on the order of 1.5 for high-income givers (Clotfelter and Steuerle, 1981).

Price sensitivity of corporate and estate giving

There is considerably less information on the price sensitivity of giving to the arts by corporations and from estates. Evidence on the price elasticity of giving by corporations suggests that the price elasticity of corporate giving to all forms of charity may range from 0.40 to 1.1, while evidence on giving from estates suggests that the price elasticity of bequests to arts organizations ranges from approximately 0.20 to 0.50.[13]

The Financial Importance of Charitable Contributions

Data on revenues received by nonprofit arts organizations indicate the potential value of the indirect subsidy that these organizations receive from the ability to receive tax-deductible contributions. These data are shown in Tables 8.3 and 8.4 which show the amount of contributions from all private sources received by the nonprofit arts organizations in the NCCS file. Roughly two-thirds of these contributions represent gifts from individuals or corporations, while the other third represents contributions that come from private foundations.[14]

Overall, the organizations reported receiving more than $4 billion in private contributions, or more than four times the reported amount received in direct government aid. Just as the data in Tables 8.1 and 8.2 provide evidence of relatively limited direct government support for the arts, Tables 8.3 and 8.4 show that private contributions are an important source of financial support for many arts organizations: more than nine out of ten arts organizations reported receiving at least some private support;

Table 8.3 Amount and relative importance of private contributions to the arts

	Number of organizations	Percentage reporting private gifts	Amount of private contributions reported on IRS Form 990 ($)				Private contributions as percentage of total revenue			
			Mean	Median	Lower quartile	Upper quartile	Mean	Median	Lower quartile	Upper quartile
All organizations	7322	92.3	599762	71365	17327	244424	38.7	33.6	11.6	61.1
Media and communications	280	88.9	1459308	171086	42596	518382	58.5	66.8	21.0	94.4
Film & TV	520	85.1	1403630	128017	13621	572851	44.7	42.2	5.1	80.2
Publishing	488	80.7	296403	54220	1563	207258	38.1	25.6	1.3	74.6
Radio	232	93.5	693179	176010	53117	479065	60.1	69.7	30.0	92.8
Visual arts	185	87.0	308056	62500	5025	160320	34.5	26.6	4.2	60.3
Museums (multipurpose)	843	96.2	440378	82959	24255	285050	46.5	44.2	17.9	74.9
Art museums	384	95.1	2201810	180494	45394	879658	45.1	45.6	23.4	66.8
Performing arts	699	90.7	478920	61119	15584	197303	35.9	29.2	9.9	58.9
Dance companies	484	95.7	339307	46529	11756	160133	30.3	25.9	8.9	47.2
Theaters	1378	94.9	271144	53699	16220	166004	30.6	23.8	10.2	46.1
Music not elsewhere classified	407	90.2	269097	48112	11830	121843	35.5	31.8	9.8	56.3
Orchestras	553	97.3	755206	122794	54563	348664	43.1	42.8	29.2	57.4
Opera companies	201	96.5	794500	150863	34021	737030	40.8	41.3	22.1	56.8
Choral groups	280	97.1	97100	41724	14658	92984	33.1	29.1	13.1	47.5
Bands not elsewhere classified	142	83.1	155937	25053	2545	103485	29.8	22.1	2.4	48.2
Music schools	204	90.2	278082	41030	6935	144852	21.2	13.0	3.4	32.9
Arts not elsewhere classified	42	97.6	196448	48522	15557	147643	36.9	32.5	6.7	63.3

Source: NCCS/PRI digitized database of IRS Form 990 returns.

Table 8.4 Amount and relative importance of private contributions to the arts, by age and size

	Number of organizations	Percentage reporting private gifts	Amount of private contributions reported on IRS Form 990 ($)				Private contributions as percentage of total revenue			
			Mean	Median	Lower quartile	Upper quartile	Mean	Median	Lower quartile	Upper quartile
All organizations										
Organization age										
Five years or less	867	90.4	373008	54198	12000	162765	46.9	41.8	12.1	84.9
More than five years	6475	92.6	629424	73757	18350	259713	37.6	32.9	11.5	58.7
Organization size ($assets)										
Less than 100000	2737	90.6	64261	32915	8000	79732	35.7	28.1	7.9	57.0
100000 to 500000	2258	92.3	146357	72516	18217	187901	38.7	33.2	11.6	62.1
500000 to 1000000	695	93.4	301420	133572	29936	408219	41.6	38.6	13.1	64.4
1000000 to 5000000	978	94.2	687119	352043	101388	959752	42.8	40.8	18.5	64.7
More than 5000000	654	95.2	4592685	1510343	367057	4466663	41.3	38.9	20.0	61.7

Source: NCCS/PRI digitized database of IRS Form 990 returns.

private contributions made up at least one-third of all revenue for one out of every two arts organizations and at least three-fifths of all revenue for one out of four organizations. The data also indicate that the distribution and financial importance of private support for the arts varies with the type of artistic activity, ranging from three-fifths of revenue received by non-profit radio producers to just over one-fifth of revenue received by non-profit music schools.

Table 8.4 shows how direct public support is distributed among arts organizations by their age and size. The data indicate that new arts organizations are almost as likely to receive private contributions as their more established counterparts, but rely more on such contributions as a source of revenue. The importance of private contributions also generally increases somewhat with organization size. (These relationships continue to hold when one controls statistically for the type of arts organization.)

The data in Tables 8.3 and 8.4 measure the importance of private contributions as a source of support for arts organizations, but do not measure the effective amount of subsidy received by these organizations. This amount, which is shown in Tables 8.5 and 8.6, is defined to be the additional contributions received by an organization as a result of its ability to receive tax-deductible charitable contributions.

The estimates of the effective tax subsidy value shown in Tables 8.5 and 8.6 were obtained in several steps. First, because the total amount of private contributions includes contributions from nontaxable private foundations, the amount of total private contributions received by each organization was multiplied by two-thirds to estimate the amount of contributions that could reasonably be attributed to taxable individuals, corporations or estates. The resulting amount was then apportioned into estimated amounts contributed by individuals (86 per cent), corporations (5 per cent) and estates (9 per cent), using data on corporate and individual giving from the Joint Committee on Taxation and the Internal Revenue Service.

The budgetary cost of each component was then estimated by applying an estimated marginal tax rate to the three components of private giving. In the case of individual contributions, the marginal tax rate equaled 33 per cent plus the top marginal income tax rate of the state in which the non-profit organizations was located provided that deductions against state income for charitable contributions were allowed.[15] In the case of corporate contributions, the marginal tax rate equaled the federal corporate tax rate of 34 per cent plus an assumed 6 per cent average tax rate for state corporate income taxes. In the case of the contributions from estates, the applicable marginal federal estate tax rate was assumed to equal 45 per cent.

The last step in the process was to estimate the portion of the budgetary

Table 8.5 Amount and relative importance of tax incentives for private contributions to the arts

	Number of organizations	Tax expenditure value of charitable tax deductions ($)				Tax expenditure as percentage of total revenue			
		Mean	Median	Lower quartile	Upper quartile	Mean	Median	Lower quartile	Upper quartile
All organizations	7322	140412	16521	3971	56836	9.0	7.7	2.7	14.3
Media and communications	280	331773	39223	10209	126371	13.7	15.8	4.9	20.7
Film & TV	520	335285	29156	3067	134925	10.6	9.9	1.2	1.9
Publishing	488	70530	12590	372	47731	9.0	5.8	0.3	17.2
Radio	232	167741	39399	11863	104984	13.9	16.1	7.0	20.5
Visual arts	185	76488	13104	1245	39286	8.1	5.6	1.0	14.2
Museums (multipurpose)	843	102472	19518	5766	63512	10.8	10.2	4.0	17.1
Art museums	384	521189	42461	9613	205295	10.5	10.4	5.3	15.6
Performing arts	699	111892	14118	3555	45610	8.4	6.9	2.2	13.5
Dance companies	484	78646	10752	2827	38877	7.1	6.1	2.1	10.5
Theaters	1378	63028	12474	3718	39040	7.2	5.5	2.4	10.8
Music not elsewhere classified	407	59915	11035	2926	28759	8.2	7.3	2.4	12.8
Orchestras	553	172261	28541	12875	86326	10.0	9.8	6.4	13.2
Opera companies	201	184360	36669	8092	168745	9.6	9.4	5.2	13.7
Choral groups	280	22599	9102	3,424	22331	7.6	6.7	3.0	11.0
Bands not elsewhere classified	142	38150	5692	614	25514	7.0	5.2	0.5	10.8
Music schools	204	65631	9432	1494	34787	5.0	3.0	0.8	7.6
Arts not elsewhere classified	42	46349	10057	4294	35990	8.7	7.3	1.7	13.1

Source: NCCS/PRI digitized database of IRS Form 990 returns.

Table 8.6 Amount and relative importance of tax incentives for private contributions to the arts, by age and size

	Number of organizations	Estimated tax expenditure value of charitable deductions ($)				Tax expenditure as percentage of total revenue			
		Mean	Median	Lower quartile	Upper quartile	Mean	Median	Lower quartile	Upper quartile
All organizations									
Organization age									
Five years or less	847	88001	12820	2802	38235	11.1	9.8	2.8	19.4
More than five years	6475	147268	17051	4188	60802	8.7	7.5	2.6	13.7
Organization size ($assets)									
Less than 100000	2737	15015	7655	1825	18274	8.4	6.5	1.9	13.2
100000 to 500000	2258	34258	16938	4156	43259	9.0	7.7	2.6	14.4
500000 to 1000000	695	70823	31286	7020	94151	9.7	8.8	3.0	15.1
1000000 to 5000000	978	162060	82220	23562	218285	10.0	9.7	4.3	15.2
More than 5000000	654	1073291	341757	80076	1024809	9.6	8.6	4.4	14.2

Source: NCCS/PRi digitized database of IRS Form 990 returns.

cost that constituted an effective subsidy to the arts organization. Drawing on the above discussion of the price elasticity of giving, the effective subsidy attributable to individual contributions was assumed to equal 100 per cent of the budgetary cost of allowing tax-deductible individual contributions, reflecting an assumption that the individual price elasticity of giving to the arts is (at least) unity. Similarly, because the evidence indicates that the price elasticity of corporate and estate giving is less than unity, the effective subsidies from corporate contributions and bequests from estates were assumed to be 75 per cent and 30 per cent, respectively, of the estimated budgetary cost.

As may be seen by comparing the estimates in Table 8.5 with those in Table 8.1, the overall average effective subsidy that nonprofit organizations receive from tax-deductible charitable contributions ($140 thousand) is roughly the same as the average direct government subsidy ($141 thousand). But, as may be seen by comparing the *distribution* of the estimated effective subsidies with the distribution of government grants, the effective subsidies that are provided by tax-deductible contributions benefit a wider range of nonprofit organizations than do direct subsidies from government grants. This can be seen by comparing median, lower and upper quartile values in Table 8.5 with those in Table 8.1.[16] Table 8.6 indicates that the effective subsidy rate (the ratio of the effective subsidy to nonprofit organization revenues) is higher for new arts organizations than it is for established organizations, and increases weakly with organization size.

Tax Exemption of Nonprofit Organizations

The tax-exempt status of nonprofit arts organizations also increases the financial resources that such organizations can devote to their artistic missions. As tax-exempt entities, nonprofit arts organizations do not have to pay federal and state corporate or trust income taxes; and these organizations are also typically exempt from local property and sales taxes (as well as sales taxes on purchases).

In addition to the charitable contribution deduction and entity-level exemption, the federal tax system also subsidizes charities by granting them the ability to issue section 501(*c*)(3) bonds, the interest income on which is exempt from tax. We do not, however, impute a subsidy value to this provision because only 59 organizations in the entire sample reported tax-exempt bond liabilities on their 990 returns.

Exemption from Corporate Income Taxes

Three-quarters of the arts organizations included in the NCCS/PRI database reported receiving more than $2 billion in revenue in excess of their expenses. It is tempting to estimate the value of the nonprofit exemption from income taxes by applying an appropriate business income tax rate to this amount, but, although the size of the nonprofit surplus has sometimes been seen as an indicator of the economic importance of the corporate income tax exemption (Congressional Budget Office, 1997), it is inappropriate to do so.

One important reason is that the surplus between revenue and expense that is garnered by a nonprofit organization will generally not correspond to a measure of profit as accountants and economists would understand the term. For example, donations are appropriately treated as a source of funds to a nonprofit organization for purposes of computing its surplus. But although donations could, in theory, be counted as a taxable receipt for purposes of determining taxable profit, given the stated rationale for organizing as a nonprofit organization, this seems rather unlikely. Indeed, in the NCCS/PRI arts sample, if government grants and contributions are taken out of total revenue (and total expense is reduced by the cost of raising grants and contributions), the estimated 'nonprofit surplus' turns into a deficit for three out of four arts organizations.

Another reason for not applying a tax rate to the nonprofit surplus is that, despite its potential economic value to nonprofit organizations, the federal exemption from corporate income tax is not even officially scored as a tax expenditure (Joint Committee on Taxation, 1998; emphasis added):

> With respect to . . . charities, tax-exempt status is not classified as a tax expenditure because the non-business activities of such organizations generally must predominate and their unrelated business activities are subject to tax. *In general, the imputed income derived from nonbusiness activities conducted by individuals or collectively by certain nonprofit organizations is outside the normal income tax base.*

In other words, tax exemption does not constitute an implicit tax subsidy because the income from the 'nonbusiness' activities of nonprofit organizations never rises to the level of taxable income in the first place.

Thus it is not straightforward to assign an implicit subsidy value to the nonprofit tax exemption from business taxes, either in practice or perhaps even conceptually. Nonetheless, despite the statement from the Joint Committee on Taxation, even federal tax law does not grant an absolute tax exemption to all forms of nonprofit revenue, but rather exempts only income that is deemed to be 'related to the organization's primary exempt purpose', or income, such as much investment income (Fullerton, 1991), that is deemed to be unrelated to the organization's main purpose, but nonetheless excluded from taxation. Thus one could, in principle, define the 'potentially taxable income' of nonprofit organizations to be the profit earned on activities that are not related to the organization's primary artistic mission, but instead are undertaken with the specific intent of earning income to support the organization's mission-related activities.[17]

The amount of potentially taxable income is not directly observable from the financial data that are provided by nonprofit organizations, but a crude estimate can be made by summing the amount of investment income received by nonprofit organizations plus the gross profit that such organizations report earning on sales of goods. The amount of taxes that would normally be collected on such income could, then, reasonably be considered to be a form of implicit tax subsidy.

State and Local Property Tax Exemption

As in the case of exemption from income taxes, the exemption that nonprofit arts organizations receive from state and local property taxes was initially not granted as an economic subsidy to these organizations, but may have stemmed more from a historic desire on the part of governments to respect the boundaries between the government and nonprofit activities at a time when the latter were primarily undertaken by religious bodies.[18]

Nonetheless local and state governments have increasingly come to view the property tax exemption, not as an automatic entitlement of nonprofits, but rather as a tax preference that is subject to review. Indeed, in some localities, nonprofits have been pressured politically to accept agreements under which they make 'payments in lieu of taxes'. Moreover the nonprofit property tax exemption is treated as an explicit tax expenditure item in the tax expenditures budgets of a number of states.[19]

Economic Value of Tax Exemption

Tables 8.7 and 8.8 present estimates of the implicit subsidy that tax-exempt status confers on nonprofit arts organizations. The estimated amounts represent the additional financial resources that arts organizations have at their disposal by virtue of being exempt from having to pay federal and state income taxes on their 'potential taxable income' and local (and state) property taxes on land and buildings owned by them.

The value of the income tax exemption is estimated by first adding together the organization's interest, dividend and net rental income plus capital gains from sales of securities and other assets plus its gross profit on sales of goods. This amount is then multiplied by a combined federal–state tax rate of 40 per cent.

To estimate the value of the property tax exemption, organizations were first classified as owning taxable real property if they reported a gross

Table 8.7 Amount and relative importance of tax exemption for nonprofit arts organizations

	Number of organizations	Estimated value of income, property & sales tax exemption ($)				Value of tax exemption as percentage of total revenue			
		Mean	Median	Lower quartile	Upper quartile	Mean	Median	Lower quartile	Upper quartile
All organizations	7367	114697	1940	172	17225	3.9	0.8	0.1	4.2
Media and communications	282	286115	6394	433	25594	3.8	1.7	0.2	4.9
Film & TV	521	120003	4485	272	32971	3.3	1.1	0.1	4.4
Publishing	493	61504	2625	258	15371	4.2	1.0	0.1	4.4
Radio	232	41016	9508	330	26787	4.0	2.2	0.2	4.8
Visual arts	185	33941	2596	406	12953	4.6	1.4	0.3	4.9
Museums (multipurpose)	846	85755	10541	1607	46857	8.7	4.7	1.0	11.6
Art museums	389	866286	22993	2021	165128	8.9	5.0	1.2	13.8
Performing arts	702	92869	790	58	9145	3.3	0.0	0.0	2.6
Dance companies	490	24061	303	5	2550	1.4	0.2	0.0	1.0
Theaters	1386	29613	919	67	11692	2.8	0.4	0.0	2.8
Music not elsewhere classified	413	21589	887	168	3771	2.4	0.6	1.3	1.9
Orchestras	555	146244	2280	402	11639	2.7	0.7	0.2	2.3
Opera companies	201	92437	2268	282	31694	2.7	0.7	0.1	2.6
Choral groups	283	5669	443	107	1582	1.3	0.3	0.1	0.9
Bands not elsewhere classified	144	16625	588	45	2734	2.0	0.4	0.4	1.7
Music schools	203	72693	1548	208	25045	2.9	0.8	0.1	3.0
Arts not elsewhere classified	42	15916	1739	372	10140	4.2	1.0	0.3	3.9

Source: NCCS/PRI digitized database of IRS Form 990 returns.

Table 8.8 Amount and relative importance of tax exemption for nonprofit arts organizations, by age and size

		Estimated value of income, property & sales tax exemption ($)				Value of tax exemption as percentage of total revenue			
	Number of organizations	Mean	Median	Lower quartile	Upper quartile	Mean	Median	Lower quartile	Upper quartile
All organizations									
Organization age									
Five years or less	860	9006	220	0	2215	1.5	0.1	0.0	0.9
More than five years	6507	128665	2557	252	20630	4.2	1.0	0.1	4.7
Organization size ($assets)									
Less than 100000	2740	806	145	0	600	0.8	0.1	0.0	0.5
100000 to 500000	2261	5964	2678	748	8103	3.3	1.2	0.3	3.5
500000 to 1000000	695	18769	15205	6918	25113	7.0	3.4	1.0	8.4
1000000 to 5000000	979	63659	46016	23654	81360	8.3	4.5	1.8	9.7
More than 5000000	692	1089465	229721	79841	679596	9.5	6.0	1.8	12.5

Source: NCCS/PRI digitized database of IRS Form 990 returns.

(book) value of land, buildings and equipment of more than $250 000. For organizations that were thus classified as owning property, the reported value of land, buildings and equipment reported on the 990 return was then multiplied by an average rate of 2.5 per cent, which is the midpoint of effective commercial property tax rates levied in the largest cities of each of the 50 states, as reported by the Minnesota Taxpayers Association (2000).[20]

Overall the estimates shown in Tables 8.7 and 8.8 indicate that the implicit subsidy resulting from income and property tax exemption is quantitatively less important for many, perhaps most, organizations than the implicit subsidy from tax-deductible contributions. In the aggregate, however, the tax exemption is estimated to be worth roughly $840 million, which is comparable to the value of government grants ($1.05 billion) and the implicit tax subsidy from deductible contributions ($1.03 billion). The results also show that the tax exemption may be of considerable value to some arts organizations, such as art museums, and to larger arts organizations generally.

The Partially Subsidized Muse

The estimates presented in Tables 8.1, 8.5 and 8.7 imply that in 1999 nonprofits arts organizations received direct and indirect subsidies worth on the order of $3 billion. Figures 8.6 to 8.8 and Tables 8.9 to 8.13 bring these estimates together to present an overall picture of the level and distribution of total direct and indirect public subsidies to nonprofit arts organizations.

Figure 8.6 shows that almost 500 organizations received direct and indirect subsidies equal to 50 per cent or more of their total revenue, while an additional 696 organizations received total subsidies of between 33 and 50 per cent. Figure 8.7 shows that about 60 per cent of the 'output' of the nonprofit arts sector (as proxied by organization spending) is provided by enterprises that receive public subsidies of less than 25 per cent of revenue. Figure 8.8 shows that direct government grants are the dominant form of subsidy among arts organizations with a relatively high rate of total direct and indirect public subsidy.

Table 8.9 shows that three out of four arts organizations received estimated direct and indirect public subsidies equal to almost 10 per cent of their total revenues, while one in two nonprofits received estimated public subsidies of 20 per cent or more. Tables 8.10 and 8.11 show that the degree of subsidization does not vary systematically with organization age, and increases with organization size, in large part because the effective subsidies from the tax exemption benefit larger organizations. (These relationships remain when one statistically controls for the form of artistic activity.)

Tables 8.12 and 8.13 show further that the current set of policies have the

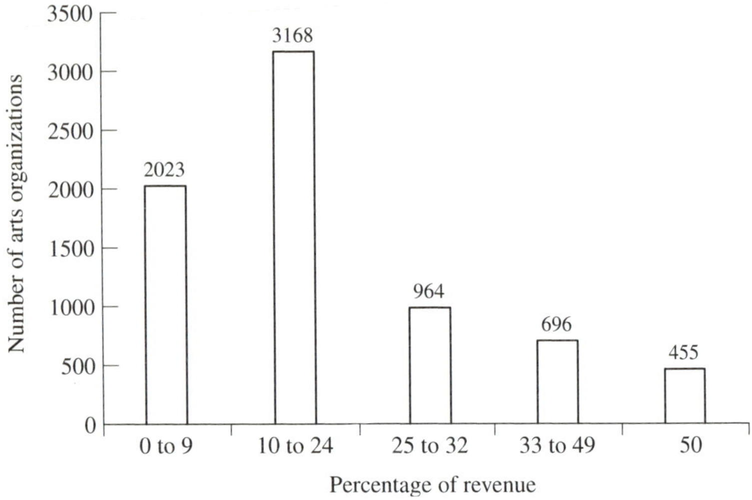

Figure 8.6 Direct and indirect subsidies as a percentage of revenue

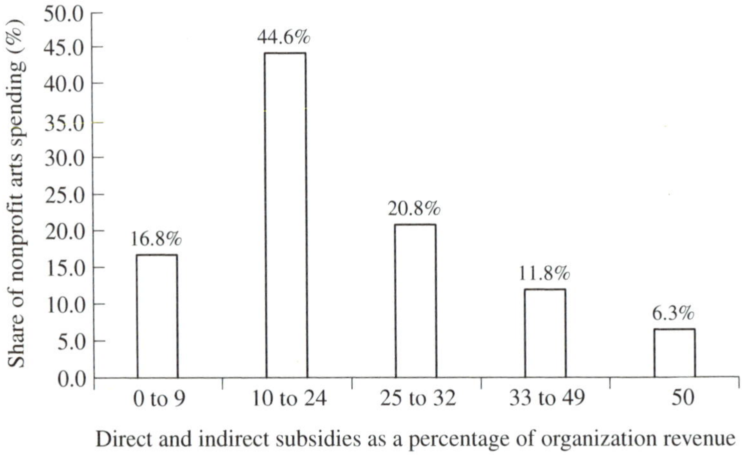

Figure 8.7 Direct and indirect subsidies as a percentage of organization revenue

effect of favoring some types of artistic activities, such as media and communications activities and museums, relative to others, such as the performing and musical arts. In the case of the 'media-related' arts activities, this reflects the fact that these organizations receive a disproportionate share of direct government contributions. In the case of arts museums, this outcome reflects the fact that art museums receive a disproportionate share of tax

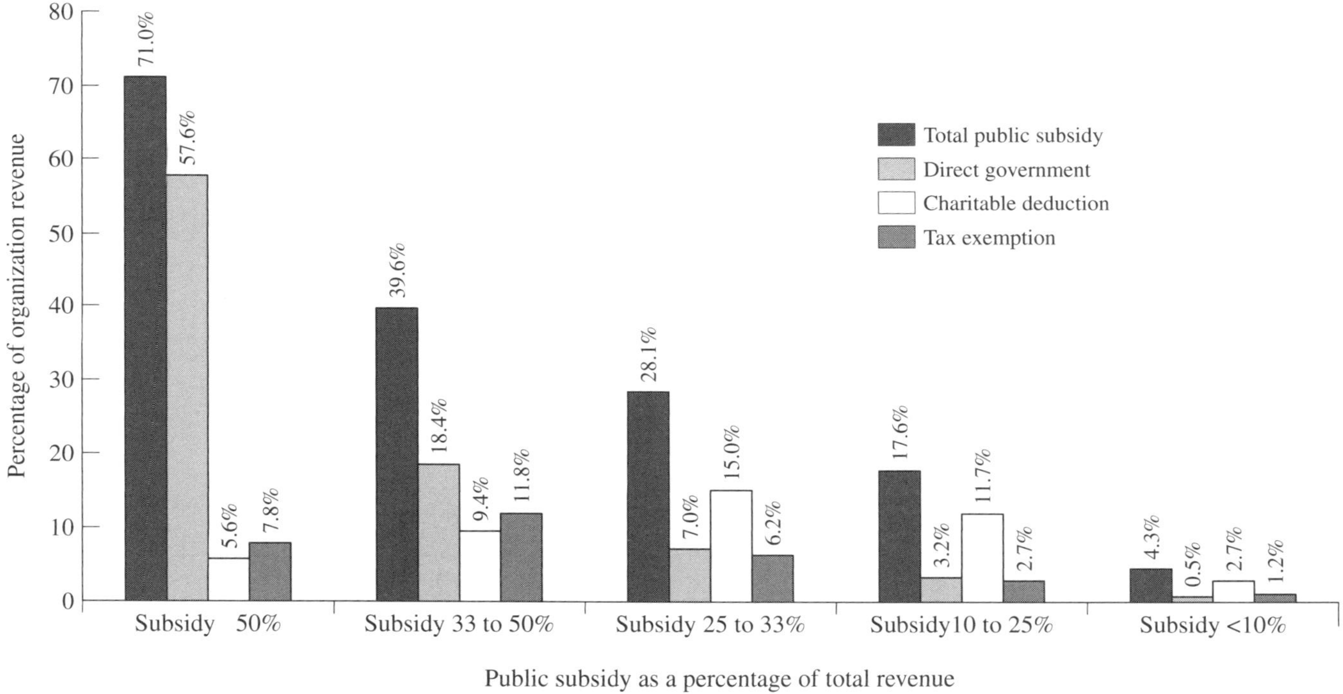

Figure 8.8 Sources of public subsidy

Table 8.9 Amount and relative importance of direct and indirect subsidies for the arts

	Number of organizations	Estimated amount of direct and indirect subsidies ($)				Direct and indirect subsidies as percentage of total revenue			
		Mean	Median	Lower quartile	Upper quartile	Mean	Median	Lower quartile	Upper quartile
All organizations	7306	398392	39331	12451	132179	20.7	17.8	9.0	26.3
Media and communications	280	1731576	75444	22422	197723	24.1	23.4	16.0	28.2
Film & TV	516	698634	90844	25516	387147	29.1	23.6	13.0	37.1
Publishing	488	164929	35624	10929	89930	17.7	15.4	5.8	23.9
Radio	231	390450	79100	27612	192184	26.7	24.0	18.1	31.6
Visual arts	185	139771	37175	8900	92982	21.9	20.1	6.9	30.1
Museums (multipurpose)	839	289589	55553	21583	182330	29.4	24.1	16.9	35.4
Art museums	384	1817427	142781	32877	589706	28.8	27.4	20.4	35.8
Performing arts	698	333447	37251	11529	124713	20.7	17.2	7.9	26.8
Dance companies	483	157884	26611	7539	87794	16.4	13.1	5.6	23.0
Theaters	1375	156884	31643	10244	95738	17.2	13.9	7.1	23.1
Music not elsewhere classified	407	126381	22510	6292	49839	15.8	14.9	6.0	22.1
Orchestras	553	401534	50213	23210	129424	18.4	16.4	12.4	22.1
Opera companies	201	353587	54765	16326	254694	17.2	16.1	10.4	22.8
Choral groups	280	41456	15971	6688	36193	13.2	12.2	5.5	17.6
Bands not elsewhere classified	142	72018	11076	2410	41091	13.9	11.0	2.8	21.0
Music schools	202	156272	21385	4562	87686	11.7	8.3	2.5	16.9
Arts not elsewhere classified	42	124864	29206	12581	90126	24.7	23.9	9.1	34.9

Source: NCCS/PRI digitized database of IRS Form 990 returns.

deductible charitable contributions, and benefit disproportionately from the nonprofit tax exemption of property and income. Conversely nonprofit drama groups and, to a lesser extent, orchestras and opera benefit less than proportionately from subsidies, especially direct government grants.

POLICY IMPLICATIONS

In the concluding chapter to *The Subsidized Muse* Dick Netzer writes: 'Public policy toward the arts in the United States tends to be the sum total of many separate responses to narrowly defined questions rather than the result of a few decisions about broad policy issues.'[21] A similar general point can be made about the estimates of arts subsidies that have been presented above.

The estimated amounts and patterns of direct and indirect arts subsidies result from a host of decentralized decisions made by three different levels of government, private donors and nonprofit arts organizations. The result of this decentralized process is a set of subsidies with the following broad characteristics.

- As when *The Subsidized Muse* was published, tax incentives are a major source of public subsidy to arts and culture. Roughly two-thirds of the estimated total public support received by the arts organizations examined in this study were in the form of tax incentives and tax preferences. In terms of breadth of coverage, and also effective subsidy value, the charitable tax deduction remains as the single most important source of subsidy for most nonprofit arts organizations.
- Despite the importance of indirect support, the results also indicate that direct government support is financially important for many, if not most, nonprofit arts organizations.
- Much of the direct government support for the arts is financed by state and local government rather than the federal government.
- A disproportionate share of total direct and indirect arts subsidies are estimated to be received by some arts providers, which, apart from art museums, do not include organizations engaged in providing what some might describe as 'high art or culture'.
- On balance, the overall pattern of subsidies seems neither to favor nor to penalize the entry of new nonprofit arts providers. Direct government grants provide about the same overall rate of 'subsidy' to new as to established organizations. Private contributions provide higher effective rates of subsidy to new than to established arts

Table 8.10 Amount and relative importance of direct and indirect subsidies for the arts, by age and size

	Number of organizations	Estimated amount of direct and indirect subsidies ($)				Direct and indirect subsidies as percentage of total revenue			
		Mean	Median	Lower quartile	Upper quartile	Mean	Median	Lower quartile	Upper quartile
All organizations									
Organization age									
Five years or less	846	168 203	23 619	6471	66 890	20.7	18.2	6.8	25.3
More than five years	6460	428 537	42 160	13 736	144 138	20.7	17.7	9.2	26.6
Organization size ($assets)									
Less than 100 000	2735	29 911	15 469	4592	35 680	17.2	13.8	4.7	23.0
100 000 to 500 000	2253	71 014	35 967	14 040	83 368	20.1	16.9	8.9	25.5
500 000 to 1 000 000	693	144 765	79 080	31 681	176 190	24.3	20.7	13.8	28.3
1 000 000 to 5 000 000	975	393 135	208 574	92 714	444 840	26.4	23.2	15.2	32.4
More than 5 000 000	650	3 361 847	937 614	433 367	257 939	25.7	24.4	15.7	32.9

Source: NCCS/PRI digitized database of IRS Form 990 returns.

Table 8.11 Direct and indirect subsidies for the arts

	Number of organizations	Subsidies as a percentage of total revenue: Total	Govt grants	Tax incentives for giving	Tax exemption
All organizations					
Organization age					
Five years or less	846	20.7	8.0	11.1	1.6
More than five years	6460	20.7	7.8	8.8	4.2
Organization size ($assets)					
Less than 100000	2735	17.2	8.0	8.4	0.8
100000 to 500000	2253	20.1	7.8	9.0	3.3
500000 to 1000000	693	24.3	7.6	9.7	7.0
1000000 to 5000000	975	26.4	8.1	10.0	8.2
More than 5000000	650	25.7	6.6	9.6	9.5

Source: NCCS/PRI digitized database of IRS Form 990 returns.

providers, but this is counterbalanced by the fact that established arts providers benefit more from the nonprofit exemption from income and property taxes.

- The system provides larger total effective subsidies to larger than to smaller arts organizations. The difference, however, results mainly from the fact that larger organizations are more apt to benefit from the various nonprofit tax exemptions rather than from a systematic tendency for government grants and the charitable deduction to benefit larger organizations.

The decentralized nature of public support for the arts in the United States is quite similar to patterns of public support in many other areas of American social policy (Howard, 1997; Zimmer and Toepler, 1999; Salamon, 2002). Critics of decentralization and reliance on tax incentives will note that the subsidy patterns described above, especially those that tend to favor some forms of art over others, would be unlikely to be replicated by a more direct program of subsidy to the arts that was of equal magnitude. These same critics would argue that this outcome is inferior to one that would result from more centralized, direct public subsidies that were 'better' aimed.

Advocates of more support for the arts would also recognize that relying

Table 8.12 Direct and indirect government subsidies for the arts

	Number of organizations	Subsidies as percentage of total revenue			
		Total	Govt grants	Tax incentives for giving	Tax exemption
All organizations	7306	20.7	7.8	9.0	3.9
Museums (multipurpose)	839	29.4	10.0	10.8	8.6
Film & TV	516	29.1	15.2	10.6	3.3
Art museums	384	28.8	9.4	10.5	8.9
Radio	231	26.7	8.8	13.9	3.9
Arts not elsewhere classified	42	24.6	11.9	8.7	4.2
Media and communications	280	24.1	6.5	13.7	3.9
Visual arts	185	21.9	9.2	8.1	4.6
Performing arts	698	20.7	9.1	8.3	3.3
Orchestras	553	18.4	5.7	10.0	2.7
Publishing	488	17.7	4.5	9.0	4.3
Opera companies	201	17.2	4.9	9.6	2.7
Theaters	1375	17.2	7.2	7.2	2.8
Dance companies	483	16.4	7.8	7.1	1.4
Music not elsewhere classified	407	15.8	5.2	8.2	2.4
Bands not elsewhere classified	142	13.9	5.0	7.0	1.9
Choral groups	280	13.1	4.2	7.6	1.4
Music schools	202	11.7	3.7	5.0	2.9

Source: NCCS/PRI digitized database of IRS Form 990 returns.

Table 8.13 Distribution of arts subsidy, by type of artistic activity

	Percentage of organizations	Percentage of expenditures	Percentage of total subsidies	Percentage of govt grants	Percentage of tax subsidies	Percentage of tax exemption
Media and communications	3.8	10.1	16.7	30.0	9.0	9.5
Film & TV	7.1	15.8	12.4	12.0	17.0	7.4
Publishing	6.7	5.6	2.8	1.5	3.3	3.6
Radio	3.2	3.4	3.1	4.0	3.8	1.2
Visual arts	2.5	1.2	0.9	0.5	1.4	0.7
Museums (multipurpose)	11.5	6.1	8.4	8.2	8.4	8.6
Art museums	5.3	13.8	24.0	15.5	19.5	39.8
Performing arts	9.6	9.3	7.9	8.4	7.5	7.7
Dance companies	6.6	4.1	2.6	2.6	3.7	1.4
Theaters	18.8	12.3	7.4	8.5	8.4	4.9
Music not elsewhere classified	5.6	1.9	1.8	1.7	2.4	1.1
Orchestras	7.5	9.5	7.6	4.4	9.3	9.6
Opera companies	2.8	3.9	2.4	1.5	3.6	2.2
Choral groups	3.8	0.7	0.4	0.4	0.6	0.2
Bands not elsewhere classified	1.9	0.5	0.4	0.2	0.5	0.3
Music schools	2.8	1.6	1.1	0.3	1.3	1.8
Arts not elsewhere classified	0.6	0.2	0.2	0.3	0.2	0.1

Source: NCCS/PRI digitized database of IRS Form 990 returns.

on the tax system to achieve public purposes (in this case in the arts) can be a two-edged sword (Brody and Cordes, 1999). On one hand, it permits subsidies to be provided that are relatively open-ended and hence are less susceptible to public scrutiny. On the other hand, providing subsidies indirectly through tax incentives and preferences instead of through direct grants makes the value of such subsidies depend on parameters of the tax system, such as marginal tax rates and/or changes in tax base, that may change over time for broader reasons of tax and economic policy. A pertinent current example is the reduction in the value of the tax subsidy to giving resulting from changes in the federal estate tax.

Some scholars have also expressed concerns about the tendencies of some arts organizations to seek increasingly commercial sources of revenue.[22] Although the impulse to undertake commercial ventures in the hope of garnering extra income is not solely driven by the fact that nonprofit organizations are able to keep the full *pre-tax return* earned from such activities, this would clearly seem to be a factor.[23]

One could surmise that Dick Netzer himself would take a mixed view of the current system. The conclusion to *The Subsidized Muse* offers a carefully argued case for modest expansion of direct public support for the arts that was properly directed. This becomes more difficult the more decentralized the system of subsidies becomes. In the final analysis, however, moving toward a more centralized system of direct subsidies for the arts would require the political system to negotiate a number of contentious issues that have arisen, and will continue to arise, about what constitutes art that is worthy of public support.[24] An advantage of the current system is that it gives private individuals, corporations and local governments considerable rein in deciding what art is to be supported.

NOTES

1. For a recent assessment of the impact of the subsidized muse on the field of cultural economics, see Blaug (2001), Schuster (1999) and Zimmer and Toepler (1999).
2. On a personal note, I fondly remember being asked, as a freshly-minted assistant professor, to write a review of *The Subsidized Muse* for a local literary magazine. The reward for the work was a free copy of the manuscript, which graces my bookshelf to this day.
3. See U.S. Census Bureau (2000) for a description of activities included in the information sector of the Economic Census.
4. In the database of nonprofit arts producers that is analyzed later in the chapter, nonprofit organizations engaged in media-related activities account for just 400 out of more than 7000 organizations.
5. Netzer (1978, p.6). Note that, in using the phrase 'From this perspective', Netzer was signaling that he did not necessarily share the presumption that the normative case for direct public support of the arts on a European scale was necessarily a compelling one.
6. See Zimmer and Toepler (1999).

7. Under the Economic Growth and Tax Relief Reconciliation Act (EGTRRA), taxpayers that are currently in the 28 per cent federal tax bracket would face a 25 per cent tax rate in 2006 and beyond. For a thorough discussion of EGTRRA, see Gale (2002).
8. Under current law, the maximum estate tax rate is set to decline from 50 per cent in 2002 to 45 per cent in 2010, when, at least technically, the Estate Tax is scheduled to be restored with a top rate of 55 per cent, and then to expire altogether in 2010.
9. This calculation is based on a formula in Fullerton (1991) in which the after-tax cost of donating \$1 in appreciated property is given by $P=(1-t-a\cdot g)$, where t is the personal income tax rate, g is the tax rate on capital gains, and a is the discounted ratio of capital gain to appreciated value. The illustration makes the extreme, though not entirely implausible, assumption that all of the asset's value represents price appreciation so that $a=1$. Fullerton uses a value of $a=0.2$ as applying 'on average' to all gifts of appreciated assets. If a is 0.2, the after-tax of giving *a* \$1 of appreciated asset would be \$0.71 instead of \$0.55. It should also be noted that the donor may not 'zero out' income with charitable gifts.
10. See Eller (1999).
11. This calculation assumes that federal tax expenditures are estimated by applying a blended individual and corporate marginal tax rate of 33 per cent to evaluate the tax expenditure cost, and uses an average state personal tax rate, calculated from the file of nonprofit arts organizations, that equals 5.75 per cent. This estimate is likely to overstate the aggregate state revenue cost somewhat because not all states allow deductions for charitable contributions.
12. This section draws heavily on Cordes (2001).
13. Joulfaian (1991).
14. The IRS 990 form does not require nonprofit organizations to indicate separately whether a private contribution was received from an individual, a corporation or a foundation. Estimates from the Census Bureau, and from *Giving USA* (2000), however, suggest that foundation contributions account for a third of all contributions.
15. I am grateful to Helen Ladd for pointing out that not all states permit charitable deductions. To determine which states allowed charitable deductions, I drew on information provided by State of Wisconsin (2001).
16. Note that lower quartile values are not reported in Table 1 because they were all found to be \$0 or 0 per cent.
17. Moreover scholars who have written on arts policy generally view the tax exemption as a form of indirect support. See Zimmer and Toepler (1999).
18. See Brody and Cordes (1999), Brody (2002) and Steinberg and Bilodeau (1999).
19. Cordes *et al.* (2001, 2002).
20. Because the amount of land and number of buildings reported on the IRS 990 return are book values, the approach described in the text may understate the value of the property tax exemption. At the same time, the unique character of buildings that are owned by arts organizations might well cause them to be assessed at 'less' than their stated market value if such property were to be subject to tax. (See Cordes *et al.* 2001.) Using this approach results in an average estimated value of the property tax exemption equal to roughly 5 per cent of revenue among arts organizations that are classified as likely to own taxable property in the first place.
21. Netzer (1978, p.178).
22. Anheier and Toepler (1998) and Toepler (2001).
23. Cordes and Weisbrod (1998).
24. Cordes and Goldfarb (1996).

REFERENCES

AAFRC Trust for Philanthropy (2000), *Giving USA: The Annual Report on Philanthropy for the Year 1999*, New York, AAFRC Trust for Philanthropy.

Anheier, Helmut and Stefan Toepler (1998), 'Commerce and the muse: are art museums becoming commercial?', in Burton A. Weisbrod (ed.), *To Profit or Not to Profit: The Commercial Transformation of the Nonprofit Sector*, Cambridge: Cambridge University Press, pp.233–48.

Brody, Evelyn (ed.) (2002), *The Nonprofit Tax Exemption: Mapping the Battlefield*, Washington, DC: Urban Institute Press.

Brody, Evelyn and Joseph J. Cordes (1999), 'The Nonprofit Tax Exemption: A Two-Edged Sword', in Elizabeth Boris and C. Eugene Steuerle (eds), *Nonprofits and Government: Collaboration and Conflict*, Washington, DC: Urban Institute Press.

Clotfelter, Charles (1991), 'Government Policy Toward Art Museums in the United States', in Martin Feldstein (ed.), *The Economics of Art Museums*, Chicago, IL: University of Chicago Press.

Clotfelter, Charles and C. Eugene Steuerle (1981), 'Charitable Contributions', in Henry J. Aaron and Joseph A. Pechman (eds), *How Taxes Affect Economic Behavior*, Washington, DC: Brookings Institution.

Congressional Budget Office (1997), *The Potential Effects of Tax Restructuring on Nonprofit Institutions*. Washington, DC: US Congressional Budget Office.

Cordes, Joseph J. (2001), *The Cost of Giving: How Do Changes in Tax Deductions Affect Charitable Contributions?*, Washington, DC: Urban Institute Press.

Cordes, Joseph J. and Robert S.Goldfarb (1996), 'The Value of Public Arts as Public Culture', in Arjo Klamer (ed.), *The Value of Culture: On the Relationship between Economics and Arts*, Amsterdam: University of Amsterdam Press.

Cordes, Joseph J. and Burton A.Weisbrod (1998), 'Differential taxation of nonprofits and the commercialization of nonprofit revenues', in Burton A. Weisbrod (ed.), *To Profit or Not to Profit: The Commercial Transformation of the Nonprofit Sector*, Cambridge: Cambridge University Press, pp.83–105.

Cordes, Joseph J., Marie Gantz and Thomas Pollak (2001), 'The Value and Distribution of the Nonprofit Property Tax Exemption Among Nonprofit Organizations', *National Tax Association Papers and Proceedings: Ninety-Third Annual Conference 2000*.

Cordes, Joseph J., Marie Gantz and Thomas Pollak (2002), 'How Much is the Nonprofit Property Tax Exemption Worth?', in Evelyn Brody (ed.), *The Nonprofit Tax Exemption: Mapping the Battlefield*, Washington, DC: Urban Institute Press.

Eller, Martha (1999), 'Charitable Bequests: Evidence from Federal Estate Tax Returns', *Statistics of Income Bulletin*, Washington DC: Statistics of Income Division, Internal Revenue Service.

Froelich, Karen, Terry Knoepfle and Tom Pollak (2001), 'Financial Measures in Nonprofit Organization Research: Comparing IRS 990 Return and Audited Financial Statement Data', *Nonprofit and Voluntary Sector Quarterly*, **29** (2), 232–54.

Fullerton, Don (1991), 'Tax Policy Toward Art Museums', in Martin Feldstein (ed.), *The Economics of Art Museums*, Chicago, IL: University of Chicago Press.

Gale, William with Sammara Potter (2002), 'An Economic Evaluation of the Economic Growth and Tax Relief Reconciliation Act of 2001', *National Tax Journal*, **55** (1), 133–86.

Howard, Christopher (1997), *The Hidden Welfare State: Tax Expenditures and Social Policy in the United States*, Princeton: Princeton University Press.
Joint Committee on Taxation (1998), *Estimates of Federal Tax Expenditures for Fiscal Years 1999–2003*, Washington, DC: US Government Printing Office.
Joulfaian, David (1991), 'Charitable Bequests and Estate Taxes', *National Tax Journal*, **44** (2), 169–80.
Minnesota Taxpayers Association (2000), *50-State Property Tax Comparison Study, 1998 Update*, Saint Paul, Minnesota.
National Assembly of State Arts Agencies (2001), *State Arts Agency Public Funding Sourcebook*, Washington, DC.
Netzer, Dick (1978), *The Subsidized Muse*, Cambridge: Cambridge University Press.
Salamon, Lester (2002), *The Tools of Government: A Guide to the New Governance*, New York: Oxford University Press.
Schuster, Mark (1999), 'The Other Side of the Subsidized Muse: Indirect Aid Revisited', *Journal of Cultural Economics*, **23**, 51–70.
State of Wisconsin, Legislative Fiscal Bureau (2001), *Individual Income Tax Provisions in the States*, Madison, WI: State of Wisconsin Legislative Reference Bureau.
Steinberg, Richard and Marc Bilodeau (1999), *Should Nonprofit Organizations Pay Sales and Property Taxes?*, Washington, DC: National Council of Nonprofit Associations.
Throsby, David (1994), 'The Production and Consumption of the Arts: A View of Cultural Economics', *Journal of Economic Literature*, **32**, 1–29.
Toepler, Stefan (2001), 'Culture Commerce and Civil Society: Rethinking Support for the Arts', *Administration & Society*, **33** (5), 508–22.
U.S. Census Bureau (2000), *Sources of Receipts or Revenue: 1997 Economic Census, Arts, Entertainment and Recreation*, Washington, DC: US Department of Commerce.
Zimmer, Annette and Stefan Toepler (1999), 'The Subsidized Muse: Government and the Arts in Western Europe and the United States', *Journal of Cultural Economics*, **23**, 33–49.

APPENDIX 1: ARTS ORGANIZATIONS ANALYZED

The arts organizations selected for analysis were drawn from the Arts, Culture and Humanities general category in the National Taxonomy of Exempt Organizations (NTEE). The types of arts organizations within that category that were included in the subsample are described below.

Arts, Culture and Humanities

Organizations or activities in the general category include those that promote enjoyment or understanding of the visual, performing, folk or media arts, or the humanities (archaeology, art history, modern and classical languages, philosophy, ethics, theology and comparative religion); communications organizations (film, video, publishing, journalism, radio, television); and organizations that promote the appreciation or understanding of historical events, including historical societies and genealogical or heredity-based organizations (for example, Sons of the Revolution, Daughters of the Confederacy, and so on). Included are museums and halls of fame; historic preservation programs; groups of or services to artists, performers, entertainers, writers or humanities scholars; programs which promote artistic expression of or within ethnic groups and cultures; and art and performing art schools, centers and studios. Not included are services that promote international understanding and friendly relations among nations through cultural programs; libraries and reading programs; botanical gardens or nature centers; or zoos.

Subsample of Nonprofit Arts Organizations

Arts multipurpose

A20 Arts, cultural organizations – Multipurpose; organizations that promote, produce or offer access to a variety of arts experiences encompassing the visual, media and performing arts.

Media/communications

A30 Media, communications organizations; organizations that produce, disseminate or provide production facilities in one or more media.

Film/TV

A31 Film, video: includes holography.

A32 Television

Publishing

A33 Printing, publishing: includes newspapers, literary journals and other publishers.

Radio

A34 Radio: includes radio reading services.

Visual arts

A40 Visual art organizations, services, not elsewhere classifield (N.E.C.)
A41 Architecture centers/services
A42 Photography
A43 Sculpture
A44 Design centers/services
A45 Painting
A46 Drawing
A47 Ceramic arts
A48 Art conservation

Museums

A50 Museums, museum activities: general museums covering arts & sciences use.

Art museums

A51 Art museums: includes museums and galleries in fine, decorative or textile arts.

Performing arts, multipurpose

A60 Performing arts organizations, activities
A61 Performing arts centers

Dance

A62 Dance
A63 Ballet
A64 Choreography

Theater

A65 Theater N.E.C.
A66 Playwriting
A67 Musical theater

Music NEC
A68 Music N.E.C.

Orchestras
A69 Symphony orchestras

Opera
A6A Opera, light opera

Choral groups
A6B Singing, choral

Bands NEC
A6C Music groups, bands, ensembles N.E.C.

Performing arts schools (music schools)
A6E Performing arts schools

Arts NEC
A99 Arts, culture, humanities N.E.C.

COMMENT

Helen F. Ladd

This chapter by Joe Cordes represents a useful updating of some of the data in Dick Netzer's seminal work, *The Subsidized Muse*. Cordes uses a new data set on the financial characteristics of 7000 nonprofit arts organizations to estimate the magnitude of subsidies to the arts as of 1999. He measures three components: direct government support, indirect subsidies in the form of the tax deduction for charitable giving, and indirect subsidies in the form of exemptions from the corporate income tax, the local property tax and the estate tax. Together the components amount to about $3 billion, with the indirect subsidies accounting for about two-thirds of the total. The estimates seem reasonable although it is important to note the absence of direct support from local governments, which is difficult to estimate. In addition, Cordes does not mention an additional category included by Netzer, namely the indirect subsidies to the arts that operate through unemployment insurance.

These new estimates by Cordes are a useful contribution to the current literature on public financing of the arts. The numbers themselves are obviously of interest. In addition, Cordes has included a careful discussion of many of the methodological issues, such as the reliability of the data and the relationship between the budgetary cost of tax subsidies and the amount of added giving that is stimulated by those tax subsidies. He makes a sensible, evidence-based case that the price elasticity of giving to arts organizations approximates -1, which implies that the budgetary cost of tax expenditures equals the amount of revenue received by the arts organizations.

Now that Cordes has provided us with the more recent information, the challenge is to understand better the context and the significance of the findings. Cordes includes some useful discussion at the end of the chapter on the significance of the use of tax subsidies. He correctly points out that subsidies that work through the tax side of the budget are likely to generate a different distributional pattern across the types of beneficiaries than that which would occur with a direct subsidy program of equal magnitude implemented through the expenditure side of the budget. In addition indirect subsidies can be a two-edged sword. On the one hand, the subsidies are open-ended and are often hidden from public scrutiny. On the other hand, changes made to the tax code for unrelated reasons, such as the current proposal to eliminate the estate tax, can adversely affect the amount of subsidies to the arts.

The new figures raise additional evaluative and policy issues that, in my view, deserve more attention. The first is whether the public subsidies are large or small. As Netzer cautioned in *The Subsidized Muse*, there is no way to determine the 'right' amount of subsidy for the arts. Instead the best one can do is to compare those subsidies with public subsidies in other sectors. It would be nice to know, for example, how the $3 billion in arts subsidies compares to public subsidies in other sectors such as sports, higher education or hospitals, and to have some discussion of how one might understand and justify the differences.

The second issue is the appropriate roles for the various levels of government. Cordes documents that federal support has fallen quite precipitously since the late 1970s, that state support has in general risen, and that local support (on which he had limited data) has also probably grown. This pattern is not inconsistent with Netzer's earlier call for a larger state and local share. The question of interest is whether this decentralization of support is appropriate. One argument against the heavier reliance on state and local governments is the likely sensitivity of their spending to the economy. Because state governments are required to operate within balanced budgets, the loss of revenues that accompanies a slowdown in the economy is likely to lead to reductions in areas of nonessential spending, including spending on the arts. That pattern emerges clearly from the data presented by Cordes in Figure 8.5, in that state support fell dramatically during the recession of the early 1990s. Consistent with that decline, arts funding is again coming under attack in many states during the current period of economic slowdown and state budgetary crises.

A third issue is the role of barriers to entry, a topic that Cordes refers to briefly in the concluding section and which presumably serves as the justification for disaggregating some of the analysis into subsidies for established and new institutions. What sort of barriers should policy makers be concerned about and how might they operate? In particular, what is the role of public subsidies in either exacerbating such barriers to entry or lowering them? One possibility is that subsidies to established institutions could present a barrier to the establishment of new institutions. However the conditions required for such an outcome would need to be spelled out. For example, if competition occurs in the same market, the extent to which the subsidies permitted the established firms to charge lower ticket prices would put new and emerging institutions at a competitive disadvantage. Alternatively, to the extent that the arts are public goods and the subsidies increase general interest in the arts, that increase would benefit both the new and the established institutions. A related question is whether it is appropriate to interpret equal public subsidies as a share of revenues as the criterion for no barriers.

In sum, the paper has accomplished what the author promised by the title, namely the careful estimation of the value and incidence of public support received by nonprofit arts organizations. It would be a fitting tribute to Dick Netzer for other researchers now to use these new figures as the starting point for additional policy analysis of the appropriate role for public subsidies to the arts.

REFERENCE

Netzer, Dick (1978), *The Subsidized Muse*, Cambridge MA: Cambridge University Press.

Index